# DIANA

## THE PEOPLE'S PRINCESS

Also by Nicholas Davies:

*Diana: The Princess and Her Troubled Marriage*
*Queen Elizabeth II: A Woman Who Is Not Amused*

# DIANA
## THE PEOPLE'S PRINCESS

### NICHOLAS DAVIES

A Citadel Stars Book
Published by Carol Publishing Group

A Citadel Stars Book
Published by Carol Publishing Group
Citadel Stars is a registered trademark of Carol
Communications, Inc.
Editorial, sales and distribution, rights and permissions inquiries
should be addressed to Carol Publishing Group, 120 Enterprise
Avenue, Secaucus, N.J. 07094
In Canada: Canadian Manda Group, One Atlantic Avenue, Suite 105,
Toronto, Ontario M6K 3E7

Carol Publishing Group books are available at special discounts for
bulk purchases, sales promotion, fund-raising, or educational
purposes. Special editions can be created to specifications. For details
contact: Special Sales Department, Carol Publishing Group,
120 Enterprise Avenue, Secaucus, N.J. 07094

Manufactured in the United States of America
10  9  8  7  6  5  4  3  2  1

ISBN 0–8065–8013–5 (pbk.)

Cataloging data for this publication can be obtained from the
Library of Congress.

*To Thomas*

———❦———

# Contents

# Author to Reader

❧

FOR THIS UNAUTHORIZED BIOGRAPHY of Diana, the Princess of Wales, I have drawn on my sources and my friends over a period of seventeen years since I first met Diana on the polo grounds of Windsor in 1979.

Since that day Diana's name has barely been out of the headlines, and the friends and courtiers who have surrounded her in those years have changed time and again. But those who have left often remain in touch with their successors, for the courtiers and staff who advise and serve the Royal Family seem like members of an illustrious club, privileged to have been of service to the Royal House of Windsor.

Amongst those "club" members I have won a number of friends through the years, and it is to these men and women that I owe a debt of gratitude, without whose help this book could not have been written. When much speculation appeared in the national press, these people kindly provided me with their own accounts of circumstances as they actually happened.

Most of these people served both Prince Charles and Princess Diana at one time or another and witnessed the daily events: the triumphs and the tragedies, the arguments and the happiness, and their love for their sons Prince William and Prince Harry.

Other valuable sources volunteered to help, including a number of friends whom Princess Diana had become close to during the past three years, assisting her with advice, giving encouragement, and offering their services to someone who they felt needed their support.

The majority of the men and women who helped in researching this book talked to me on the understanding of absolute confidence and complete anonymity. None wished to endanger their relationships with members of the Royal Family or members of the respective royal households they served. So their names do not appear.

# Diana's Last Battle

ONE COLD WINTER'S DAY toward the end of February 1996, Princess Diana drove purposefully out of Kensington Palace, threading her way through the busy afternoon traffic on the mile-long journey to Buckingham Palace. As she parked her car and hurried inside, a flurry of snow filled the air.

"Good afternoon, ma'am," came the quiet voice of the footman as he bowed his head to Diana.

"Good afternoon," she said. "I believe I'm expected."

"Yes, ma'am," came the reply. "This way."

Diana set off behind the palace footman on one of the most important journeys of her life. Later she would tell how her mind raced back sixteen years to the February day when she had been in Buckingham Palace, squeezing the arm of Prince Charles, blissfully happy after announcing their engagement to the world. That, too, had been a cold winter's day—but she remembered the sun had shone as they posed together on the palace lawns and the cameras clicked away.

Now she was desperately trying to save her marriage, to prevent divorce, a divorce that she never wanted and that she feared would mark the beginning of an estrangement from her beloved Wills and Harry.

Throughout January and February 1996 Diana gambled that she could ignore the demands her mother-in-law had sent in a letter, urging Diana to divorce Charles as soon as possible. Diana hoped that if she did so she could face down Prince Charles by simply refusing to attend to the matter, giving her solicitor, Anthony Julius, no instructions.

The Queen, however, had different ideas. She had no intention of permitting her daughter-in-law to manipulate the Royal Family and instructed the royal solicitors, Farrer & Co., to press the Princess of Wales to comply with her demands that there should be a speedy divorce settlement.

Anthony Julius had informed Diana that she would have to give him instructions, that she could no longer ignore the demands of the Queen herself. During her visit to Pakistan in February 1996 Diana decided to take one final gamble, to seek an interview with the Queen to try to dissuade her from pushing for a divorce, so that the family could remain together, though in name only.

On her ten-minute drive to the palace, Diana had rehearsed, as she had a dozen times already that day, precisely the argument she would put forward. Diana was ushered into the Queen's first-floor drawing room, and the doors were closed behind her.

Their conversation would last just ten minutes. Diana argued eloquently that her marriage to Charles should be allowed to continue for the sake of the two princes. She contended that it would be in their best interests if Charles and she remained married, though they would continue to live separate lives.

Diana then played her ace, telling the Queen in a quiet, dignified voice that neither Wills nor Harry wanted their parents to divorce and had come to terms with the life they now led, sharing time between their father and mother, understanding that their parents were living apart, separated but still married.

The Queen hardly said a word but simply sat and listened, which infuriated Diana. She had hoped to start a conversation in which she might have been able to involve the Queen, trying to persuade her that divorce could not be good for the boys.

After Diana had finished her argument and sat nervously on the edge of a large easy chair, her fingers twisting together, the Queen told Diana that she would promise nothing but would think over what she had said and would discuss her request with Prince Charles.

As Diana curtsied and left the room she felt that there could be some hope in that her mother-in-law had not denied her request outright. But Diana had also felt that coldness in that warm room, the Queen offering very little, simply sitting opposite her, listening to her pleas, and looking directly into her eyes.

Twenty-four hours later the Queen informed Diana that she should seek a meeting with Charles and discuss the matter with him. Before that meeting with Diana would take place, Charles was briefed about what had happened during the secret meeting at the palace and was informed that the Queen still believed that a formal divorce was best for the children, the monarchy, and the nation. Charles had been left in no doubt that his mother expected him to push for a divorce.

Charles immediately wrote a short, formal letter to Diana suggesting a meeting, informing her that the Queen and Prince Philip were urging him to reach a settlement with her as soon as possible.

At four-thirty on the afternoon of Wednesday, February 28, Diana and Charles met by arrangement in Charles's private rooms in St. James's Palace, two hundred yards from Buckingham Palace. Charles opened the discussion by telling Diana that there was no way back, that the Queen and Prince Philip had demanded that they move toward a divorce because of the effect the long-drawn-out affair was having on the image of the monarchy.

Diana made one final plea to Charles. She begged him to reconsider the decision to divorce. She pleaded with him "for the sake of William and Harry" not to divorce her. She urged him to stand up to his parents and do the right thing by their two sons—because *they* didn't want their parents to divorce.

With tears in her eyes, Diana told Charles in a voice barely more than a whisper, "You know that I loved you. Now I want you to know that I will always love you, because you are the father of William and Harry."

But Charles would not be swayed. He replied that the matter had gone too far, that there was no turning back; the divorce would have to go through.

Diana unfurled a piece of paper she had taken into the meeting, an offer in case her pleas fell on stony ground. She showed the paper to Charles; in it she agreed to yield her HRH (Her Royal Highness) status, effectively removing her from the official front rank of the Royal Family. Diana knew that the Queen would never permit her to keep the prefix HRH.

She accepted that after the divorce she would be officially titled Diana, Princess of Wales. But she demanded that she keep her royal apartments in Kensington Palace for the sake of the children, so that they would not feel they were being thrown out of the family home. And she suggested that she should keep her small suite of offices in St. James's, next to Charles's large office apartments.

However, she surprised Charles by suggesting that they should agree to a public divorce, covered by live television cameras, so that the entire nation could witness the formal end of their marriage, just as the entire nation had witnessed their wedding in July 1981. Charles was flabbergasted by the suggestion, and he told Diana that he thought the idea was "crass and stupid," that he was totally against it and wanted nothing to do with it. Diana argued that such a nationwide broadcast would offset their public image, that of a couple continually bickering.

Within minutes of the secret meeting, Diana decided to tell the world the details of what had happened. She told her new media adviser, Jane Atkinson, a woman who had held the job for only a matter of weeks, to issue a formal statement.

The statement read: "The Princess of Wales has agreed to Prince Charles's request for a divorce. The Princess will continue to be involved in all decisions relating to the children and will remain at Kensington Palace with offices at St. James's Palace. The Princess of Wales will retain the title and be known as Diana, Princess of Wales."

Prince Charles, the Queen, senior aides of both the Queen and Charles were taken completely by surprise at Diana's official announcement—for nothing had been agreed between Charles and Diana. They all believed the meeting had been in secret, the discussion absolutely private. They understood the princess had simply stated her demands for her solicitors to follow up, now that she had agreed to a divorce.

The whole affair became increasingly messy. After Diana gave a briefing to Anthony Julius, her solicitor, about her meeting with Charles, Buckingham Palace received a statement from Mr. Julius stating that divorce negotiations could be jeopardized if the Princess's version of events was not confirmed. He said, "If we cannot rely on agreements that have been made, it would be unsafe to continue our negotiations."

Wrong-footed once again, the palace instructed their solicitors, Farrer and Company, to put an end to the public wrangling and make sure that all future negotiations were conducted in absolute secrecy. In private the Queen was seething with anger that Diana had debased the divorce proceedings by the public statements, desperately trying to seize the initiative in matters which should have been kept entirely private.

No one knew the precise demands that Diana would make on the Royal Family. But some close to her suggested that she had demanded a one-time sum of $23 million, or annual payments of $2 million. These sums of course would be for her personal expenses. Charles, or the Queen, would also have to provide a home in London and another in the country, pay all staff salaries, run her cars, pay for the upkeep of her homes, and of course pay all the costs of the two princes.

Diana had thrown her last dice and lost. Now she would take everything she could for herself and for the boys. She already knew the measure of the loneliness which faced her but was determined to maintain the loving relationship she had with Wills and Harry. But in her heart she wondered how long it would be before her sons were seduced away from her by the ruthless power of the House of Windsor.

# DIANA
## THE PEOPLE'S PRINCESS

# 1

## The Christmas That Made Diana Cry

———⚜———

In SILENCE, Princess Diana walked through the suite of rooms of her Kensington Palace apartment looking at the Christmas decorations. She entered the bedrooms of Wills and Harry and looked around, everything once again tidy, their Christmas decorations still in place, in the hallway the large Christmas tree a blaze of color, the tinsel and crackers reflecting the colored lights on the tree. But it was the deathly silence that unnerved her for she wasn't used to such peace and quiet in her palace home.

Only twenty-four hours before, the apartment had been a hive of activity, Wills and Harry rushing around, playing games, and talking nonstop of the presents to come, enjoying the time with the mother they adored, the staff going about their business though most had already left for the Christmas break.

Now Diana walked through the palace alone. Her sons would be at Sandringham with Charles, the Queen, and Prince Philip and one or two other members of the family who had decided to celebrate Christmas, 1995, at the family's Norfolk estate, one hundred miles north of London.

The tears began to flow as thoughts of despair and loneliness raced through her mind. It had only been a matter of days since she had received the news from her mother-in-law urging her to divorce "as soon as possible." She had eaten a cold salad for lunch, sitting alone in front of the television set, watching but not bothering to take in what was on the screen. She had decided to spend Christmas alone, to feel the trauma of loneliness, and had even told the duty staff to go off to their respective families and friends and enjoy themselves.

With some trepidation, she walked into the kitchen and opened the refrigerator door, the bright light momentarily dazzling her. It was half-full. Before she had taken in what food was there, Diana slammed shut the door and walked quickly away, back to the television set and the film she had been idly watching.

Later, Diana would say that she could not remember how many times that day she had gone to the fridge, intent on raiding it, wanting to eat everything she could see for the comfort she knew it would bring her. That Christmas day Diana fought many battles trying desperately not to slide back down to the depression that had controlled and wrecked her life for three long years when she had suffered from the awful effects of bulimia.

But only to one person, her trusted psychotherapist Susie Orbach, did Diana confess everything of what happened that Christmas day when she had never felt more lonely. She had revealed to a select few that Christmas had been "a difficult time," but she had tried to shrug it off, not wanting to reveal the extent of her misery and the daunting, shuddering specter of bulimia that had haunted her.

The Queen, her mother-in-law, had invited her to bring Wills and Harry to Sandringham on Christmas Eve, stay the night in a house on the estate, attend church with them the following morning, and stay for the turkey dinner. But Diana had declined the invitation, not wanting to spend that much time with the family she knew had turned against her, pretending to the nation that all was well despite the pending divorce she had not sought and did not want. She knew the whole episode would be a ghastly sham, the Queen and Prince Philip smiling for the cameras on Christmas morning as though the Royals were once again a happy family.

Nor did Diana want to see Prince Charles, the man whom

she had come to despise and sometimes hate, making an attempt to be a fun-loving father for Wills and Harry, merrily cracking jokes around the Christmas dinner table. From past years Diana knew the whole day would be a stilted, formal occasion bereft of real happiness and enjoyment, lacking spontaneity and fun, and with every member of the family sitting around that table pretending that she, Diana, was welcome.

During Christmas day Diana phoned numerous friends, wanting to share Christmas with someone, a telephone link being better than nothing. As she flipped through the pages of her personal phone book, Diana realized how few friends she now had. A number of her former close friends who had helped her through many crises during her marriage had faded from the scene. Kate Menzies, daughter of a wealthy Scottish family, Catherine Soames, the ex-wife of the Armed Forces Minister Nicholas Soames, and Julia Samuel, wife of banker Michael Samuel, were three of Diana's staunchest allies who had helped her through her marriage breakdown and separation. They would see Diana three or four times a week, take her to lunch, give parties for her, introduce her to friends. But during the past twelve months they had hardly been in evidence.

The three remained good friends, but Diana had moved away from them. Indeed, to the surprise of many, Diana was in Lahore, Pakistan, in February 1996 when Kate Menzies, once Diana's closest friend, married her longtime lover, restaurateur Simon Slater, who had also been counted among the Diana set of the early 1990s. A year earlier Diana would have been the principal guest at their wedding. But the relationships that had supported Diana in her hours of need had withered and died.

Diana knew the truth. A friend explained, "All Diana would ever talk about was her personal life, her problems, the misery of her marriage. It simply became too much for them. They had tried to help Diana in every way possible, but the Princess only had one topic conversation, herself."

However, she would make one important call that Christmas: to Susie Orbach, the woman who had in the past helped Diana battle her bulimia.

Almost in tears Diana asked whether it would be possible to see her the next day, Boxing Day, although she realized full well it would be a great imposition. Diana explained that Christmas had become a crisis that she could not cope with alone. But the person who had given Diana so much support and advice would never for a moment turn down such a cri de coeur. And the following day Diana drove over to Susie's house for an hour-long session.

Diana had needed Susie's expert help for some time. She had come to rely on Susie, to trust her, in a way that she had never been able to trust any other therapist. For Susie gave Diana the vital part of her character she had lost as a child and never regained, her self-confidence. In the eighteen months she had been treating Diana, Susie had succeeded in guiding her royal patient in her metamorphosis from victim to the almost mythical strongwoman she appeared to be in her famous hour-long television interview in November 1995.

Her Christmas crisis had, once again, been a question of confidence. The sense of elation she had felt following her sensational television interview had evaporated within weeks, leaving her demoralized, physically shaken, her confidence shattered as she realized all she had been striving to achieve had gone awry.

Only a month earlier Diana had given her extraordinary and moving interview to the BBC *Panorama* program in which she talked of her postnatal depression and bulimia, her miserable marriage, and her adultery with an Army officer. She pulled no punches in attacking the Royal Family and the Establishment while casting doubt on Charles's willingness to become king. She had also demanded that she be given a new wide-ranging ambassadorial role for Britain, arguing that she wanted to become "queen of people's hearts" rather than queen of England.

Princess Diana was determined to adopt that role whether or not she received permission from the Queen or the Foreign Office. She believes she has a unique ability to comfort the dying, the ill, the disadvantaged, and the homeless. In her interview, Diana had revealed an almost saintly image, amplifying the nation's concept of her as a generous and suffering young woman.

Within days of her interview twelve thousand people had written to her almost all supporting her decision to speak out about her life, her marriage, her adultery, and her bid to become a royal ambassador. Diana had thrown down the gauntlet in a way that surprised not only the courtiers, who never believed she would have the courage or the gall to challenge their authority, but also Prince Charles and other members of the Royal Family, who were quietly seething at Diana's obvious intention of causing as much trouble as possible.

"Now they know what I really want," she said after her BBC interview, a steely determination in her voice. "Now they know I mean business. And they know that I won't go quietly."

This was the Diana the world never sees. She all but spat out the words, and the look in her eyes told those to whom she was speaking that most of the nation and the Royal Family had totally misjudged the sweet, innocent virgin who had made such a shy impression on everyone sixteen years before. But that was the young Diana, before her miserable, loveless marriage and her years of incarceration, of isolation and loneliness in a royal palace.

Only Charles, some of her staff, and some close palace aides know the real Diana. The great majority of people believe the Princess of Wales to be the innocent victim of a broken home and a tragic marriage, her husband cheating on her, sleeping with his old mistress before the ink was dry on the marriage certificate. They understand Diana's cries for love and emotional security fell on the closed ears of the hard, unyielding Royal House of Windsor, committing her to the depths of despair, postnatal depression, and bulimia.

But Diana is no longer an innocent.

A few days after her BBC interview, when Diana spoke of her midnight visits to the sick and dying, she was on a high, convinced that by her interview she had outwitted Charles, the Queen, Philip, and their senior courtiers and would soon realize her ambition of becoming a royal ambassador, touring the world as "queen of people's hearts."

"I've got them on the run," she would jubilantly say. "I'm winning. They can't refuse me this time, they can't refuse me now."

So determined had Diana become to achieve her ambition that she began to make claims that did not bear scrutiny.

Shortly before midnight, on a cool, late November night in 1995, a dark blue BMW convertible drew up outside the Royal Brompton Hospital in West London. At the wheel sat Diana in jeans, a pink top, and a blue baseball hat with the numbers 492 emblazoned in white. She parked her car, clambered out, locked the vehicle, and walked toward the main entrance as two photographers approached from the darkness. She smiled happily as she stopped to talk to them.

Chatting to photographers was quite extraordinary behavior for the Princess of Wales for she usually walks on past them, often with her head down making it more difficult for them to get the shot they want. For years photographers have been the bane of her life, following her every step in public, and never ceasing to take pictures of her wherever and whenever possible. This November night, however, Diana not only stopped and posed for the photographers but waited while one of them answered a call on his mobile phone.

"Who is it?" she inquired.

"Our royal reporter," he replied.

"Could I have a word with him?"

The photographers were taken aback once more for the Princess of Wales never gives impromptu interviews to journalists on the streets.

"Yes, I'm sure he would be only too happy," the photographer replied, handing over the phone.

Diana at first asked the reporter from Rupert Murdoch's Sunday tabloid the *News of the World* not to mention the name of the hospital she was visiting, then happily chatted for a few minutes. It would be one of the most bizarre interviews Diana had ever given, for she will never even answer reporters' questions, let alone volunteer to talk.

She explained that she was in the habit of making midnight visits, on the spur of the moment, to several London hospitals two or three times each week, spending three or four hours a night chatting to sick and dying patients: "I hold their hands. I talk to them, tell them that everyone is on their side. Whatever helps."

The patients were total strangers. "They are not people that I know but they all need someone," Diana said. "I try to be there for them."

The tip-off to the *News of the World* that the Princess would visit one of two hospitals late that night came earlier in the day from a woman who said she was calling from Kensington Palace. When asked for name or more details, she hung up.

It seemed extraordinary that such information should have come from Kensington Palace unless Diana herself ordered the call to be made. The idea that the Princess of Wales would spend three or four hours a night, from 11 P.M. until 3 A.M., three times a week, walking around darkened hospital wards waking total strangers for a chat seemed most bizarre.

In Britain today, where there are usually between six and twenty-four patients in any single ward, hospitals only employ skeleton staff at night. Most patients are sound asleep around midnight, and even close relatives of the dying are not encouraged to spend those hours at their loved one's bedside chatting away for fear of disturbing other patients.

Diana had been photographed that November night outside the Royal Brompton Hospital at 11 P.M., saying she would be spending some hours inside. She was seen to return to her car parked in a side street outside the hospital four hours later, but she had not been visiting any patients in the hospital. In fact, she had not even been in the hospital but was visiting an old friend who lived nearby.

"We have no record whatsoever of the Princess of Wales visiting this hospital at that time," said a hospital spokesman.

"In fact we have no record of the Princess ever visiting this hospital late at night or during the early hours of the morning. It is not something that we would encourage."

Two other major hospitals in the immediate area, the Royal Marsden, where Diana is the president, and the Chelsea and Westminster, which handles 20 percent of the entire nation's HIV and AIDS cases, also had no record of the Princess of Wales visiting that or on any other night. Hospital authorities, doctors, and the Royal College of Nursing found the idea of Diana's midnight visits somewhat strange and hard to believe. Yet such was the mood of the country at that time, supporting Diana in her quest to bring comfort to the sick and disadvantaged, that her story of nocturnal hospital visits was taken as yet another example of her angelic character.

Some newspapers invited readers to phone with details of friends or relatives who had woken from surgery to find Diana at their bedside, helping and comforting them. None phoned.

This naive idea would be part of Diana's plan to seize and keep the initiative, to confuse the Royal Family's senior courtiers, forcing them to accommodate her demands, rather than finding ways to deflect her determination to become a roving ambassador. On this occasion, however, she was simply acting on the spur of the moment without thinking through what she said. Very ill patients do not need total strangers, not even the Princess of Wales, to comfort them, especially since many would be recovering in intensive care beds. Their great need would be expert nursing.

One week later Diana would continue pressing her claims to be taken seriously, speaking out stridently and emotionally in support of the homeless. This time, however, she would go too far upsetting cabinet ministers for what seemed to be her wholehearted support of a Labour attack on government policies. Some ministers were furious, accusing Diana of "meddling" in politics. She even warmly applauded the shadow home secretary, Jack Straw, who appeared on the same platform that day attacking the government's policy toward the homeless. There is a strict rule that members of the Royal Family stay totally clear of politics, on all occasions.

Diana gave her speech at the annual meeting of Centrepoint, the youth housing charity where two years before she had made her sensational announcement of her withdrawal from public life.

In her 1995 speech she said with much conviction in her voice, "Society must ensure young people are given the chance they deserve. I have listened to many young people whose lives have been blighted by their experiences. Teenagers are forced to resort to begging, or worse, prostitution, to get money in order to eat.... It is truly tragic to see the total waste of so many young lives, of so much potential. We, as part of society, must ensure that young people, who are our future, are given the chance they deserve."

Within hours of making her Centrepoint speech, Prime Minister John Major was forced to defend the government's housing policy during question time in the House of Commons.

Tory members of Parliament were angry that the Princess of Wales had become involved in political controversy, sharing a platform with someone clearly trying to score political points. Diana had not even cleared her speech with ministers, earning herself another bad mark. One outraged Tory MP, Sir Patrick Cormack, said, "We now have the Princess, who is a rather headstrong and willful young lady, on a platform in a preelection period on a highly contentious subject with a highly partisan politician. It is very, very unwise and it undermines the constitutional neutrality of the monarchy."

Most Tory newspapers used Diana's speech to point out her naïveté and lack of political skill, emphasizing that the Princess of Wales has no training in politics or diplomacy and should therefore not be permitted to carry out any ambassadorial role.

Diana would read the criticism with horror, realizing that she had made a serious mistake. She called her secretary, the much-maligned Patrick Jephson, into her room. "Why the hell didn't you warn me," she screamed at him. "You read the speech and you let me make it, you idiot. Now look what you've done."

The tirade would continue, off and on, through the day as Diana repeatedly reread the criticism and realized that one speech could have ruined everything she had worked for during the previous six months.

"Shit, shit, shit," Diana would be heard repeating as she stormed around her apartment. She would remain in a furious mood throughout the day.

Diana's mood swings are legendary in Kensington Palace. She will appear happy and relaxed one minute, joking and laughing with staff; the next moment Diana will change, a flash of anger will cross her face, and she will turn on whoever has upset her. Diana will yell at her personal dressers, at maids, at office staff; no one will be spared her venom.

Staff will know there is no point in arguing with the Princess of Wales when she is in that mood. Any reply will be met with a tirade of abuse from Diana, peppered with coarse words.

When Princess Diana had only been married a matter of months, she would ask one of her senior secretaries, half-laughingly, "Do you think I'm a bitch?"

"No, not at all," came the genuine and honest reply.

"Do you think I ever will be?"

"Yes."

"Why do you say that?" Diana asked, disappointed, yet she seemed eager for the answer.

"Because this is your life now. When you have had some years of having everything you want, whenever you want it, when you understand that if you want a car at midnight, one will arrive, when you know that you can give any order to anyone and that order will be instantly obeyed, you will not be able to stop yourself becoming a bitch."

"But I'm not a bitch yet?"

"Not yet."

"Thank you," Diana said. "I'll try to remember that."

Some who work close to Diana believe that she may now have earned that singularly brutal accolade. But she has never again questioned the man with whom she had that conversation back in the early 1980s.

She knows that Prince Charles thinks she is a bitch. During their warring days Charles would call Diana a "bitch" when the going became rough, and Diana hated the description. In return she would usually call him a "shit" or a "bastard," nearly always for the same reason—deserting her and the boys to run off to his mistress.

But the sledgehammer that felled Diana and crushed her self-assurance came in a personal letter from the Queen delivered to her by hand at Kensington Palace a week before Christmas. Though written elegantly, diplomatically, and sympathetically the letter in fact demanded an immediate divorce.

Diana's first reaction was fury that the Queen, the grandmother of Wills and Harry, would write such a letter to her hours before the boys' Christmas holidays. Throughout their most acrimonious battles, both Charles and Diana had tried to keep their marital rows away from their sons. At boarding school both boys were protected, to a certain extent, from the acres of column inches in the newspapers detailing the latest juicy revelations of both Charles and Diana.

Now the Queen had sent letters demanding a divorce that she knew would be splashed over every newspaper, would be read and reread on every television and radio news bulletin for days, exposing Wills and Harry to the publicity from which Diana had sought to shield them.

"How could she do such a thing?" Diana cried in anger in her office. "She knew the boys were breaking up this week. How could she? And what a Christmas present for them, their parents' divorce, on the orders of their own grandmother."

Contemptuously Diana added in anger, "Have they no feelings? Have they no blood in their veins? My God, they make me sick."

Before she read the news and the comments in the papers, Diana knew that her BBC interview had brought about the ruthless riposte from the Queen, the Establishment, and the senior courtiers, many of whom had wanted Diana sidetracked for some time, away from the spotlight where she could do little or no damage to the monarchy.

Diana knew in her heart that the Queen's intervention into her marriage was an act of vengeance. For in her interview Diana had challenged the Queen, describing those ranged against her as "the enemy" and even expressing doubts that Charles would ever be king, in what was seen as the most extraordinary and damaging royal statement since the abdication of Edward VIII in 1937.

She knew from her own aides that Buckingham Palace had been so shocked, and the Queen and Philip so angry, by the vitriol in her interview that they had decided the time had come to move against the Princess of Wales fearing what further damage she might inflict on the crown. Yet Diana was still surprised by both the speed and the timing of their actions.

Before deciding to give her interview Diana had thought long and hard about whether she should go through with her plan. She had also determined how tough she should be in the statements she would make. In the end she decided to gamble all, to reveal her true feelings and her ambitions for the future, for she realized that she had nothing to lose.

She realized that England's Establishment, including the Queen and Prince Philip, would never permit her to be crowned Queen, and that she would be moved aside.

Diana had been forced to tape her interview secretly because she knew, from bitter experience, that the Queen and the Establishment would have prevented such an interview from ever being broadcast. She would say, "Everyone was shocked that I did it secretly, but I had no option. I had to tell everyone what had happened in my life, to tell them the truth, as well as trying to seek a role for myself, as a charity worker. I had tried carrying out that role before, but nearly every invitation I was handed was withdrawn at a later date, after pressure from the palace."

Of course Diana had known divorce would one day occur,

yet neither she nor Charles had ever raised the matter. Diana knew pressure had been on Charles for him to divorce her so that the Establishment could begin to create the gulf they believed necessary, so that when Queen Elizabeth died, Charles's sole right to become king would not be challenged or even questioned. But Diana had hoped a divorce could be postponed for perhaps three or five years. That was why she stated, categorically, in her interview that she did not want a divorce.

Her eldest son and the heir to the throne, young William, now nearly fourteen, had begun to study constitutional history and the monarchy in September 1995. Courtiers believe within a few years William will fully understand the role he will be called on to play one day, and that role will not include his mother.

"I know the game they're playing," she said to one of her new, close male friends before her BBC interview, later shown on ABC in the United States. "I know they will freeze me out if they can. Well, they might have another think coming. It might not be that easy."

The nation perceives a rivalry between Diana and Charles as they campaign for the hearts of the people. But Diana knows she wins those battles with ease. The overwhelming majority of British people are not only convinced that Charles is responsible for the breakdown of their marriage, but that Diana is totally innocent of any wrongdoing.

Senior Tories and members of the Establishment believe the monarchy to be severely damaged by the continued warfare between the two. They perceive that Charles's office wages a subtle, dignified but rather sly campaign against Diana while she confronts them head-on, taking the war to the enemy, challenging Charles and the Queen publicly, on the streets, on TV, and in the media. Thus far, Diana has won the propaganda war with ease, a point that infuriates Buckingham Palace officials, who seem unable to dampen her ever-growing popularity.

While Diana took her eighteen-month sabbatical away from

the limelight to recharge her batteries, Charles was busy
creating a new image for himself, increasing his staff and
advisers, and completely filling his appointment diary. Quietly
Charles set about rehabilitating himself and his tarnished
relationship with the people who will one day be his subjects.

But the last few years of strain and emotional turmoil have
taken their toll. At forty-seven he appears more careworn, the
face thinner, the furrows deeper; the face has noticeably aged
during the past two years. And he seems to smile far less, the
laugh more forced. In December 1995, Prince Charles began
visiting a well-known, highly respected psychiatrist, Dr. Alan
McGlashan, in London's West End. But his aides would not
confirm, deny, or comment on the visits, leaving the public to
judge for themselves if they believed the heir to the throne now
required the assistance of a psychiatrist, following in the
footsteps of Diana, who had sought psychiatric help when her
marriage was in turmoil.

And Charles has taken heed of Diana's remarkable success
with ordinary people, those with whom Charles had never felt
at ease and found great difficulty in establishing a natural
rapport. His humor would appear forced, his demeanor awkward, his habit of constantly holding the cuff of his sleeve
revealing how uncomfortable he felt. Now, Charles has lost his
hesitancy and has become more friendly and understanding,
particularly with the young people he meets. One of the reasons
is the hugely successful Prince's Trust, a charity for the young,
unemployed, and disadvantaged, including many teenagers,
which he launched ten years ago and which has created twenty-
five thousand small businesses across the nation.

Prince Charles spends at least one day every week with the
Prince's Trust and the directors who run it, still personally
involved with selecting many of the projects the Trust supports
and funds. Those thousands who have received grants from the
Trust—mostly funded by big business—all agree their involvement with Charles has brought pleasure, hope, and fulfillment.
Yet, the world hears little about them and the national TV
stations and newspapers virtually never mention them.

Diana, on the other hand, knows full well that she only has to step out of Kensington Palace, walk down a street, visit a hospital, pick up an ill child, and her photograph will be blazoned across the front page of every tabloid in the land.

Today, however, Diana has no sympathy for her husband. "He will get everything he deserves," Diana told a family friend whom she visits frequently. "He behaved like a shit and I will never forgive him nor will I ever forgive that bitch Camilla."

After Camilla and her husband, Brig. Andrew Parker Bowles, announced their divorce in January 1995, Diana commented, "Now wait and see what happens. In no time she will be seen in public on Charles's arm. She has been out to catch him for years and she thinks she has all but succeeded."

Every photograph of Camilla in the newspapers would be seen and commented on by Diana. Camilla dieted, changed her hairstyle, wore smarter outfits, appeared more in public, and began visiting Scotland for short breaks with Charles and stayed openly at Charles's country home, Highgrove. Diana would watch every move like a hawk, and her comments would emphasize the bitterness she feels toward the woman she believes stole her husband.

Despite her increasing number of public appearances where Diana, quite often, looks stunning, the charity work where she looks concerned and caring, the official engagements where Diana now appears serious and attentive, and her daily workouts at the gym where she looks fit and healthy, there is nevertheless an undercurrent of worry felt by those who know her well.

Diana will still burst into tears for no apparent reason, still purse her lips when her confidence wanes, and will look lost when in a gathering of people, many of whom will be her friends. With her boys away at boarding school, her sisters away from London with their families, her mother in Scotland, Diana seems only to become involved with people with whom she can hide, never wanting to be seen with them in public where she could exude some confidence and appear as a loving person in a wholesome, fulfilling relationship.

Ever since the public became fully aware of her life estranged from Charles, Diana has cut a lonely, unhappy figure. Her public persona now seems more forced, the smile less natural, her behavior and body language more deliberate and less spontaneous. It is not surprising. At home, in the privacy of the palace, she will frequently become distraught, crying in anger and frustration at her unhappiness, believing that no one really cares for her and loves her, save for the public at large.

For the past two years Diana has faced an unenviable dilemma to which only now she believes she may have found a partial answer. She may be unhappy with her present circumstances, but she has no clear sense of direction for her future. Her situation is exacerbated because she has no male or female role model or mentor to guide and advise her. Following her father's death, she seems to have grown apart from her mother, Mrs. Frances Shand Kydd, and also from her brother, Charles, the Earl of Spencer.

Perhaps this failure to chart a new direction is leading her to erratic behavior and swift changes of mood. On some days Diana will now speak with enthusiasm about her pending divorce or talk of seeking a new life outside Kensington Palace. On other occasions she will stridently refuse to take part in any divorce talks with her lawyers and tell them she has no intention of leaving Kensington Palace.

In the same vein she will request no public duties for a particular week and then, overcome by anxiety, change her mind, deciding to visit one or two of her charities. She often changes her mind because she suddenly feels lonely and knows that seeking out the public, feeling their respect and admiration, will give her back the self-confidence she still frequently finds slipping away.

At times she feels living in the country would give her a new perspective, away from the cameras and the bright lights. She will be happily discussing this idea with someone and then immediately change her mind, saying, "That's a stupid idea. I could never live outside London. I would be so terribly lonely and utterly bored."

Another example of her swift changes of plan occurred in December 1995. She had announced that, as in the previous two years, she would accept the Queen's invitation to spend twenty-four hours at Sandringham with the Royal Family. Everything had been arranged when, exactly one week before Christmas, Diana decided that she didn't want to spend any time at Sandringham and told the Queen she would simply arrive with her sons on Christmas Eve and drop them, returning immediately to London.

It was typical Diana. It is part of her nature to react instantly to events and situations. One of the bugbears of royal life, which caused her real problems, had been coming to terms with royal protocol, the necessity of keeping appointments, come what may, always arriving on the day, at the exact time, dressed correctly for the occasion, at the spot that had been decreed months before. And always smiling and looking happy and cheerful no matter how awful she felt.

Now Diana is living through what she refers to as "her twilight period," not absolutely sure what she wants to do with the rest of her life, not certain that she wants another man to marry because her first husband made her life so miserable.

Within minutes of receiving his letter from his mother urging a swift divorce, Charles had issued a statement agreeing with his mother's suggestion, relieved that she had taken the responsibility of urging a divorce. Charles's immediate acquiescence surprised Diana for her husband had never once mentioned to her that he was seeking a divorce, only a separation.

"He has never said no to his mother in his life," Diana said scathingly after reading the news in the press. "Typical that he has to get his mother to carry out his dirty work."

Diana had always known that her bid to keep the marriage intact, though in name only, would end one day. But she didn't believe even the Queen would be so ruthless as to demand an immediate divorce when Diana had explained to her on numerous occasions that she thought it better for Wills and Harry if they were a few years older and better able to cope with their parents' divorce.

She knew the "gray men," as she called them, had wanted
her out of the way, removing her from the family and the
monarchy so that her influence and popularity would slowly
but inexorably diminish. Now she knows that they have got rid
of her officially, but she is determined that her influence and her
presence will be felt for many years to come.

# 2

# A Furious Diana

─────◦◦◦◦◦─────

From the moment of her separation from Prince Charles in December 1992, Diana flew the royal nest, putting space between herself and Charles and the House of Windsor. During her first year of freedom she felt constricted by the requirements of the occasional royal duty, but continued her ever-increasing number of charity commitments. She wasn't quite sure what role she should play or how independent of the Royal Family she should become.

The separation had made Diana realize for the first time ever the burden of duty that she had had to accept as a Royal. Previously, she had never fully understood the strict code of duty that made Charles seem so distant and disciplined, but had believed, perhaps naively, that her life, as a wife to the heir to the throne and a mother to two young princes, would never be subject to the same strictures of royal life.

During those first blissful five months in 1981 as she prepared for her fairy-tale wedding to her beloved Charles, Diana had been too involved with her new royal life to realize just how much time Charles had to spend attending to his numerous royal duties. She had accepted that he would kiss her goodbye each morning and maybe return during the day, but more often than not, he would leave her again in the evening to attend some royal function.

She didn't realize that he had the Duchy of Cornwall to run, in itself a multimillion-dollar estate; speeches to write; the

Prince's Trust to organize as well as an ever-increasing work-load as he took over more official tasks from his mother's heavy schedule. Diana had been blind to the pressures on his time and his lifestyle because she had been swept off her feet, infatuated, some thought obsessed, by the man she believed could do no wrong.

However, only a matter of months later, after she discovered she was pregnant, Diana found that she needed Charles around her far more than before the wedding. She could not understand how a man who loved his wife could leave her to attend to some boring royal duty when she so obviously wanted him to be with her. During Diana's first pregnancy the principal issue that would destroy their marriage began to emerge. The second vital issue, the reemergence of his mistress Camilla, would occur some months after the birth of Prince Harry.

Charles's understanding of and commitment to duty had been drilled into him since birth. He knew that he had to live up to the motto of the Prince of Wales, *Ich Dien* (I serve), whatever else happened in his life. Duty would be paramount, above marriage, fatherhood, or family. Diana would never understand that Charles lived by that code of conduct, as later she, too, would be expected to do.

But Diana had not been brought up in such a strict regime. She had been allowed to run free, though not wild, during her childhood and teenage years with little discipline in her life and no duties. When Diana was only six years old, her mother, Frances, had fled the family home, meaning that Diana had grown up with no maternal influence, a severe handicap for someone who would be expected, without argument or dissension, to put duty to the crown above all other considerations for the rest of her life.

Diana's understanding of life as a member of the Royal Family would be seen at close hand by Michael Colborne, who had served with Prince Charles in the Royal Navy for four years and then worked in his private office for six years. When Diana married, Charles asked Colborne to become her secretary to teach her the ways of royal life. He stayed in the job for three years.

"Throughout those years the Princess of Wales never seemed to understand that being a member of the Royal Family meant that duty came before everything else," Colborne said. "She did not understand that Charles had no option but to carry out his duties. It would never enter his mind that he ever had an option, but Diana could not understand how the Prince of Wales could not do whatever he wished. She could not grasp that Charles's life was far more disciplined and ordered than anyone else in the entire kingdom. He couldn't say no, he couldn't do what he wanted for duty came first.

"And that is what lead to the rows and arguments, the tears and the tantrums that eventually ended with the breakup of the marriage."

Colborne would witness their close, loving relationship fall apart when Diana realized that she, too, would have to put duty before all else. "Nearly all the rows that I witnessed were about the fact that Diana didn't see why she and Charles should carry out whatever was in the day's diary of events, come what may. That the only exception would be illness, but not simply a cold or cough, and never a diplomatic illness.

"Diana's objection to carrying out royal duties would escalate from discussion to argument to tantrums and, finally, to a total refusal to take part. No matter what I said or tried to explain, or what other senior courtiers suggested or Charles tried to explain, Diana would never accept that duty came before her wishes."

That basic failure to accept duty as paramount was also one of the reasons why Diana accepted Charles's request for a legal separation, though initially she felt panicked by it. They both knew their marriage had ended sometime in 1987 when they stopped sharing a bed. Diana was angry and mortified that Charles had left her to return to Camilla, a woman who she believed had behaved like a snake, deliberately ruining their marriage so that she could have Charles for herself. Diana's desperate unhappiness and her need for emotional security, someone to love her, had driven her into the arms and the bed of Capt. James Hewitt in that same year, 1987.

But when Charles finally suggested to her that they should separate, Diana didn't argue for she had been expecting that suggestion for two or three years, though she had never asked for a separation nor demanded one, not even in her wildest moments of anger. She believed that remaining the Princess of Wales would keep her closer to her sons and would mean she had more say in their schooling and upbringing. And she feared that without her around, the boys would lack the warmth of a mother's love, something she holds so dear because of her own horrid childhood when her mother left her husband and children. She only asked what would happen to her and the boys for she had no idea what the estranged wife of the Prince of Wales was supposed to do, how she was supposed to live or behave.

"Don't worry," Charles had told her, "you and the boys will not be thrown out of KP [Kensington Palace] to fend for yourselves."

He then explained that nothing would alter in her life nor in the lives of the boys. She would still live at Kensington, still have the same staff, the same privileges, and would retain her title. He assured her that she would continue to enjoy the same financial arrangements as before. Understandably, Diana felt relieved.

And there would be some positive benefits from a separation. She knew that by separating from Charles she would escape the awesome burden of royal duties, most of which she had come to hate. Diana hoped that being free of the Royal Family would permit her to live the life she wanted, enjoying as much time as possible with her growing sons, carrying out charitable duties whenever she desired.

She had not, however, considered the other pressures that would crowd her single life. Pressure from the media became almost unbearable as they eagerly sought to chronicle every waking moment of Diana's new life as a single mother. In Diana's eyes her decision to live a life apart from Charles had been taken by the media to mean she could be pursued and photographed, constantly asked for comments and sound bites, making her life miserable.

"Please, please leave me alone," Diana would plead as the paparazzi followed her down a street, off shopping, driving in her car, or out with her children, forever clicking away as she arrived or left any event, whether public or private. Sometimes they might oblige by leaving her alone for a day or more, but they would return with a vengeance.

"Oh, come on Di," they would call. "Just one picture, Di." "Smile, Di, for God's sake give us a smile." "Just one more, Di." The demands for her to pose for pictures never ended.

She understood that their primary interest was to photograph her chatting or meeting, dining or even walking, with a new man, a potential lover. Diana would occasionally meet old friends, both male and female, but she took the greatest care to ensure she was not caught in any compromising situations. Throughout her three-year affair with James Hewitt, the great might of Fleet Street and the cunning paparazzi had never caught her with him. She was equally determined that they would never catch her with any other lover.

Diana believed that Charles and the Royal Family as a whole had decided the monarchy would be better off without the woman they viewed as a potential "basket case," someone in whom they could never have faith or confidence. A separation had been agreed to in secret conversations among the Queen, Prince Charles, and senior courtiers. Of course, constitutional lawyers had been consulted and had offered their opinions. They were invited to suggest if the separation and possible future divorce would cause any problems for the crown. Diana had been totally unaware of these deliberations. She was never consulted and was only informed after agreement had been reached. To Diana, it seemed extraordinary, unfair, and hurtful that after twelve years of marriage she was not even entitled or permitted to be included in such discussions.

In the autumn of 1992, Sir Robert Fellowes, the Queen's private secretary, had talked to Diana, explaining the legal process and also informing her that she would still continue to be the Princess of Wales, still live at Kensington Palace, and still enjoy all the privileges that she had since the day she married.

Later, Diana would say to one of her older female friends, "I was not surprised but yet I was still taken aback by what I was being told. It's not very nice simply to be informed that you are to be separated from your husband, that you have no say, no rights, that your opinions are not sought on any matter. I just said thank you and walked out. In a matter of minutes my whole life had been shattered, but it was none of my doing. I had been cast aside, thrown out like an old coat. I felt sick, physically sick with fear and apprehension."

She stayed at home in Kensington Palace that night and the tears never ceased as she contemplated a life with no family. She wondered whether Charles and the Establishment would now try to have her removed from the palace and, worse still, whether they would try to restrict her access to the boys. The very thought brought more tears. That night she kept trying to reassure herself. "They can't do that," she would repeat in front of a group of people who had come to visit. "Charles wouldn't be that cruel."

And yet there was a nagging suspicion at the back of her mind that, though she doubted Charles would try to keep her sons, she knew others in Buckingham Palace might argue that it might be better for the boys if they were taken away from the influence of their mother because, as they would say, she is rather unstable. And she knew Charles did not have the backbone to fight such a move. Diana had on too many occasions witnessed Charles agreeing totally with something his mother had said, and yet she had known that, in his heart, he took a diametrically opposed view of the matter. Charles would never disobey his mother.

Diana would phone Charles to reassure herself that her worries were unfounded, and he did try to reassure her. In essence, he said, nothing would change. He also confirmed that he would never, under any circumstances, refuse her access to William and Harry and tried to reassure her that the suggestion had never even been discussed. Somehow Diana managed to push all these worries and fears to the back of her mind as she realized she had to get on with her life. That weekend she saw the boys, then aged ten and eight, and loved every moment she spent with them.

"I found myself wanting to hug and kiss them all the time," she confessed later. "But they have rather passed that stage. I kept reminding myself that they were nearly young men who didn't want to be kissed and hugged by their mother too much."

She had hoped the separation would give her a freedom she hadn't known since becoming engaged to Charles in 1981, twelve years before, free from the constant pressures on her life as a public figure. That brief illusion disappeared the first time she set foot outside Kensington Palace. From that moment the pressure intensified until she felt she had no life of her own and precious little privacy except when closeted inside the palace, her luxurious ivory tower, which had become a prison for Diana. Understandably, she became fed up, frustrated, and dejected with her restricted life and, a year later, in December 1993, made her famous announcement that she was reducing her time spent in public life.

Diana was trying to regain some privacy while removing herself from the strictures of royal life. One of her first actions would be to fire her ever-present armed police bodyguard. The Royal Protection Squad guards all members of the Royal Family, and these bodyguards had become Diana's shadows ever since her engagement to Charles in February 1981. She had never grown used to their presence and hated the fact she was never permitted to go anywhere alone. Their presence had quickly become another royal shackle she ended up hating with a passion. On occasions, Diana would plead with them, in her inimitable doleful manner, to let her go shopping, to walk down a country lane alone, or drive in her car. Every time the answer would be the same: "You know, ma'am, that we are not permitted to leave you alone, not for one moment."

Despite warning of the possible dangers from courtiers at

Buckingham Palace and senior police officers, Diana dismissed her bodyguards. The Princess of Wales felt like a new woman, freer and happier, able to do what she wanted whenever. She did, however, tell her girlfriends how awful it had been to always have a police officer at your side. And with a smile she added, "Whatever you do, don't even think of marrying a prince. It's not worth it. Take it from me. For if you do, your life will never again be your own."

From January 1, 1994—the date Diana decided to become truly independent—the Princess of Wales all but changed her official identity. When she booked seats on flights or at the theater she would give her name as "Ms. D. Spencer," her maiden name. She wanted to remove all reference to the fact that she was Diana, the Princess of Wales, or a member of the Royal House of Windsor or that she was a married woman with two growing sons. She knew that writing *Ms.* would make people realize how independent she had become.

She would say, "I much prefer people to know me as my father's daughter, a member of the Spencer family, rather than being seen as some sort of appendage to the House of Windsor. People tend to forget that by using the name Ms. D. Spencer I am simply using my maiden name. Anyway, I prefer it to Windsor because that sounds so dreadfully pretentious."

Diana wants to have as little contact as possible with Prince Charles because of the marriage scars that have still not healed, despite the fact they have been living apart since 1987. During the years that followed they would undertake official royal duties together as the Prince and Princess of Wales, but Diana hated every second that she was forced to live that lie, pretending all was well with the marriage.

Today, Diana still finds it extremely difficult even to be pleasant toward Prince Charles. She feels a bitterness bordering on revulsion for she believes that the man she adored never really loved her. She felt that he cheated her, not just sexually, by continuing his affair with his old flame Camilla, but in a far more insulting way by pretending to love and cherish her.

At home one night at Kensington Palace, in the early 1990s,

Diana told one of her lovers, "I don't despise Charles because he went off and had an affair. I despise him because he lied to me and the boys. I don't believe he ever loved me and yet he made me think that he did. He deceived us, making a mockery of our marriage, and I felt ridiculed, betrayed by his duplicity. Any woman treated like that will tell you the pain is so destructive to one's confidence, one's relationship, and one's whole inner being. I felt eaten away inside."

As one of Charles's private secretaries recalled, "At one stage in the 1980s virtually every weekend they stayed down at Highgrove, there would be violent arguments, often ending with two or more flower vases being smashed, hurled in anger by Diana at her husband."

Diana first began throwing things at Charles one night in November 1982 at Kensington Palace when she decided at the last moment she didn't wish to attend the solemn Annual Festival of Remembrance at the Royal Albert Hall in honor of those who died in the two world wars. Diana walked down the stairs to a waiting Charles and announced, "I'm not going."

"What do you mean you're not going?" Charles asked.

"I mean that I'm not going. I'm fed up of being at everyone's beck and call. I'm not going."

Charles would attend the Festival of Remembrance, come what may. Charles looked at Diana in astonishment, for not only did her insistence shock him but he realized that both the Queen and Prince Philip would be there.

At first Charles tried to humor Diana. "Oh, come on, we've got no option. We have to go."

"I'm not going," she replied.

Charles quickly lost his temper. "Don't be so bloody silly. There's no question of not going. We have to go. Now come and get in the bloody car this instant."

"Don't you dare talk to me like that," Diana shouted.

"I'll talk to you how I like, especially if you're going to behave in such a bloody silly, childish way."

"Don't patronize me. You're behaving like a shit. Just go and leave me here."

"Don't be so bloody stupid," Charles yelled. "And get in the bloody car, now."

That did it. "Don't you ever speak to me like that," Diana said, and, bending down, took off her shoe and hurled it at Charles. The shoe missed Charles, hitting the wall.

"Right. This is your last chance because I have to go. We're late."

"I have no intention of going," Diana said, turning and walking up the stairs, "and I'm certainly not going with you."

On that occasion Charles left on his own, but Diana thought twice about her actions and arrived ten minutes later, causing quite a stir because her chair in the royal box had been discreetly removed. It was quickly replaced, but the media soon learned the truth: the Waleses had had some sort of tiff.

From that time on Diana took to hurling anything she could lay her hands on during heated arguments with Charles. And the more the marriage disintegrated the more severe were her physical attacks. She would throw shoes, books, glasses, magazines, and table mats, but her favorite items were flower vases.

One of Charles's staff at that time recalled listening to one Highgrove incident in 1985: "Charles and Diana were in the drawing room and I happened to be next door. I could hear raised voices, and then they became louder and Diana seemed to be becoming hysterical. On that occasion Charles, too, lost his temper. I cannot recall the reason for the argument. They both seemed to be hurling insults at each other, the air blue with swear words.

"Suddenly I heard Charles shout, 'No, don't, for God's sake, Diana, put it down.... No... don't be so bloody stupid.' Then I heard an almighty crash of glass splintering and realized she had thrown another vase at him.

"For a moment there was silence. Then Charles said in a shaky voice I could hardly hear, 'You must stop throwing things. That very nearly hit me.'

"The door flew open and a red-faced, angry Diana stormed out, running up the stairs to her room. I waited a couple of minutes, then went into the room. Charles was on the floor gently picking up the pieces of what had been a beautiful cut-glass vase. He said nothing but looked at me with a look of resignation on his face.

"'Can I help, sir?' I asked.

"'If you wouldn't mind,' he replied. And together we picked up all the pieces, which had splintered across half the room."

On another occasion, Charles would not be so fortunate. Diana herself told the story to one of her girlfriends: "He had made me so furious. He had spent hours on his own in his fucking garden and then came in and said he wanted to listen to some music on the radio. I had been down there mooching around Highgrove all day on my own with no one to speak to and he didn't care a damn. I just saw red and went for him. He turned to walk away and I picked up a vase and threw it with all my might at his back. It hit him on the back of the head and he just went down in a heap.

"I began to shake as I ran towards him believing I had killed him. The vase had shattered. I thought, 'Thank God it wasn't a heavy cut-glass one but only a porcelain vase.' I turned him over and he began moaning and I felt a wonderful sense of relief. But I was still shaking because I realized how near I had been to killing him. Charles came round and realized I had thrown a vase at him. He looked at me as if he would throttle me. I stood watching, not knowing whether to help, but he got to his feet, then immediately sat down on a chair holding his head in his hands, still stunned. I knew I had gone too far, but for an instant I thought I had killed him. He just went down and lay there, not moving."

Diana confessed that the shock stopped her from throwing anything at Charles for some months, but she did return to her favorite form of attack sometime later. Nothing remotely as serious ever happened again because Diana believes she no longer tried to hit Charles with any heavy object, just throwing them near him to frighten him into understanding how angry he had made her.

And Diana will also recall how cold Charles would act

toward her and the effect that had on her: "After the wonderful few months we spent together before the marriage, it seemed that after I became pregnant, three months after the wedding, Charles rarely came near me. The warmth he had shown evaporated, and I don't think it ever came back. That hurt. On occasions, of course, things were good, but never great again as they had been before the wedding."

The colder Charles acted toward Diana the more she yearned for someone to love her, but her need for a lover, a companion, a man who would care for her, would lead Diana into a number of unfortunate and embarrassing relationships.

# 3

## *Bold and Wild*

———— ❧ ————

AFTER DIANA DISCOVERED the truth about Camilla Parker Bowles, sometime in 1986, the gulf between Charles and Diana widened dramatically. Soon after, she fled into the arms of Capt. James Hewitt, a man who had shown her respect and kindness, who seemed to love her passionately and who offered to marry her and give her a baby. Diana had believed every word Hewitt had told her for she wanted to hear those sentiments. Above all, she needed love and someone to care for her.

When the affair with Hewitt ended three years later, Diana immediately began the search for another all-embracing relationship in which she could love and be loved. When that didn't occur, she would throw herself into some new sporting activity or pamper herself with some new therapy. She would tell herself that she could be happy on her own with no male companion.

But then, out of the blue, she would meet someone to whom she felt some attraction, some *simpatica*, and a new relationship would take off. The great majority fizzled after nothing more than a couple of dinners, or an invitation for drinks at Kensington Palace. She would suggest that she didn't need a man or a lover in her life. Those comments were a little white lie, for Diana has been keeping the proverbial eye open for the right man ever since her disastrous three-year affair with James Hewitt.

I have spoken to two men, both married, who admitted to having affairs with Diana in the early 1990s. Because they are still married, neither would talk unless I agreed to honor their anonymity. Both had remarkably similar stories to tell.

The first became Diana's lover in 1992. He was a former Cavalry officer, who worked in the City and had been married for some years. He first met Diana at a house party in the late 1980s. He recalled, "We were instantly attracted to each other. We flirted madly that first evening and we both agreed to see each other again. Of course I felt flattered that the Princess of Wales seemed to fancy me. Nothing happened and I thought it wrong to follow up such an involvement because she was married to the Prince of Wales. But we met by chance some years later, and with a glint in her eye, she invited me for drinks at KP. She knew I was married but it all seemed perfectly innocent.

"From the moment I walked into her drawing room it seemed obvious to me that Diana wanted a relationship. After a couple of drinks we went out to dinner to a little restaurant and kissed as soon as we returned to KP. We had more drinks, listened to romantic music, which Diana selected, and before midnight we were in each other's arms.

"She didn't want me to leave, but when I left, sometime after two A.M., I knew that we would become lovers. We arranged to meet early the following week. I arrived around ten P.M. and we had some wine and Diana rustled up a cold snack from the kitchen. We listened to music again, drank some more, and began kissing.

"Diana was unbelievable. I felt as though I had been hit by a hurricane. She left me absolutely breathless with her passion. We moved from the drawing room to the bedroom and we made love in her bed. I anticipated that she would want me to leave shortly afterwards, but she wanted me to stay. We must have made love four times in the next three hours, and she still didn't want me to leave her, as though frightened to be left alone. She kept pleading for me to stay with her, to make love to her again, and she seemed so fearful that I would leave her and she would be on her own. Finally, around five A.M. I did leave, exhausted, somewhat bewildered, and feeling rather guilty.

"Two weeks later we had another date, and I sensed from the first few moments that the evening would end up with the two of us making love again. We had a wonderful time fooling around in the drawing room, drinking and listening to music. She seemed on a wonderful high, laughing and giggling, looking shy and embarrassed and then becoming absolutely wild in her lovemaking, demanding more and more. But I didn't think it was me that she craved. It seemed that she had become desperate for company, and she wanted to share herself and her body with someone who would love her in return."

After several further visits to Kensington Palace, the man, three years older than Diana, felt the guilt of cheating on his wife and the Prince of Wales. He began to discuss his unease with Diana. "I don't want to know," she replied, "I don't want to know. All I want is you."

Two weeks later he decided the affair could not continue. He phoned Diana. "'I know what you're going to say,' she told me, 'I understand. Goodbye.' The phone went dead and I could not believe she could have become so dispassionate where she had been so romantic, so tender, and so demanding only a few days before."

In the summer of 1993, Diana met an older man, in his middle forties—about the same age as Charles—who attracted her greatly. They had seen each other on occasion during the past few years but had never really had the chance to talk. He was married with three children and worked as a banker in the City of London.

"We began to talk when we met at a cocktail party in 1993," he said, "and I found myself unbelievably attracted to her. I knew she was flirting with me, removing a hair from the shoulder of my jacket, asking me to find her a drink, offering me petit fours to eat, and one minute appearing shy, even coquettish, the next looking me straight in the eye as if daring me to kiss her.

"I wasn't sure how to react and whether this was the flirting Diana I had read about, the Princess who loves to tease, to toy, to play the vamp when talking to men she finds attractive. At the end of the evening Diana suggested that we should have lunch or dinner together to chat, and to get to know each other better.

"The encounter and her straightforward approach had surprised me, but I agreed. I wanted to find out more, to discover what made her tick and to see whether her apparent sexual interest was for real or simply a ruse to attract. I would soon discover that Diana's innocent appeal was no fantasy but the prelude to remarkable passion.

"Our affair lasted two months, during which time she proved a completely different person to the one I imagined. Diana would be both bold and wild and, at other times, gentle, loving, and sometimes tearful. What I found remarkable would be her passion, not just sexual, but in everyday matters that she felt important. I also noted an underlying bitterness towards Charles and the Royal Family in general, which surprised me. It seemed that she had been unable to forgive anything that had happened, continuing to feel cheated by Charles.

"At one point I wondered whether Diana was making love to me as a way of punishing Charles for his involvement with Camilla. It seemed that she wanted to make love to get her own back against Charles, and I began to feel that I was there to be used, as part of this macabre game she was playing in her mind. That feeling unnerved me, and although we had wonderful times together and Diana made me feel she wanted me emotionally as well as physically, I thought that whatever we had between us was not for real. I didn't like that.

"Diana must have sensed that, too, because the phone stopped ringing and my calls were no longer returned. We never actually ended the affair. We never said farewell or good luck. She just stopped phoning as though she knew the game was over and she wanted no further embarrassment. That is what I believed happened and I respected her wishes and never tried to contact her again. I just hope she manages to sort out her problems."

Diana had turned to sport, swimming, and playing tennis

so that she could burn away her excess energy while taking her mind off her search for the "ideal man."

Diana wondered whether she was searching for a father figure, who would replace the one person she had always loved and trusted, her father Viscount Johnny Althorp, who became Earl Spencer on the death of his father. Diana's father died in 1992, only months before her official separation. She knew she had always been attracted to older men, finding younger ones, such as her former lover James Hewitt, rather juvenile in their thinking.

Diana, however, bore no deep love for her mother. Diana had been too young to remember her really well for she had been only six years old when Frances Spencer had left her husband and their four children to live alone in London. From when she first understood what had happened, Diana would never wholly forgive her mother, even if she did try to understand why she had left her family for no apparent good reason.

Frances Spencer's second marriage in 1969 to Peter Shand Kydd, a paint millionaire, would also end in divorce some twenty years later. Frances would move to Scotland, open a gift shop, and settle down to a quiet, almost nunlike existence. She had a few friends and a few interests and a growing involvement with the Roman Catholic Church, which surprised Diana. In 1991, Frances sold the small Highland shop she had bought as an interest and an investment and, three years later, bought a larger house in the same area. The stone house had been a bed-and-breakfast residence, but Frances had no intention of taking in paying guests. She refurnished and redecorated the house and settled down to a quiet, rather lonely existence.

A year later Diana's mother announced her decision to embrace the Roman Catholic religion, having attended services at the Catholic cathedral in nearby Oban for six years. Diana wanted to find out more about the Roman Catholic faith to better understand her mother, whom she confesses she has never really understood. Some years earlier, Diana had met Dom Anthony Sutch, headmaster of Downside, Britain's pre-

mier Roman Catholic school, who had previously worked as a
layman in the hard-nosed City of London, and she asked if they
could meet in an effort to help her understand her mother's
interest in Catholicism. They would meet and talk privately on
a number of occasions.

Whatever had happened between her beloved, warmhearted
father and her high-spirited mother, Diana could never imagine
anything that could have been so terrible that her mother found
it necessary to walk out, leaving her husband and four small
children to fend for themselves. Diana never forgave her mother
for what she perceived had been an act of desertion, leaving her
elder sisters, Sarah and Jane, and her younger brother, Charles,
who was only three at the time. Despite the dramatic traumas in
her life, Diana has found it difficult to turn to her mother for
help or advice.

Diana had often wondered why both of her mother's
marriages had failed, and it worried her that her marriage to
Charles might have failed because of some flaw in her and her
mother's makeup, perhaps a weakness or a defect that made it
all but impossible for them to have long-term relationships. She
would try to put such thoughts to one side, dismissing them as
unwarranted, yet a doubt would always remain. She wondered
whether her mother's conversion from the Anglican religion to
Catholicism might in some way help her, and it crossed Diana's
mind that perhaps one day she, too, might convert.

Though Diana believes in God, she is not a religious person.
She doesn't say her prayers at night or in the morning; she
wouldn't go to church of her own volition, except to celebrate
Christmas, a wedding, or as a duty. She has not, until now,
thought too deeply about religion, but her mother's conversion
did make Diana wonder whether she might find some solace,
some peace of mind, in religion in her later years as she hopes
her mother has done.

At the time of her conversion, in October 1995, Frances
Shand Kydd said, "If Diana has inherited anything from me, I
hope it's what I was given in childhood by my father. He was
quite simply the most compassionate, caring, sensitive person I

have ever met. He would hold our hands and teach us about caring, literally. I tried to do that in bringing up my children, and I think Diana has the gift of compassion, and she uses it."

Frances Shand Kydd, however, would not succumb to Diana's charms. Many women have suggested that Frances and her daughter could not become close because they were so alike, and their personalities would clash.

A friend of Frances Shand Kydd's, an older woman, commented, "When they meet, they are fine together for the first couple of hours, but then, invariably, an argument will develop. They know each other too well. They pretend to get on when there are other people around, but they both know they could not live under the same roof for one minute. Many so-called experts have asked why Diana had never rushed to her mother for advice to talk over the traumas in her marriage or her dreadful eating problems. The reason is that Diana would, more than likely, have received short shrift from Frances if she had done so. Frances would have been tough on her daughter and probably told her to return immediately to her family, concentrate on enjoying life as the Princess of Wales, and make sure she was a good wife.

"It didn't matter that Frances had never been able to do that herself, but she knew that Diana should have bitten her lip and learned to enjoy the privileged life she had been handed on a plate. She also believed Diana had a duty as the mother to the heirs to the throne to stick with her marriage, come what may. Diana knew her mother would react like that to her appeals, and that was the reason she kept her distance."

It seemed that Diana's mother had deliberately moved herself out of the limelight and away from her children, and there were no reports of her being visited by any of her four children or grandchildren. The fact that Diana never enjoyed a close relationship with her mother meant there was no older woman to whom the Princess of Wales felt she could unburden her troubles, whether they were marital, emotional, or the disturbing eating problems she experienced.

Diana's various problems continued and so did her numerous disastrous love affairs, only some of which the media discovered. Diana knew full well that she had to find a new interest in life other than searching in vain for a new man. She searched for other avenues of escape and discovered that one of life's pleasures was spending money.

As a teenage bachelor girl both in the country and in London, Diana semingly didn't care about fashion or clothes. She was happy wearing jeans and a shirt, a long skirt and a sweater, and all her clothes fitted comfortably in a single wardrobe and a small chest of drawers.

Her grooming after marrying Charles changed, and after Wills and Harry were born, she found that shopping for clothes was rather fun. She had an American Express card that would automatically be paid every month by the Duchy of Cornwall no matter how much she had charged. Whenever she felt miserable, she would pop off to Harvey Nichols or Harrods to buy a little something to cheer herself up.

Then she grew more adventurous and her advisers, including some friends at *Vogue,* introduced her to different and more exciting designers. At first, she was persuaded to support British designers to help British export sales, but this, too, would change as she became her own woman and she would fall in love with a variety of European and American designers.

With her photograph appearing on magazine covers around the world Diana became more confident and her clothes more adventurous. Diana was spurred on by those who hailed her as a fashion leader of the Western world. She loved that accolade. Today, wherever she travels, whether in Britain or abroad, the fashion experts as well as ordinary young women love to examine what the Princess of Wales is wearing and, if possible, to emulate her.

For some years now Diana recognizes that she has become a fashion icon. Originally, under the tutelage of *Vogue* fashion experts and Buckingham Palace, Diana played for safety with Catherine Walker, Tomasz Starzewski, and Amanda Wakeley, who dressed her in long jackets, short skirts, and overelaborate evening gowns.

But from the moment of her separation Diana felt like a new person, who could wear whatever she wanted with no one to raise an eyebrow if she appeared with or without stockings in the summer, with no husband to approve what she wore for royal duties, with no mother-in-law to look disapprovingly if she stepped out of line.

But she would go to the other extreme, flirting with very short skirts, acres of thigh, and rather glitzy German-style designs, as though trying to show how daring the real Diana could be. Some women pointed out that Diana's new dress code seemed to be a rather immature way of showing any available man what was on offer.

Throughout most of 1994 it appeared Diana wanted to show off her legs at every possible opportunity, even, for example, when collecting her sons from school. She began donning skirts that split to the upper thigh and arrived at church on Christmas day wearing a split skirt.

It seemed that Diana had completely lost her magic touch of never making a fashion error, for her split skirts had been the rage of the fashion runways two years earlier in 1992. During the following twelve months the split skirt electrified Main Street sales, irresistibly combining the demure appearance and security of the maxi with the freedom of movement and sheer sex appeal of the mini. Twelve months later fashion-conscious women banned them from their wardrobes and moved on, for they realized the split skirt would, on windy days, reveal far more thigh than intended, sometimes exposing the wearer's panties. The fashionable declared the split skirt cheap-looking, unladylike, and too risky.

But Diana persisted, wearing the revealing skirts and reaping the criticism, even the opprobrium, of the fashion world. Some fashion writers believed Diana's persistence could only be attributed to her determination to return to the public arena with dramatic effect, making the most of her physical assets like any showgirl returning to the limelight.

Journalists recalled Diana's penchant for using her body when she wanted to upstage Charles, or to show the world what a great body he had left behind when he quit Kensington Palace for the tranquillity of Highgrove and a woman with none of the physical beauty Diana possessed. As an example, they recalled the night Charles confessed on television to his adultery with Camilla Parker Bowles, when Diana appeared at an art gallery wearing a revealing thigh-skimming, figure-hugging black cocktail dress. Diana knew she was inviting the media to compare the sexy, gorgeous Princess in a stunning number with the older, ample-framed Camilla, who would never have been able to get away with wearing such an outfit. It was a perfect counterattack, which was not lost on the rest of the world.

In Kensington Palace the following morning a happy Diana spread out all the morning newspapers, examining them in detail. Every paper, from the broadsheets to the tabloids, had printed Charles's confession on its front page alongside a photograph of a radiant, sexily clad Princess. "Look at that!" she said ecstatically a dozen times to her staff whom she invited to see the front pages. "Fantastic, great. He's always hated me upstaging him. That'll show him."

Though few understood the true psychological battle going on inside Diana's head, some remonstrated with her to return to her more demure, less sexy, but more alluring dress sense that had won her so many plaudits from the fashion world. Diana ignored their advice. She saw that the newspapers continued to print large photographs of her dressed in split skirts, high heels, and figure-hugging outfits. She would continue to wear a black suit adorned with gold elephants (an ensemble from the up-market German fashion house of Escada, a safari collection costing $1,600). Or she would squeeze into ultratight black leather trousers, sport stilettos under tight jeans and apply her makeup too obviously. On occasion Diana would wear a black belt whose buckle depicted a pair of elephants mating!

She was thirty and for the first time was able to wear what she wanted, when she wanted. And Diana wanted to experiment, to wear not only her British designers when she felt like it but also to explore foreign designers. She chose to wear

Chanel, Saint Laurent, Armani, Valentino, Escada, and her all-time favorite, Versace.

When Diana finds a dress that she loves, she will sometimes buy two or three of the same design, but in different colors. Despite some criticism, Diana believed that her famous white, Versace, figure-hugging number, with thigh-high hem and plunging neckline, made her look twenty-five again, so she bought another in black. She also bought three lizard clutch bags in red, yellow, and black ($1,800 each) from Asprey, the Bond Street jewelers, to ring the changes with the dresses. Some critics wondered whether Diana should be seen wearing the same dresses in different colors. Diana didn't care. She was convinced the dress looked stunning on her.

On occasion Anne Beckwith-Smith, her secretary for eight years and now her chief lady-in-waiting, will ask Diana if she thinks her choice of a particular outfit is really wise.

"Why not?" is Diana's usual reply. "What's wrong?"

Anne will reply that perhaps the outfit is not "entirely suitable" for whatever function the Princess is attending.

"Is it that bad?" Diana will ask.

"No, not that bad. But we've seen better."

"If it's not that bad, then I'm going to wear it." And more often than not Diana will add, "Anyway, if it shocks them at the palace, all to the good. It's what they need."

The fashion writers urged Diana to return to tailored suits and silk blouses, suggesting the stylish and simple fashions of Ralph Lauren, DKNY, or Nicole Farhi rather than expensive, ostentatious styles. But Diana had given away scores of her tailored suits, which she had worn on official royal duties before she quit the public stage. She invited seven girlfriends to Kensington Palace and told them to take their pick while Diana entertained their children with tea and cakes.

The fashion writers, however, openly attacked Diana, describing her as an "Essex girl," a manifestly rude, even insulting description, for Essex girls (from the County of Essex, near London) are ridiculed as having the worst manners, appalling bad taste, an addiction to cheap, flashy clothes, and no morals.

Initially, Diana dealt with such criticism by telling her friends, "They're just jealous. I take no notice. They have always criticized me, no matter what I wear." And Diana would mischievously give the single-finger sign, with some feeling in the upward thrust of her hand.

The upper-crust *Tatler* magazine even took up the cudgel of criticism, showing Diana wearing outfits similar to those of TV soap stars. "It proves that if you dress five years out of date you look 'dead common.'" The article continued, "There are times when Diana gets it right, when she can be marvellous but we have endured terrifying taste blunders. Take the appliquéd jumpers, the court shoes with jeans, the almost permed marmalade hair and flesh-colored pop-socks."

And in a vicious summing up, *Tatler* added, "Will the real Diana please sit down and dress like a princess."

That attack, written in March 1994, stung Diana to the quick. Photographs, deliberately selected for their shock appeal by the tabloids, showed Diana wearing a number of unflattering outfits. They also liked to show a photograph of Diana sitting in a straight-backed chair, in front of an audience, sporting a short skirt that revealed a great expanse of inner thigh and all but revealed her panties. This, they noted, was the same Princess who took exception to snatched pictures showing her dressed in a leotard and exercising at a gymnasium, the LA Fitness Club. On that occasion, Diana had been photographed, by a camera secreted in the ceiling by the club's owner, with her legs wide apart pulling on a rowing exercise machine.

The photographs, published in the tabloid *Daily Mirror,* angered Diana and she sued the newspaper and the club owner, a New Zealander, Bryce Taylor, for breach of confidence and breach of contract. She also won an injunction ordering them to hand over the photographs, copies, and negatives and never to reproduce them again.

Diana was determined to win the case and told her lawyer,

Lord Mischon, that she was eager to take the witness stand to defend her honor since some people had suggested she had deliberately posed for the shots. Diana was strongly advised to settle out of court. Her lawyers knew that a topflight barrister would quite likely have caused the Princess severe embarrassment by the type of questions she would have been called on to answer. Her advisers worried that Diana had no idea of the intense pressure involved in answering tough questioning for a number of hours. At the last moment, just days before the case was to be tried in February 1995, Diana accepted the advice and settled. If Diana had taken the stand, she would have been the first Royal to have done so for more than a century.

# 4

# *A New Man to Love*

~~~❧~~~

PRINCESS DIANA walked into the reception room at Windsor Castle during Ascot week in the summer of 1985 to meet the guests with whom she would be having lunch prior to that afternoon's racing at nearby Ascot. Every year Queen Elizabeth, a keen racing enthusiast, owner, and breeder, gives pre-race lunches at Windsor to which privileged guests are invited.

Standing in the light of a magnificent window overlooking the castle lawns, with the sun cascading into the room, Diana saw a young man, with rather long, dark, wavy hair, not very tall but dressed immaculately in a morning suit, the traditional Ascot dress. Diana looked again and noticed how handsome, relaxed, and friendly he seemed to be. Many in the room, most of them strangers to Diana, seemed nervous, not sure how to conduct themselves as they waited for the Queen to walk into the room.

But not this dark stranger. He smiled and laughed with the people who chatted with him. Diana noticed the laughter lines around his eyes and the twinkle in his eye and wondered who he was. By his side stood a young woman, perhaps a little older than Diana, who the Princess noted was most attractive and dressed in a beautiful silk, printed summer dress. She wondered whether they were married for they seemed eminently suited, both attractive, sophisticated, and at ease in the daunting surroundings of Windsor Castle. The man was Oliver Hoare, a millionaire art dealer, specializing in Iranian art and antiquities, then thirty-nine; the woman, his wife, Diane, then thirty-seven, the daughter of a French heiress, the Baroness Louise de Waldner, one of the Queen Mother's closest friends, who lived in a magnificent château in the heart of Provence in southern France.

Charles joined Diana, and accompanied by the Queen Mother, they went over to chat with Oliver Hoare and his wife. Diana remembers feeling rather shy when she shook Oliver's hand, not sure whether to look into his eyes, for they appeared so blue, attractive, and warm. She found herself looking into his eyes and smiled broadly, and he returned the smile.

Diana began talking to Diane and found they had much in common. Oliver and Diane had three children, two sons and a little girl, Olivia, then two. Prince Harry was then one year old. Diana recalls telling Diane that she would love one day to have a daughter, especially, like her, after two sons. The two women became quite close that day, neither terribly interested in the racing at Ascot, preferring to talk about other matters. Diane was of course well aware that Diana had a great interest in fashion, as she did, too.

The two men also chatted comfortably with each other. Charles would always attend the four days of racing at Ascot each year under some duress for he cannot abide the sport. However, he is under orders from the Queen to join her and chat with her guests. Charles would always leave before the last race so that he could prepare for the polo matches that are traditionally played at Windsor Great Park in the evening of Royal Ascot race days.

Charles, three years younger than Oliver, found him most interesting for when he discovered Oliver was an expert in Islamic art and antiques, the two had much to discuss. Charles was no great authority on Islamic art but had always been fascinated by the subject and was eager to learn more. Charles also rather appreciated Oliver's sophistication and air of confidence.

Oliver Hoare was born in July 1945, son of Reginald Hoare, a civil servant employed in the War Office in London. His mother, Irina, was a member of the Kroupensky family, who had come to Britain from Moravia, a onetime province of Czechoslovakia. In his family background Oliver Hoare could boast the Earl of Coventry, and distantly the famous Quaker Hoares, one of the families that had founded Barclays Bank, a major British bank. The Hoares, however, had little money and struggled to educate their children, though Oliver did finally attend Eton College, where Prince William now boards. When Hoare was only nineteen, and enjoying a student life at the Sorbonne in Paris, his father died suddenly, leaving exactly $2,500!

At that time many Iranians were living in Paris, and fortunately for Oliver, he came under the wing of a wealthy Iranian princess some years older than him, the famous Hamoush Azodi-Bowler, a woman who loved all forms of Islamic art. She would invite the handsome, dashing twenty-two-year-old student to study art in her Tehran mansion where she presided over and encouraged a circle of intelligent, artistic young men, many of them from England.

Those years in Tehran formed Oliver Hoare's life. There he learned everything about Iran and its art. He would tour the country, sometimes residing in palaces and mansions, at other times staying in peasant-style hotels in the far reaches of the mountainous country.

Through Hamoush, Oliver also met a host of young people with brilliant social connections, many from celebrated families, some of whom would become wealthy and famous in their own right. Some are still his close friends. In Tehran, Oliver met Prince Charles's lifelong friend, Nicholas Soames, now a minister of the British government; Victoria Waymouth, daughter of the Earl of Hardwicke; and David Sulzberger, the man who became Oliver Hoare's business partner, and whose family owns the *New York Times*. In the evenings the young people would gather for stimulating debate on art, music, and poetry while drinking wine and eating the wonderful Iranian dishes prepared by Hamoush's servants. It was here that Oliver found his spiritual home and his destiny.

Hamoush recalled, "Oliver came to study and excavate and to read Arabic and Persian script. He was a brilliant scholar. In a matter of months he read them perfectly. Often I would find him in the house, late in the evening, studying while the others were out in the town enjoying themselves."

Oliver was a serious, rather studious young man, but he would later learn to relax and enjoy life to the hilt. His one relaxation at that time was playing the guitar, which he mostly taught himself. Late into the evenings a group of Hamoush's young protégés would sit around while Oliver would play, often to songs he had written himself.

Hamoush continued, "After a while people would invite him to the most sophisticated social parties and invite him to play and sing. His voice was stunning. Many suggested that he should become a pop singer, playing and writing his own music and words. He didn't want to. His style, his music, his voice, and his looks, however, meant that he rapidly became the object of many young women's attention. I can remember many young women, of different nationalities, openly admitting they wanted an affair with Oliver. He was so romantic, untouchable, wonderfully artistic, some would say gifted. And very, very good-looking. Many also wanted to marry him.

"They would tell me," Hamoush said, "'He is so, so sexy.' And I would smile and wish them luck."

Hamoush would say of her young protégé, "Oliver is half child and half old man. Like a child he is impressed by unimpressive things. He has something that probably God never gave him, a tranquillity of life."

I met Oliver Hoare sometime at the end of the 1970s when he came to my London apartment with the Russian ballet star Rudolf Nureyev. They became close friends and were part of the wild brigade of brilliant, artistic, world-renowned, wealthy young men and women who at that time were enjoying life to the full—infamous for sex, drugs, and rock 'n' roll—among them pop stars like Jimmy Page of Led Zeppelin and Mick Jagger and Laura Nelson, the talented Hollywood writer whom they all loved as a sister.

They all adopted pet names that they would use on phone calls and messages so that their identities would remain anonymous from anyone listening to the calls, taking their messages, or wanting to crash their circle. Oliver Hoare became part of that privileged in-crowd.

Nureyev asked Oliver to decorate his Paris apartment, No. 23, Quai Voltaire, on the banks of the Seine. Oliver Hoare found the task challenging and rewarding. Later, Nureyev could boast of one of the most magnificent apartments in the French capital, beautifully designed, the artifacts treasures from around the world, and the nearly one hundred paintings Nureyev purchased showed images of the male torso, some in exaggerated poses, others more erotic. There were also various tortured poses in bronzes.

Oliver took Nureyev, the actor Terence Stamp, and another dancer, Richard Collins, to visit Hamoush in Tehran. Hoare and Nureyev would enjoy wild times together, and years later Oliver would tell these stories to an enchanted Diana, who would ask him to recall his moments with the stars she had read about and admired from afar, but never met.

Hoare would later tell Diana how he had begun work, helping customers at the front desk at Christie's, the London art dealer. Later, his knowledge led him to specialize in Islamic art. But in 1976 he quit his full-time job to break out on his own, opening a small gallery in Kynance Mews in Chelsea with David Sulzberger.

Soon they moved to larger premises in Belgravia, London, launching the Ahuan Gallery, named after an Iranian caravanserai—a traditional Persian inn and watering hole—owned by Hamoush. She had planned to give her caravanserai to Hoare as a gift, but it was confiscated by the mullahs when the Ayatollah Khomeini came to power in 1979 following the revolution that overthrew the Shah.

In 1976, Hoare had married the beautiful Diane after a year-long romance. But their marriage, too, would have its share of problems. While Charles had rekindled his love affair with Camilla Parker Bowles, cheating on the beautiful Princess

Diana, Oliver Hoare was becoming seriously involved with another woman, Ayesha Nadir, another Islamic art expert, the estranged wife of the disgraced tycoon Asil Nadir.

But the relationship between the Waleses and the Hoares blossomed. Within a matter of a few weeks of that first meeting at Windsor Castle, Charles and Diana invited the Hoares to dinner at Kensington Palace. Again they got on remarkably well. Diana found both Oliver and his wife charming, with interests she, too, could relate to, a far cry from the usual guests Charles would invite to dinner, many of whom Diana would privately call "boring old farts."

Friendship between the four of them developed, and both Charles and Diana visited the Baroness's Provence château from time to time. Charles particularly loved to fly to the south of France to rest and paint in the peace and seclusion of the estate. As the Waleses marriage disintegrated in a blaze of arguments, verbal abuse, and tears, Charles would flee to the tranquillity of the Provence château for peace and quiet.

The Hoares knew that Charles and Diana were having major problems in their marriage for Diana began to confide in Diane, seeking advice. Diane would listen to what the Princess said and offer encouragement. She knew that simply by listening to the torrent of abuse Diana would describe she was helping in some small way to ease Diana's anguish. On occasions, Diana would phone her in tears, and Diane knew that the Princess, thin and hardly ever eating, was suffering from depression and a most unhappy marriage.

Oliver Hoare broached the matter with Charles and offered to act as a go-between if, or when, necessary, telling Charles that his marriage with the lovely Diane had also had its share of problems.

"Thank you," Charles said, "I think that might be useful."

During the protracted drama that went on behind the scenes as Charles and Diana edged toward a formal separation in 1990 and 1991, both Oliver and his wife tried to help them. Princess Diana knew that Charles had great confidence in the older Oliver, believing him to be a man of the world who had the self-confidence to advise Charles honestly and straight-forwardly.

When Charles and Diana stopped speaking to each other, she turned to Oliver Hoare. He would spend hours with her at Kensington Palace, much of the time listening to Diana's anger and frustration at what she saw as a most unfair situation.

She would talk for an hour or more pacing up and down the drawing room in Kensington Palace, sometimes calm, at other times wringing her hands, her eyes filled with tears of utter sadness.

On other occasions she would rail at Charles for walking out on her and their sons, living a life on his own in Highgrove with his mistress, Camilla Parker Bowles. She would become infuriated whenever she visualized Camilla in the double bed at Highgrove making love to Charles while Diana was meant to say and do nothing but care for Wills and Harry in London.

In part Diana favored Oliver Hoare as an intermediary because one of his great friends for many years had been Camilla. Hoare and Camilla had met earlier in the late 1970s, and she, too, had enjoyed his company, his sophistication, and his wit. Later, Charles and Camilla would dine with the Hoares at their London mansion, but Diana would not be told of that.

Diana wanted to know every tiny piece of information about the woman she believed had stolen her husband, the woman she would, more often than not, refer to as "that bitch." Diana would repeatedly probe Oliver, asking a hundred questions about her rival.

Hoare found himself in an impossible position. He was close to both Charles and Diana and did not wish to be seen taking sides in their wrangling. He told Diana what he thought he should about Camilla without going into any great detail. That of course was not enough for Diana for she wanted every possible tidbit of information, gossip, and speculation.

"But why," Diana would repeatedly ask, "why on earth would Charles want her? What's so special about her? What's her secret? She looks like a horse."

And Hoare would tell Diana that he had found Camilla to be a warm, intelligent companion who loved the country, horses, dogs, and the life of a country woman who had the money to enjoy the best of life.

Diana knew Camilla well herself. She and Charles had stayed at her home in Gloucestershire before they became engaged. Later, Diana would learn that it had been Camilla who had pushed Charles into marrying her after refusing Charles's offer of marriage years after she became Mrs. Parker Bowles. She knew the enormous, perhaps catastrophic implications to the monarchy that would follow if Charles married a divorced woman. Only forty years ago King Edward VIII had sacrificed the throne for his love of a divorced woman, the American Mrs. Wallis Simpson, who would become the Duchess of Windsor.

Charles had first proposed to a deliriously happy Diana in the cabbage patch at Camilla's home. But those were the days when Diana had been hopelessly in love with Charles, her true Prince who would take her away from her unhappy childhood, and together they would live happily ever after.

Diana found that she desperately needed the presence and the understanding of Oliver Hoare. She could not survive for twenty-four hours without seeing him or, at the very least, talking to him on the phone. She became dependent on him and would become agitated if she didn't stay in constant contact with him. She had no idea that during 1992 she had become a burden to Oliver Hoare. Nor did Diana realize for many months that her demands were putting a tremendous strain on Hoare's marriage. By this time Diane and Oliver Hoare had reconciled their differences and their marriage was once again on a fairly even keel. The demands of the Princess of Wales all but dashed their relationship.

Diane accused her husband of having an affair with the Princess for he would spend one or two evenings a week with Diana, either dining out, going for long drives in the country, accompanying her to dinner parties, or spending time alone with her at Kensington Palace, sometimes not returning home until the early hours. On weekends, Diana would spend thirty minutes or more on the phone talking to Oliver, much to the growing annoyance of his wife.

Sometime during 1992 Diana realized that she had fallen hopelessly and completely in love with someone who she felt had all the attributes of a real man—strength, honor, charm, wit, and sophistication. And she had never forgotten, could never forget, that she had been physically attracted to him from the moment she first set eyes on him seven years before. Diana came to the realization that Oliver Hoare was the man she wanted.

Diana, however, was not sure whether the attraction was reciprocated. She realized that Oliver found her attractive, but she wondered if the handsome art dealer, who was having financial problems with his business, needed the additional problem of escorting the Princess of Wales, the estranged wife of Prince Charles, the focus of every photographer and royal writer in Fleet Street and beyond.

Oliver Hoare had never enjoyed the limelight. A quiet man, he preferred to lead a more sheltered, less ostentatious life, shunning rather than seeking the glare of publicity. Even his car was ordinary, a standard Volvo. She knew that she would have to tread most carefully. Hoare enjoys the company of those in high society, whether in London, Paris, or New York, but prefers to be involved with people who share his passion for Eastern and Middle Eastern culture. He also enjoys his freedom.

But Diana believes she yearns for that lifestyle most of the time. She would love to go shopping, alone and unrecognized, to swim or play tennis, and be ignored. Sometimes she doesn't want to enter a room full of strangers, especially when she is on her own, for she feels vulnerable. Even today, she will on occasion shake with apprehension when she is about to make a speech. Her fear that she will misread or mispronounce a word only compounds her lack of confidence.

When asked directly whether she would not miss the excitement of being the center of attention, Diana will look shy and a wry smile will pass her lips, knowing that she does still feel thrilled by the cheers of ordinary people. The clapping, the call of her name, give Diana an inner strength, boosting her fragile self-confidence. More importantly, the warmth she feels from people delighted to see her makes her feel wanted and loved, which is what she has missed for most of her life and what she has always craved.

During the summer of 1993, Diane Hoare reached the end of her patience with the Princess of Wales. Diane had noted that whenever she did chat with Diana for a minute or so on the phone, the Princess, who had shown friendship and warmth during their earlier meetings, now seemed brusque, as though not wanting to talk to her at all. Diane became suspicious.

The constant stream of phone calls continued and her husband would continue to visit Diana two or three times a week. Diane became convinced that her husband and the princess were having a full-blown love affair. She knew from bitter experience that Oliver was capable of having an open affair with someone else. His relationship with Asil Nadir's wife, a former Turkish beauty queen, lasted four years until it ended in 1989.

Diane began to challenge her husband, demanding that he spend less time with Diana. She also told him in no uncertain terms that he must somehow stop Diana from constantly phoning their home, sometimes three or four times a day, sometimes late at night, demanding to speak to him.

Oliver would talk to Diana about the problem. She would respond, "Doesn't she understand what I'm going through? Doesn't she know that I need your help and advice with all the terrible problems I'm having?"

Diana would continue to pour out her most intimate fears, anguish, and concerns: the grief caused by Prince Charles and his affair with Camilla, the fact that Charles was now demanding a legal separation from her, the criticism she received from the Queen and Prince Philip, as well as senior courtiers. Their criticism would sometimes make her feel physically sick and exhausted. Usually, these sessions of rage and fear for the future would end in a stream of tears.

She would cry out to Oliver, "Doesn't Diane realize that I

have no one to whom I can turn? No one whom I can trust? You are my only friend. Doesn't she relaize that I am so bitterly alone?"

The phone calls and the demands on Oliver Hoare's time continued. But now Diana would invariably never speak to Diane Hoare if she answered the phone; she would either hang up or simply say nothing. On occasions, when Oliver answered the phone, Diana would sometimes remain silent, simply hanging on wanting to hear the voice of the man she loved.

Throughout 1993 the phone calls continued, though Diana would also see much of Oliver Hoare during most weeks of that year. For much of the time Diana smiled and seemed at ease. Her friends wondered whether there was a new man in her life. Some believed that Oliver Hoare had filled that role, and they were pleased that the Princess of Wales had found a soul mate with whom she seemed happy, relaxed, and on occasions excited. Some friends thought she had recaptured a spring in her step and exuded a certain je ne sais quoi that some women who are happy with their life display.

She had even managed to remain calm when she had been informed by Sir Robert Fellowes, the Queen's private secretary, that later that week, in December 1992, Prime Minister John Major would announce to the House of Commons the formal separation of the Prince and Princess of Wales.

She had felt a thrill when John Major had told the nation that despite the separation no constitutional implications were involved, meaning that when Charles became king, Diana could still be crowned queen. It had also been stated that both Diana and Charles would be involved in the education and upbringing of Wills and Harry.

The outcome could not have been better for Diana, though she would have preferred to remain married. Polls showed that the great bulk of the nation, and particularly women, whole-heartedly backed Diana, blaming Charles for the marriage collapse. When Diana resumed her official duties, the crowds greeting her were bigger, the reception more noisy and enthusi-astic. And Diana's smile seemed more winning.

Despite her burden of official royal duties and charity functions, Diana worked out more, her tennis improved, and she swam more energetically and enthusiastically than she had for years. She seemed like a woman in love. The happiness, however, would not last.

# 5

# The Mad Caller

❦

OLIVER HOARE BEGAN TO TIRE of his role. The demands on his time and his life were becoming unbearable and his wife, Diane, insisted that he should end the relationship with Diana. His business suffered a dramatic decline and in 1993 recorded a loss of nearly $1 million. His London gallery also lost money.

The phone calls to Oliver Hoare's $4-million four-story town house in Chelsea increased. They had now become pest calls, the caller saying nothing, waiting for a minute or so and then replacing the receiver. Most calls were taken by Oliver Hoare himself for he would usually answer the phone. There would be no heavy breathing and Oliver would try to persuade the caller to speak. On most occasions his requests were met by silence. Some calls, however, were positively malicious.

On one occasion, late at night in the autumn of 1993, Diane Hoare answered the phone and was startled to hear a woman's voice screaming, "You hard-hearted bitch... you're ruining my life.... Why don't you leave me alone.... Why don't you leave your husband alone.... Why do you behave like a jealous French bitch."

"Who is that? Who is that?" Diane demanded. But her questions were ignored and the phone slammed down. Diane didn't recognize the voice, but she suspected the Princess of Wales.

Diane demanded her husband phone British Telecom and report the malicious calls. Mr. and Mrs. Hoare estimated there had been about three hundred pest calls during a sixteen-month period.

Oliver Hoare wasn't absolutely convinced that all the malicious calls came from Diana. Not only had his business fortunes suffered during the 1990s, but several people in the world of Islamic art were casting doubts about some of Oliver Hoare's business deals. He had also wondered whether he or one of his family might be the target of a terrorist attack or a possible kidnap and ransom demand. Hoare decided that he could take no further chances in case he might be putting his family at risk.

In 1989, Hoare's business came under scrutiny during the trial of a man accused of handling goods stolen from Hoare's Ahuan Gallery during an exhibition. Under cross-examination Hoare admitted that he insured some individual artworks for more than ten times the price he had paid for them. Many in the art world accepted that practice as a sound way to deal with unique pieces of art.

In 1993, Dr. Nasser David Khalili, owner of one of the world's largest private collections of Islamic art, had to return items that he had bought from Hoare, among others, after it was discovered they had been stolen from a Dublin library. No suggestion, however, was ever made that Hoare had acted other than properly.

Oliver Hoare had no option but to accede to his wife's demand to contact British Telecom. In his heart he believed some of the calls could have been instigated by Diana, but he doubted that she had begun making violently abusive phone calls, especially to his wife.

British Telecom installed sophisticated tracker equipment, and the Hoares were given a code to tap into their handset as soon as the nuisance caller came on the line. For two months there was nothing. Early in 1994, however, the calls resumed in earnest.

The first call came at 8:45 A.M. on January 13, the second at 8:49 A.M., and another at 8:49 A.M. There would be three more that day. All were silent. More calls followed until, on January

19, Hoare was shown a list of the numbers from which the calls had been made. One he recognized instantly as Diana's personal number in Kensington Palace, the number he would use to phone her.

British Telecom gave all the information to the police as they do in all such matters. The calls were traced to two phones inside Kensington Palace, Diana's mobile phone, two phone boxes near the palace, and a line at the house of her sister Lady Sarah McCorquodale.

The information was passed to Comdr. Robert Marsh, head of the Royal Protection Squad, who discussed the matter with a senior civil servant at the Home Office, who discreetly informed Buckingham Palace. The matter was handled by Diana's brother-in-law, Sir Robert Fellowes, the Queen's personal secretary. He called Diana to the palace. Nothing is known of that conversation, but the calls ceased forthwith. The police elected not to prosecute. The extraordinary affair was allowed to drop after Oliver and Diane Hoare said they did not wish to take the matter any further.

Journalists who made inquiries to Scotland Yard and Buckingham Palace were told that absolutely no comment would be made about the incident. They were also informed that the matter was now closed and that no action would be taken.

In August 1994, Diana went to Martha's Vineyard in New England for a two-week holiday with friends. She stayed with Lucia Flecha de Lima, an older woman who has been one of Diana's staunchest and most trustworthy friends for many years. Some have suggested that Lucia has become so close to Diana she is her surrogate mother.

Diana and Lucia became friends when Lucia's husband, Paulo, had been his country's ambassador to London. Indeed, when Oliver was trying to persuade Charles and Diana to reconcile their differences, Lucia would allow Diana and Oliver to use her London home for their clandestine meetings. On occasion they would spend hours there together, in private. And Diana found herself depending more and more on the calm, gentle approach of the handsome Oliver.

That August, Diana had a wonderful holiday lazing on the beach, sunning herself, swimming in the ocean waters, and eating and relaxing with friends. Throughout the two weeks not a single paparazzi would be seen.

Dressed in a smart navy blazer and Bermuda shorts, the Princess of Wales returned to London off the British Airways flight from Boston at around five-thirty in the morning of Thursday, August 18, looking rested, suntanned, and happy. Two days later Diana went as usual to her health club for a swim and a workout.

As she emerged and walked to her car, a complete stranger approached.

"Excuse me, ma'am," he said, "I would like to speak to you about nuisance phone calls over a sixteen-month period made to Oliver Hoare, an art dealer."

Diana appeared thunderstruck. "I don't know what you're talking about," she stammered, and walked quickly toward her car, leaving the young man's question unanswered.

The young man was a reporter from Murdoch's sensation-seeking Sunday tabloid the *News of the World*. Fearing the newspaper would reveal her stream of phone calls to Oliver Hoare, she contacted a journalist friend, Richard Kay, the *Daily Mail*'s royal correspondent, and urgently asked to meet him.

They met on Saturday afternoon in leafy Talbot Square, in West London. Diana drove up in her Audi sports car, disguised in a baseball hat pulled well down over her face, and wearing a jacket and jeans. Kay, in jeans and open-necked shirt, waved to Diana, who parked her car opposite his Volvo. He ran over and for twenty minutes they talked in Diana's car. They then moved from her car across the road to his Volvo and drove off. Three hours later they returned, and Kay took Diana to her car and waved goodbye.

During that time Kay phoned the *News of the World* from a public call box to explain that he was speaking on behalf of the Princess of Wales and telling the newspaper there had been a mix-up, that Diana could not possibly have made the malicious phone calls at the times stated because she had been somewhere else.

The following day the *News of the World* reported the story of the malicious phone calls and the fact that suspicion had fallen squarely on Diana. The headline screamed, "Di's Cranky Phone Calls to Married Tycoon."

Her ruse had fooled no one.

That Sunday morning Diana was besieged by newsmen and photographers as she went to play tennis at Chelsea Harbour club. She smiled happily for the cameras. She wore her favorite American-flag sweatshirt, ultrashort light blue shorts, and trainers. Diana appeared not to have a care in the world. She was also wearing dark glasses. Questions were thrown at her by the waiting newsmen, but she said nothing. Every question she met with a confident smile. And as she reached her car, she gave the photographers a one-fingered salute with her middle finger, leaving her hand lingering in the air for a full five seconds.

A worried Oliver Hoare phoned Prince Charles that Sunday morning telling him about the exposé in the newspaper and explaining what had happened. He also reassured Charles that his relationship with Diana had been entirely proper.

Hoare himself said later, "All this speculation is nonsense. There really is nothing to it. I've known both the Prince and Princess of Wales for many years. They are friends and I get on with them both."

When asked if his wife had been concerned by the publicity, he replied, "Not particularly, because she knows the relationship is perfectly friendly."

The denials, however, would not stop the rumors of a romantic relationship between Diana and Oliver.

Diana herself tried desperately to head off the appalling embarrassment of the pest calls, which she knew would make her look irresponsible and childish. She also dreaded what Elizabeth and Prince Philip would think.

Britain's newspaper lonely hearts columnists wrote open letters to Diana, advising her to seek help, talk to a counselor or to call the Samaritans, a nationwide help line, to guide her through the difficulties of working out her life.

They reminded her that isolation and loneliness was the

The engagement that thrilled a nation. Charles and Diana at
Buckingham Palace, February 24, 1981 (Photo Buckingham Palace)

Diana on an official visit to a Royal Navy base in 1988 (London News Service)

On parade at Royal Ascot and looking stunningly beautiful, June 1991 (London News Service)

The Princess of Wales on an official
visit to the principality of Wales, 1994
(London News Service)

Diana visiting sick and
disabled children with her
hostess, Jemima Khan,
during a visit to Lahore,
Pakistan. They wore
traditional Islamic dress,
February 1996.
(Express Newspapers)

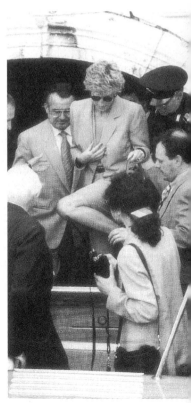

Thousands turned out to greet Diana when she visited Tokyo, February 1995.
(London News Service)

Surrounded by Italian security men, Diana steps aboard a gondola during her visit to Venice in 1995.
(Express Newspapers)

Chatting with an AIDS patient in a London hospital, 1989
(London News Service)

Diana breaks down
in tears in Newcastle
while visiting residents
in a program for
housing the homeless,
April 1991.
(London News Service)

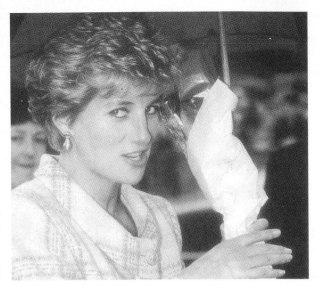

Leaving a charity event in the London rain, June 1993
(London News Service)

Diana is always happy to help other people fight their eating problems.
Here she arrives at a 1993 conference on eating disorders.
(Express Newspapers)

Diana opening the Mortimer Market Centre for Sexually Transmitted Diseases, HIV, and AIDS, December 1994 (London News Service)

Diana visits a cancer hospital for children during her visit to Pakistan in February 1996. (Express Newspapers)

Diana allegedly making midnight visits to hospital patients in December 1995. In fact, she never went to the hospitals. (London News Service)

Diana receives a kiss from a total stranger in Liverpool as she was strolling without a bodyguard or police protection. The young man was in fact a mentally disabled hospital patient who bet other patients he would kiss the Princess, July 1995. (Express Newspapers) price she would have to pay for the freedom she had demanded to live separated from her husband and members of the Royal Family.

One wrote, "No matter that you found the rigid, austere life-style stifling—or your in-laws cold and unapproachable—for ten years it was all you had and you're still trying to fill that gap."

Another's advice hit home when she wrote, "Naturally you're desperate to form new and close relationships with men and women. But most of all you want to share your life with a loving and supportive partner."

Psychiatrists suggested that Diana had made the calls to the Hoares' house because she was desperately lonely or had been rebuffed and simply wanted to hear the voice of a person she loved and trusted, perhaps someone who had in the recent past provided much warmth and support.

One of Britain's foremost psychiatrists, Dr. Dennis Friedman, commented, "Nuisance callers need to hear a friendly voice over and over again to comfort them in their loneliness. It's like taking a Valium tablet when you are in a panic. It's a comfort. But while a drug like Valium lasts up to five hours, the relief from a phone call may only last thirty minutes. That's why the caller has to repeat it, over and over again. These callers cannot control themselves. It's a compulsion. They often want to stop, and know they should, but they can't because they become addicted to the relief it provides."

Zelda West-Meades, one of Britain's foremost marriage guidance experts, said, "Constantly ringing someone but not being able to speak can be the sign of a very frightened and lonely person longing to make contact but not daring to do so. They are more likely to call someone they feel is loving and caring and who knows what they are going through, someone who has listened to them in the past or who they feel can help them. They may feel they need to talk—but are unable to acknowledge how great their own need is. And worse still, they fear if they do give voice to their emotions, the person they desperately want to talk to will be driven away. This only increases their sense of abandonment and loneliness.

Embarrassed and affronted that she should be labeled a phone pest, Diana believed that she could yet persuade the public to accept her claim that she was innocent of the allegation. She told Richard Kay she had been framed, saying, "What are they trying to do to me? I feel I am being destroyed. There is no truth in it."

And she produced her engagement diary to prove that she was elsewhere at times she was said to have made the calls. She said, "It is true that I have called Oliver Hoare, but not in the way alleged. It's not true that I've made three hundred calls, and I have never stayed silent on the phone."

Painstakingly, Diana then went through her diary to prove, as she put it, that the allegations against her were "a massive lie." She told Kay she was determined to clear herself of the slur.

On January 13, 1994, when it was alleged she made a call in the middle of the day, Diana's diary shows that between 1 P.M. and 3 P.M. she was lunching at Harry's Bar in London with Lady Stevens. The same day she is alleged to have made a call from Kensington Palace at 8:19 P.M. The diary indicates she was at the London home of a titled lady.

On January 15, 1994, she was said to have made a call at 4:55 P.M. Di's diary reports she was at the cinema watching a Clint Eastwood film with a close friend, Catherine Soames. Catherine Soames has said she could confirm the cinema date.

On January 17, Diana was alleged to have made a call at 5:33 P.M. The diary showed she was at Kensington Palace at the time having aromatherapy from Sue Beechey, who also said she could confirm the date.

On January 18, Diana was said to have made two calls from Kensington Palace at 10:41 A.M. and 11:36 A.M. But her diary says she was scheduled to be with hairstylist Paul Galvin between 9:30 A.M. and 11:30 A.M. at his West End salon.

Diana was able to quote many more examples from her diary showing she could not have made the calls that were alleged.

Despite her denials and the evidence she gave proving her

innocence, the great majority of the British public believed that Diana did indeed make those calls. But they forgave her. They thought that she had been driven to make the calls through misery and her fragile emotional state brought about by the collapse of her marriage.

The public accused Charles and other members of the Royal Family for their coldness toward her and a lack of concern for her lonely predicament. The public believed Diana needed help, and yet none appeared to be coming from Charles or the rest of the family. She had been cast adrift and left to care for herself. Women particularly demanded that Diana not be condemned for what she had done but given time and help from specialists to come to terms with her life alone.

Within days of the revelations Diana would read all the papers, particularly the tabloids, learning more about the Hoares than she had ever known. During her four-year affair, Ayesha Nadir would boast to her friends of the most intimate details of her lovemaking with Oliver Hoare. Their affair would become the talk of London, one of the worst-kept secret love affairs.

She would tell her society friends, "Oliver has the most amazing staying power. I call him Marathon Man. He is the most sensational lover. He can go on forever. He is wonderful."

But their affair would end when Ayesha became convinced that Oliver Hoare would never leave his wife, Diane, a strong practicing Roman Catholic. Ayesha would say, "I would sit at home and cry over him. In the end I couldn't take it anymore so I finished the affair."

That year, 1989, Ayesha was granted a second divorce from her multimillionaire husband, Asil Nadir, the boss of Polly Peck, which was then one of Britain's fastest-growing conglomerates. It was understood she received a $30-million settlement. The deal included an eighteenth century villa on the banks of the Bosporus near Istanbul, which had been lavishly restored. Ayesha returned to her native Turkey and reverted to her maiden name, Tecimer.

Diana and Oliver Hoare continued to see each other, but the

drama over the phone calls seemed to take the edge off their relationship.

Diana threw herself into keeping fit, playing tennis harder, swimming longer and stronger, and working out with more determination than ever. After such exertions she would feel better, believing the effort had somehow improved her mind and reinvigorated her body. But the anger remained.

# 6

## Princess in Love: Diana and the Captain of the Guards

❧❧❧

SOME TWELVE MONTHS after Prince Harry's birth in 1984, Diana wondered how she would ever escape from the strait-jacket of her royal marriage. Her misery and loneliness only added to her desperate thoughts as she battled to recover from the awful postnatal blues that had left her feeling "absolutely bloody awful nearly all the time."

This time, however, the blues seemed much worse. She felt Charles had drawn away from her, not kissing or cuddling, paying less attention and spending weeks away at Highgrove, his country home one hundred miles from Kensington Palace.

Diana told some friends how she awoke in a cold sweat one night in the autumn of 1986 and suddenly realized that Charles was having an affair. "It was pure instinct, a woman's instinct," she said. "It was cold and dark and Charles hadn't shared a bed with me for weeks. He had barely touched me. I knew in that instant that he was having an affair, and I also knew the woman must be Camilla."

During the following weeks Diana would often cry herself to sleep at night and her bulimia escalated. Rarely a day would pass without her raiding the larder and the refrigerator before making herself ill, sometimes bingeing and vomiting four and five times a day. Almost with a feeling of righteousness, she would eliminate what had given her self-indulgent pleasure. She hated what she was doing but could not stop herself, for the eating disorder made her feel better. And when she realized the bulimia had taken a firm grip on her everyday life, she felt too ashamed, too frightened, to ask anyone for help.

At first, she would seek reassurance from Charles that he was not having an affair, and he would tell her not to be so silly. He would reassure her that he only stayed at Highgrove to escape the rigors of too much family pressure. Highgrove gave him a peace of mind that he couldn't find in London. Diana tried to believe him, but the more distant he remained the more she instinctively knew that he was lying. He was staying at Highgrove because of Camilla.

About this time a dashing cavalry officer, resplendent in the uniform of a captain in the Life Guards, that most royal of all the sovereign's regiments, rode into Diana's life. His name was Capt. James Hewitt.

They met in London in the summer of 1986 at a party where Hewitt was formally introduced. During their chat Hewitt offered to help Diana overcome her fear of horse riding, something that Charles had tried and failed to carry out years before.

After their first few riding lessons, Hewitt and Diana, who were about the same age, were having coffee one morning in the deserted officers' mess at Knightsbridge Barracks in central London, half a mile from Kensington Palace. Diana desperately needed someone to pay her attention. She wondered whether the smooth-talking polo player could be that man.

Realizing Diana's needs, Hewitt gave her the attention she craved. He would later provide the passion Diana realized she had never really enjoyed with any other man, not even Charles.

Their affair began shortly afterward. Diana loved Hewitt's kind and tender ways, and how he seemed to anticipate her every need. They would spend nights together at Kensington Palace, at Highgrove, at Althorp, her family's stately home, and at Hewitt's mother's cottage in Devon. There, they would push two single beds together and make love through the night while Diana's personal detective slept in the adjoining room.

For three years the passion, which Diana had missed all her life, continued, though the amount of time they could spend together would be limited by the demands on both their lives and the fact that Diana was still married to the Prince of Wales. Hewitt was a serving officer, and Diana not only had two growing boys to care for but was also taking on more royal duties. Her charity work had escalated at an extraordinary pace as the British public took her to their hearts and her popularity soared. Charities queued for her patronage.

Meanwhile, Hewitt's regiment would be posted to Germany and months would pass when they would not see each other. They would write and call, but Diana began to realize Hewitt would never become a permanent part of her life.

At first Diana had loved spoiling Hewitt, who she knew had no real wealth but survived on his Army pay. She would buy him Savile Row suits costing $2,500, Jermyn Street shirts priced at $125 each, shoes at $1,000 a pair. In return Hewitt gave the Princess of Wales one of his old cricket sweaters and a $50 Puffa jacket to keep her warm in winter.

Diana did find herself fretting when Hewitt was dispatched to Saudi Arabia to take an active role in Operation Desert Storm. The fact that her lover was fighting in a real war added a piquancy to her passion, instilling a feeling of intense nervousness, tinged with pleasure.

On his return, Hewitt realized that Diana had cooled and that their affair was about to end. He tried to resurrect the passion, but Diana had decided that Capt. James Hewitt would not be the man to rescue her from her marriage and become her lifelong companion.

She considered he hadn't the strength of character she needed to support her, nor intellect enough to keep her happy, nor the courage to woo and win the Prince of Wales's wife. She had never been sure whether Hewitt's protestations of love had been entirely genuine, whether he really loved Diana for herself or whether he took pleasure in the affair because it bolstered his vanity that he was bedding the Princess of Wales. In her heart Diana feared it was the latter.

She recalled that on one occasion a desperate Hewitt had asked a tabloid newsman reporting the Gulf War if he could borrow his mobile phone to call the Princess of Wales. And Hewitt then carried on a conversation with Diana for three minutes while newsmen around him listened. She read about it in one of the tabloids. She wondered at the time how the man she loved could be so stupid.

She remembered Hewitt cracking jokes about making love to the future Queen of England, which made him appear vain, shallow, and insensitive. Diana was anxious that perhaps the love she had felt for Hewitt had been one-sided, but she felt she could trust the word of an officer and a gentleman. She would take comfort in the Guard's motto, *Honi soit qui mal y pense* (Shame to him that thinks ill).

Throughout their affair Queen Elizabeth had been made aware of Diana's adultery with Hewitt. Senior officers of the Royal Protection Squad informed her private secretary, Sir Robert Fellowes about what was taking place. It seems extraordinary that Diana did not realize that such actions on her part would have to be reported to higher authority.

"I hope that girl knows what she is doing," Elizabeth said. "I hope she understands that she is the wife to the heir to the throne and that she is committing adultery."

And yet Elizabeth did not warn Diana or ask anyone, either her advisers or her bodyguards, to query the princess about her adulterous affair.

Years later, some would wonder why Elizabeth hadn't intervened, why she hadn't had a quiet word with Diana, advising her, as her mother-in-law, in her capacity as the Queen, head of the Royal Family, that she was playing a most dangerous game. But that is not Elizabeth's way. She has never intervened directly in any of the love affairs of her three sons or her daughter, Anne. She believes that their private lives are their own business to sort out for themselves. She also believes that they must take the consequences for their actions.

Naively, Diana believed she could trust her personal bodyguards, Insp. Ken Wharfe and Sgt. Alan Peters. She did not seem to realize that it would have been an offense punishable by instant dismissal if they had not kept senior officers informed of all Diana's movements including the people, both men and women, she met privately and in secret. She was not permitted to leave Kensington Palace without an armed bodyguard at her side. With an IRA action against the Royal Family always possible, members of the Royal Protection Squad were never permitted to forget that the IRA had assassinated Earl Mountbatten and half his family when they blew up his fishing smack in Northern Ireland in August 1979. They could strike at any time. There was also the constant fear of a terrorist attack against the world's most celebrated royal family.

And the possibility of blackmail could never be discounted. Diana would have been placed in an impossible situation if some blackmailer had seen her or taken photographs of her during her trysts with James Hewitt.

Diana discovered that ending the relationship with Hewitt would be far easier and less complicated than she believed possible. She had made up her mind after the war in the Gulf that the relationship should end, for she found herself losing respect for him. He was always nice to her, expecting presents in return, and would flatter her with his protestations of love. Diana suggested that perhaps they should see less of each other, explaining that she had "to sort out many of the problems" in her life. It seemed to Diana that Hewitt had expected the rejection and took it rather nonchalantly. She asked that he return the letters she had sent him during the Gulf War and on other occasions. He told her that he wanted to keep them as a memento of their love for each other. Reluctantly, Diana agreed. As she drove away that day, she wondered whether she had been sensible in leaving such incriminating evidence to Hewitt's safekeeping.

Hewitt would twice fail the exam to become a major in the Guards, exams that are not difficult and that he should have passed with ease. He knew that by failing those exams his future in the British Army was virtually at an end, for there was no need for officers incapable of passing them.

Three years after their affair ended, Diana heard rumors that James Hewitt was visiting tabloid offices trying to sell the story of his affair with Diana for $1 million. She heard that he boasted to editors that the story he could write would include explicit sexual details of his romance with Diana, including a claim they had made love in Diana's bedroom with a photo of Prince Charles by the bed, that he had given Princess Diana her first orgasm, and that Diana had said making love to Charles had been a duty but with Hewitt it was pleasure.

In September 1994, Diana learned that a book, *Princess in Love* was about to be published revealing intimate details of the affair. The thought that Hewitt might reveal all their private moments together sent shivers through her. She could not believe that the man she had loved and to whom she had given so much of herself could possibly have anything to do with such a book. Ten days before *Princess in Love* was published, Hewitt phoned Diana at Kensington Palace to tell her not to worry for there was nothing of substance in it. Unfortunately, Diana had misjudged Hewitt and he had deliberately lied to her.

She feared the letters she had written to him would make it impossible for her to deny the allegation and she would be branded an adulteress. Diana tried one last time to persuade Hewitt not to publish the book, which she was convinced would ruin her in the eyes of the British public. Toward the end of September she contacted him by telephone and asked to see him, but he refused to do so.

They did in fact meet and Diana tried again to persuade him not to publish his book. Later, Hewitt boasted how, in tears, Diana had begged him not to publish, telling him, "My God, if you go ahead with this book, it's going to kill me."

Hewitt confided that he had been so shocked by Diana's reaction that he had seriously considered scrapping the book because he didn't want to upset her. Allegedly, Hewitt told others that Diana knew all about *Princess in Love* and approved.

Diana read the newspapers over the days leading up to publication with growing anxiety and fear. There were hints that *Princess in Love* would shock the nation, suggestions that

Capt. James Hewitt, the man whom four years previously this author had revealed to be Diana's lover, in my book *Diana: A Princess and Her Troubled Marriage,* would tell the world that he and the Princess of Wales had enjoyed a long, passionate affair.

Pictures of Diana in those days immediately prior to publication show her distraught, her lips pursed, her face distorted in anguish, not waving to anyone or looking at the cameras that tracked every move she made whenever she left the protection of her home.

In the privacy of her palace apartment Diana wondered why the phone didn't ring. With all the speculation she expected a call from Prince Charles or the Queen or her brother-in-law Sir Robert Fellowes demanding to know the truth about an alleged affair that had started years before. But the phone stayed silent, driving Diana into bouts of tears and terror, for she realized *Princess in Love* would brand her an adulteress. Worse still, she worried what her sons would think and what possible harm her ex-lover's revelations might cause them. She also feared for herself and her future.

During those days and nights Diana cursed herself for having been so stupid, for having been involved in a love affair that she now understood would mean nothing to her. The more she examined her reasoning the more foolish she realized she had been in trusting such a man as James Hewitt. And yet she knew why, for Diana would later say, "I adored James. I loved him very much."

"Why? Why? Why?" she kept repeating over and over when discussing the matter with one of her closest girlfriends.

Days later, in October 1994, *Princess in Love* hit the bookstores throughout Britain. It caused a sensation and the public flocked to buy it, the first seventy-five thousand copies selling out within twenty-four hours. The book had been written by Anna Pasternak, twenty-seven, a freelance journalist and friend of Hewitt's and a great-niece of the Nobel Prize–winning Russian author Boris Pasternak.

Revelations in the book stopped short of the bedroom. *Princess in Love* includes much talk of love and passion but none

of actual lovemaking. According to Anna Pasternak, the book
was based on her conversations with Hewitt, who she said had
shown her some letters from Princess Diana. It was written in
the third person under Anna Pasternak's name.

Literary critics tore the book to shreds. Susannah Herbert,
the arts correspondent of the conservative *Daily Telegraph*
commented, "From the first thrill of the lovers' meeting to the
last gasp of their final embrace *Princess in Love* is a squirm-
inducing embarrassment."

Scathingly, she continued, "The author's fondness for
slushy clichés... would be hilarious were it not for the humbug
in which both Miss Pasternak and Captain Hewitt cloak their
distinctly unromantic motives for producing this book."

In an editorial the *Daily Telegraph* noted bitingly, "Even in
an age in which Mr. Rupert Murdoch and his imitators have
reduced every moral property to sale goods, the spectacle of a
former Guards officer selling for cash his claims to have
enjoyed an intimate relationship with the Princess still com-
mands revulsion."

In the book Hewitt claimed Diana told him, "I want to
marry you and have your baby." He also claimed that Diana was
about to leave Charles and settle down with him. Lurid scenes
that took place in a bathroom, a summer house, on Dartmoor,
and in a procession of beds were detailed. And the book was
dotted with florid images when Hewitt recounted the most
intimate occasions: "Di led me trembling to her bed"; "Diana
fell into my arms in the bathroom and said, 'I need you; I want
you now.'" Yet another passage read, "Diana whispered, 'Now
no one will come.' The thrill was in being locked together so
near five hundred party guests."

The furor that greeted *Princess in Love* had never before been
witnessed for any other royal book and most of the vitriol was
aimed squarely at James Hewitt. He was variously described as
"a cad," "a bounder," and "vermin."

Members of Parliament, both Conservative and Labour,
condemned the former Guards officer who had resigned from
the regiment some months earlier with a $60,000 severance

payment and a $9,000-a-year captain's pension. "Off with his bits [meaning testicles]," demanded one MP, while many accused Hewitt of treason.

One MP suggested that Hewitt should be executed in public, others that he should be flogged, and some thought he should be made to walk the plank. Diana was called on to sue Hewitt for libel. But she did not.

The debate over what quickly became known as "the Hewitt book" remained mostly one-sided with the former Guard officer taking flak from all quarters. Captain Hewitt was castigated because he had been a professional soldier, educated at Millfield, one of England's foremost public schools, and privileged to serve in the Life Guards, the sovereign's own troops. By his education, so the argument ran, he should have acquired a sense of honor, of decency, of what is done and not done by a gentleman who cares about his reputation and those of others. Many suggested scathingly that Hewitt was so dim that he probably didn't know how an officer and a gentleman should behave.

This slur was compounded by the author herself, Anna Pasternak, in ruling out any possibility of her having an affair with Hewitt. She commented bluntly, "He is far too thick. You insult me if you suggest I would have an affair with him."

Overnight, Hewitt became an outcast. Within hours Hewitt's name was "posted on the gate," the Life Guards' expression for banning someone from their midst. There was no public posting of his name, but from that moment Hewitt had been declared persona non grata not simply among the Guards regiments but in all military circles. The reason: he had broken his honor and that of his regiment, something that would never be forgotten by the Life Guards or the Household Cavalry. He was deemed to have gone beyond the pale.

There would be more. He was made "not welcome" (a polite euphemism for being banned) at the Cavalry and Guards Club in London's Piccadilly; he was officially banned from ever again attending the Cavalry Memorial Parade; he was advised never to return to the officers' mess at Knightsbridge Barracks, one of his favorite haunts; was banned from attending the Life Guards Officers' Club annual dinner at The Savoy; and advised not to visit the Turf Club tent at Cheltenham racing festivals.

All these actions were saber thrusts into Hewitt's personal life. For fifteen years he had been most welcome at all these events, accepted as a brother officer. One of his close friends in the Life Guards commented, "We understand that he made at least four hundred thousand dollars from that damn book. He should at the very least have gone into self-imposed exile for a year to indicate some remorse or regret at what he had done. That he did nothing of the sort has gone down badly among those of us who already consider he let the side down."

Residents of Hewitt's tiny country village, Topsham in Devon, rich in antique shops and "olde-worlde" tearooms two miles from his home, were flabbergasted by Hewitt's betrayal of the Princess of Wales, whom they all adored. Many described him as "a rat."

He was banned from his favorite restaurant and wine bar, Denleys in the High Street, banned from shopping in some of the local stores, and banned from the pubs. As one regular at the Tavistock Inn at Poundsgate put it, "If he dares show his face in here, I'll kick him straight out again with my boot up his arse."

And sensibly Hewitt stayed away from his local hunt, the South Devon, with whom he used to ride two or three times a week, after it was pointed out that two local landowners had said the hunt would be banned from their land if Hewitt rejoined it.

Others, however, had little or no sympathy for Diana. Richard Littlejohn, a columnist in Murdoch's *Sun* tabloid, wrote, "Diana is the scheming little shrew who had no qualms about betraying her husband in another project so she can hardly bleat when her ex-lover dishes the dirt.... At least the Hewitt revelations have exposed Diana's carefully-honed Mother Teresa act as a complete sham.... And if Diana thinks Hewitt shouldn't make money out of his relationship with her, then it's about time she stopped living off a man whom she quite clearly despises."

Three days later, on October 8, 1994, Diana awoke, pulled on her white toweling robe, and walked swiftly through to the drawing room in Kensington Palace where she knew the morning newspapers would be neatly arranged. She flicked quickly through them, glancing at the front pages, but saw nothing to alarm her. Then she began to scan them more carefully, for she had become desperate to know the nation's reaction to the book and to her adultery.

Suddenly, the air was rent with a great whoop of joy as Diana read the headline in the *Daily Mirror:* "We Don't Blame You, Diana," it proclaimed.

She then read the accompanying story eagerly, smiling throughout. The article read, "She may have been unfaithful to her husband.... But the verdict of *Mirror* readers is loud and clear: Diana, we still back you.... Most of our readers see Diana as a woman driven into the arms of another by a cold and unfeeling husband."

The *Mirror* poll revealed that 27 percent of its readers blamed Diana for having an affair with Hewitt while 73 percent did not. Only 15 percent thought less of Diana after her affair while 85 percent said it made no difference. However, only 39 percent thought Diana should have left Prince Charles for Hewitt but 61 percent did not.

Still, the majority of the nation seemed to blame Charles for the marriage breakdown. The poll revealed that 81 percent thought Charles had driven Diana into the arms of another man; 61 percent thought Charles and Diana should divorce immediately; and a remarkable 73 percent thought that Queen Elizabeth II should be the last British monarch.

Later that day Elizabeth's attention would be drawn to the same article. She was far from amused. She had given her entire life's work to the promise that she had made to her father, King George VI, before his death in 1952—to preserve the monarchy and secure the future of the Royal House of Windsor. Now it seemed that thanks to the stupidity of her daughter-in-law Diana, all her life's work had been put in jeopardy. Elizabeth could hardly contain her anger that day as she kept seeing the figures before her. The British public had turned its back on constitutional monarchy and wanted the House of Windsor to crumble on her deathbed. The idea filled her with sadness and remorse.

The report also meant that any residual affection or compassion that Elizabeth had felt toward Diana over the breakdown of her marriage to Charles had evaporated. "Stupid, stupid girl," Elizabeth would repeat time and again. "Stupid girl."

The revelations made Elizabeth believe that the final act in Charles's marriage to Diana could not be far off. They had officially separated in December 1992, which, according to British laws, meant they could divorce without any legal problems once they had been living apart for two years. To all intents and purposes, theirs had not been a proper marriage for many more years than that. Elizabeth understood that Charles and Diana had hardly shared a bed since 1985.

Perhaps, Elizabeth mused, the time was fast approaching when Charles should take steps legally to end the marriage. Until Hewitt's book, Diana had been able to occupy the moral high ground following Prince Charles's TV confession to author Jonathan Dimbleby that he had been guilty of adultery. Now the balance in the game played by Charles and Diana seemed to have shifted in favor of Charles. No longer would Diana be able to use the Prince's confession of adultery to put pressure on the Queen to secure favorable terms.

Officially, the only comment from Diana would be, "The Princess is extremely upset by the book's account of her friendship with Mr. Hewitt. It is simply not true that we ever had sex. He wanted to, but I never let it happen. He lives in a fantasy world."

A Buckingham Palace press officer commented with the full authority of the Queen, "This is nothing but a grubby and worthless little book." He added that Buckingham Palace would not take any legal action.

The palace also insisted the book would have no bearing on Diana's renewed round of public engagements. Diana read that announcement in the morning papers, relieved that she had at last received some support from the palace. For months the courtiers had ignored her, letting her carry on with her life without any intrusion, or even acknowledgment that she was part of the Royal Family and the mother of the two princes.

The tabloids, of course, enjoyed a field day. While panning the book on the one hand, they would run numerous articles about its contents, revealing many of the intimate details as well as throwing as much mud as possible at the "rat" Hewitt. They would also track down former girlfriends of Hewitt's and discover he had been a cad on more than one previous occasion. It seemed his appeal, besides his being an "officer and a gentleman," was his physical qualities. All agreed that Capt. James Hewitt was a very well endowed young man.

Anna Pasternak would later explain her motives in writing the controversial book that had so devastated Diana. She claimed that she had resolved to write a book about Hewitt's love affair with Diana on June 29, 1994, the night Prince Charles admitted in a television interview that he had been unfaithful with Camilla Parker Bowles. Ms. Pasternak said she had been appalled at the revelation. Earlier that year she had interviewed Mr. Hewitt about his friendship with the Princess for a slightly anodyne series of interviews for the *Daily Express*. Mr. Hewitt, whom she knew to be retiring from the Army, had been paid $60,000 for the series.

After Prince Charles's announcement, Ms. Pasternak said she persuaded Hewitt to cooperate with her on a book she would write. She told him, "At the end of the day the public will respect the truth. They condemn you because they don't know the truth about how you stood by this woman through the most traumatic time of her life and her marriage."

Ms. Pasternak commented, "My motives have only ever been to try and set the record straight for both of them. I am a great fan of the Princess of Wales. I think she has had a tremendously difficult time, and this is very much a book of a woman's journey to find herself, as it were, through adversity."

She went on, "Hewitt is a very lonely, very sad man who has lost everything. He has only ever wanted the best for her. I just feel that if the public could really see the true story; if they could try to understand that really he risked his life to be with this woman, who had such a tremendous need and put that need on him, and he was able to fulfill it, then perhaps they would not judge him with such a harsh tone."

Most critics were unconvinced by the reasoning, some describing her argument as "bunkum." Other critics condemned the book, written in the style of a romantic novel, as "clogging, nauseating and overblown."

Hewitt was hounded by Fleet Street tabloid journalists and photographers who trailed him across England and France. He was finally captured on film emerging from a French pigsty on a farm where he had stayed the night, fearful of being obliged to face the awesome pack of newspaper reporters scenting blood.

The Hewitt fiasco made Diana feel less secure than ever. She realized she had made a cardinal error of judgment, but she also understood that she had to take some of the blame herself. After all, she had encouraged their affair and had thoroughly enjoyed their time together, all of which helped her to forget Charles and her marriage, which had become a hell on earth.

After the weeklong uproar and newspaper headlines that detailed the most intimate and embarrassing moments of Diana's grand passion with Hewitt, Diana wanted nothing more than to go to bed and stay there, out of the limelight. And she did just that. She called close, trusted friends on her beloved telephone, but always from the safety of her sitting room or bedroom. With some of the younger ones, such as her friend of many years Kate Menzies, she managed to laugh at her embarrassment and some of the revelations in the book. Diana would say, "Please don't tease me. I feel so awful. I keep asking myself how I could have done such things with such an awful creep. Everything I've read makes me want to curl up and die. I am so embarrassed."

One of her girlfriends, determined that Diana see the funny side of the affair, asked her, "But did you enjoy yourself, you dirty stop out?" (An English phrase meaning that a girl stayed overnight at a man's apartment for sex.)

Diana would shriek and put her hand over her face to hide the blushes. Diana would say, "I couldn't have done all those things that were in the book, could I? It's just not me to behave like that, is it?"— all but demanding that the person she was talking to take her side.

"We never knew you had it in you," some teased her, and Diana would giggle and laugh and blush, but never reply.

Others told her bluntly, "God, after all you had been through with Charles, we don't blame you one bit going for whatever you could get. It must have been terrible. All we hope is that you bloody well enjoyed yourself. You deserved it."

Diana, however, would keep the secrets of what had occurred in bed, for the book had stopped at the bedroom door. Hewitt, however, would later tell friends of Diana's sexual secrets. He would relate how she would cling to him in bed, never wanting him to let go, demanding they make love time and again so they could stay together. He would describe how Diana would talk about her sex life with Charles; how awful and boring it had been; how she had never achieved the heights of passion with Charles that she experienced with Hewitt. And she would reveal all these intimate details while she was actually making love to Hewitt. It would seem to Hewitt that Diana achieved pleasure from revealing those marital secrets of her lovemaking with Charles while having sex with Hewitt, for it would drive her to ever greater and more intense pleasure.

There would be a more serious, far more concerned attitude to the issues provoked by Diana's fling. Once again the old chestnut of republicanism became the talk at society, political, and Establishment dinner tables, though some pointed out mischievously that if marital infidelity toppled English Royals, the institution would have disappeared years ago.

Historians recalled that before Queen Victoria came to the throne to clean up the Royal Family act, her Regency uncles had mistresses and bastards stretching to the horizon, and no one thought them any the worse for doing so. And a number of their wives took lovers to entertain them in their boredom. Such royal shenanigans were the talk of the coffeehouses and filled the papers of the time, revealing intimate details of royal lovers and mistresses and the games they played.

Most, however, argued that the notion of republicanism remains in Britain an eccentric diversion because all the country's leading politicians realize that tinkering with the monarchy would spell electoral catastrophe. While the nation argued, Diana calmed down and put her misdemeanor in perspective.

In late October 1994, when she finally summoned up the courage to make her first public appearance following the Hewitt scandal, Diana found the crowds cheering and shouting for her as if nothing had happened. When she returned home that evening, she told her butler, Harold Brown, thirty-seven, who had been with her for ten years, "Well, no one threw any rotten eggs."

"I didn't think they would, ma'am," he replied. Diana had survived another disastrous love affair with her reputation barely dented. But it had been close.

# 7

## A Prince's Betrayal

---

EVER SINCE CHARLES WALKED OUT on her and the two princes back in 1988, not a single day has passed without Diana feeling something of the pain, humiliation, and anger she felt at that moment. She can never forgive that Charles had lied to her throughout those years when he was virtually living with his mistress, Camilla Parker Bowles, at Highgrove in Gloucestershire, telling Diana that he resided alone in the country for the peace and tranquillity it gave him.

Diana had trusted Charles absolutely, given her heart and her soul to him, the only man in her life, other than her father, in whom she had put her faith. To this day she has never found anyone else whom she has been able to trust in the same way, and she fears that now she never will. In Charles, Diana found her prince who could do no wrong and who would always behave, so she believed, in the most correct, gentlemanly, and respectful manner.

Even today some minor occurrence will bring Diana's thoughts crashing back to the realization that Charles had left her and the boys to fend for themselves, alone. During the 1995 summer holidays, before Will went to Eton College, Diana, Will, and Harry were leaving Kensington Palace to go to the cinema. She realized, in a ghastly moment of fear, that she had ordered three seats to be reserved and yet she had wanted to ask for four.

"I went into a state of shock," Diana recalled. "I had to go back to my room, telling the boys I had left something there. I was shaking, physically shaking. They could tell something was wrong, but sensibly they said nothing. I pretended to search my bedroom for something I had left behind, but my legs became weak and I felt I would faint. It was awful, so awful."

Diana told all this to one of her older men friends who had been trying to help her come to terms with the separation and her life of loneliness. On that occasion Diana had managed to pull herself together, take a drink of cold water, and rejoin the boys, thankful they were going to a darkened theater where she could try to sort herself out before returning home.

Diana's friend explained to me, "That was typical of the way in which the breakup still affects Diana, and yet she has had more than seven years to accept what has happened. Today, she still finds it all but impossible to forget those dark hours when she realized she had lost Charles's love, when she didn't know whether she wanted to live or to die."

On another occasion on the M4 motorway in the summer of 1994, Diana was driving her Audi sports car with Wills and Harry in the backseat. She found herself following a Range Rover with a father, mother, and two boys in the vehicle. She followed the car for more than twenty miles watching the family and thinking that Charles should have been with her and the boys, rather than spending his time with his mistress.

After that occasion, Diana would tell her mentor, "I kept telling myself I must overtake the Range Rover and put such thoughts behind me. But I couldn't bring myself to overtake the car. I felt that if I overtook the car my problems would just be left behind, that I could forget about Charles and Camilla and the breakup, yet I continued to drive immediately behind them, thinking, fantasizing all the time of what life should have been with Charles, me, and the boys. I felt mesmerized, unable to concentrate on anything but Charles and the bitch, Camilla. I could see them in my mind's eye kissing, making love, having a meal together, going for walks together, riding out together, listening to music together, doing everything together while I was alone with the boys taking them to school. I drove along with the tears welling in my eyes. But my heart was full of anger and hatred."

Experiences like that cause Diana to feel she cannot forgive Charles for what he has done to her and the boys, leaving them to cope as best they can without him.

She has never forgiven Charles for announcing to the world in his TV interview that he had never loved her. That upset and hurt Diana deeply, far more than anything else in the two-hour program. She wasn't upset for herself but for Wills and Harry. She has commented, "How could he say something like that? Didn't he realize that was something terrible for the boys to hear about the relationship between their father and mother? Making that statement showed what a selfish prig Charles has become, as though nothing in the world matters, except his feelings—not his wife, his children, or any of their memories. I could gladly have scratched his eyes out for announcing that to the world, knowing the boys would read about it later. For that one statement I will never, never forgive him."

Diana always hated the fact that Wills, in particular, had learned of his father's goings-on by reading the occasional newspaper smuggled into school. The boys had been put through the mill far too often in their young lives having to read in newspapers of their parents' breakup, their father's goings-on, and later his confession of adultery.

The boys seem to have accepted that their parents have separated, that there is no going back to a full family life. Diana is fully aware that she is the one who has been unable to come to terms with her loneliness and life without a caring man. Diana readily accepts that she had been far too young and inexperienced to marry.

It was not surprising she would tell her elder confidant, "I had no role model. I could never remember my father and mother living together as man and wife. I had no memory of them kissing or showing any affection for each other. Mother had gone before I realized what was happening. When Charles proposed to me, I felt I was in a dream, that for the first time in my life I would learn what true love could be like. I think my father loved me, loved all of us, but he was not an affectionate or tactile man. He couldn't be. I wonder if he ever knew real affection. As far as Mother is concerned, I don't know. I've never known. She left me. That's all I can ever remember. Deep down I believe that I have probably never forgiven her for walking out on us all. With Charles I expected everything to change and life would be nothing but wonderful. I thought I knew what marriage was all about. In reality, I knew absolutely nothing."

And no one took Diana to one side and gave her a foretaste, or even any information of what to expect. She had been given no sexual advice, though she had made herself read a couple of books outlining the basics, of which she knew very little when she began dating Charles. Diana had only kissed and hugged a couple of boyfriends before she first dated Charles. She was a virgin, a girl who had never dated seriously and, at eighteen, still felt shy and embarrassed in the presence of young men.

She told her friend, "Sometimes, even today, after everything that has happened, I will laugh at my naivety at that time. I had no experience whatsoever, hardly any passionate kisses even, let alone anything else. I was eighteen years of age and very, very young for my age, an innocent. I would keep thinking that some girls had had a couple of babies by the time they were my age and knew far more about sex and life than I ever did."

Diana would read newspaper stories claiming that she and Charles had not enjoyed their honeymoon together because of his approach to sex. "Rubbish, all rubbish," she would say. "They simply didn't know that Charles and I had enjoyed the most wonderful time together during our six-month engagement when I spent nearly every night sharing his bed in Buckingham Palace. I was innocent but it didn't matter. I felt I was on cloud nine simply because I was in the arms of the man I adored and that I believed loved me. It was truly wonderful and I believed that feeling would continue forever."

Today, Diana sometimes blames herself for expecting far too

much of Charles and, also, of marriage. But then, in an instant, her mood will change, her eyes will flash, and she will find herself in a cold rage simply thinking of the deceitful way Charles behaved toward her when she needed him so much. She now accepts that she knew nothing of what to expect from a royal marriage, especially a marriage to the future king. She didn't really expect that he would have to spend so much time away, inspecting troops and factories, making speeches day and night, chairing meetings about a hundred different matters, and welcoming strange heads of state she had never heard of from foreign countries she never knew existed.

"I just couldn't cope," she would say. "I couldn't understand what was happening and didn't want to understand. I didn't trust anyone, except for Charles. I thought everyone was against me—all Charles's highly intelligent staff and his personal friends. I thought they didn't like me, that they didn't respect me because of my intelligence and my awful education. I felt so vulnerable, so lost."

Diana would be criticized by senior palace aides for seeking out the domestics, the cooks and the cleaners, the secretaries and the footmen, to chat to, people who she felt would want her to be their friend. From some she would even ask advice. At first, these were the only people she felt at ease with, whom she could talk to freely without being made to feel inferior and uneducated.

A few months after her wedding Diana received a rude shock. She had wandered into the kitchens at Balmoral to chat to the staff, smiling broadly and saying hello to everyone, happy to be among people she felt respected her as a friend. One of the senior butlers walked up to Diana, looking most serious.

He asked, "Can I have a word please, ma'am [pronounced "marm" as in *marmalade*]?

"Of course," Diana replied.

"I must warn you to stop coming into the kitchens. The staff do not like it, none of us do."

Diana was taken aback, startled, by the tone of his voice and the dressing-down he was giving her.

He continued, "You must understand, ma'am, that there are us and them. You are a Royal, one of them, and we should never mix. We don't want to mix with your lot, ever. We know our place and we expect you to know yours. I am afraid I must ban you from ever visiting the kitchens again."

Dumbfounded and forlorn, Diana turned on her heel and walked away, totally taken aback, tears in her eyes. She had believed they welcomed her friendly face in the kitchens, not dreaming for a moment she would not be welcome, for she had never understood the concept of being a Royal. But she had learned a lesson. And she vowed never to return to a royal kitchen until she had a house of her own.

Later she would say, "That was so painful. I had never looked at it like that. I thought they liked me popping into the kitchens for a chat. I felt desolate after being ticked off. Suddenly I felt even more lonely than before. But I understood they were right. That was their world and I had invaded it."

Diana told one of Charles's confidants with whom she had developed a good understanding in those early days, "No one talks to me. I stand around at every official gathering not knowing what to do, what to say, or where to look, worried that I might be doing something wrong. When people do speak to me, they seem to treat me like some schoolgirl, asking me how I am. I feel like a fish out of water all the time and can't wait for the whole thing to finish so I can go back to the apartment."

Charles's former Royal Navy colleague Michael Colborne would become Diana's secretary, but more importantly Diana would come to treat him as her "unofficial uncle," and they would become close friends. Twenty-five years older than Diana, he would become her principal adviser for the next three years, explaining the thousand and one different matters she would need to know about the Royal Family, the monarchy, and the way she would have to conduct herself.

Except for Colborne, there were few others Diana would ever trust. She believed that most of Charles's former aides didn't like the fact that their cozy little all-male world had been shattered by her arrival. They hoped everything would continue as before, with all-male meetings most mornings, polo or hunting in the afternoons, and quiet, reflective chats and drinks in the evening before dinner. And Lady Susan Hussey, one of the Queen's ladies-in-waiting, would phone offering help and advice, but Diana became suspicious of her and everyone else at the palace and found it impossible to seek their counsel. Eventually, the phone stopped ringing.

Later she would tell one of her girlfriends from her bachelor days of the problems she had had with Charles's staff: "They would never let me see Charles alone. They would keep him closeted in meetings as though I had no call on his time whatsoever, expecting me to stay in the background, the little woman whose duty was to be seen occasionally but certainly not heard. Most of them didn't like me around, and they hated it if I ever had the audacity to interrupt one of their cozy meetings. When I would pop into the room where they were chatting with Charles, all men together, they would look at me as though I was something the cat had brought in. They were really awfully rude to treat me like that. Unfortunately Charles never seemed to notice, though I did tell him how they treated me. He would just tell me that they all loved me, admired me, and that I was imagining things. That was why they had to go. If I hadn't made a fuss, I don't think I would have ever seen Charles."

Diana would have a particularly bitter experience with one of Charles's most experienced advisers, a man she knew to be gay. She said, "He told me when I first became pregnant with William that I could now be proud of myself, that I had done my duty by the crown and that I should be thrilled that I had been privileged to carry the child of the Prince of Wales. It seemed to me at the time that after giving birth he would have preferred for me to disappear into the nursery and only come out again if another child was required. "On that occasion I went to my room and wept, feeling that I wasn't wanted at all. I remember wondering whether Charles felt that way towards me. It frightened me."

Diana would later be accused of getting rid of all Charles's former aides and old friends. During the first four years of their marriage a remarkable number, forty or so of them, resigned, quit, or were fired. Diana always refused to accept that she deliberately went out of her way to have them dismissed or to make their lives so miserable and awkward that they had no recourse but to leave.

Challenged about that now, Diana will say, "I think that's a little far-fetched. Some simply left because the scene changed; Charles was no longer a bachelor."

However, with an impish twinkle in her eye and a wry smile she will admit, "I may have had something to do with some of the departures, but not all of them. Some of them were just hangers-on and others wanted to stifle both Charles and myself. I think Charles would admit that some had passed their sell-by date."

Diana had hoped that the arrival of William, a male heir to the throne, would win the hearts of Charles and the entire Royal Family, for many jokes had been made about the need for the marriage "to be blessed" with children as soon as possible.

Charles had decided to marry following the assassination of Earl Mountbatten, blown apart when an IRA bomb exploded in his fishing smack in Ireland in August 1979. Until that tragic moment Charles had no real intention of settling down, marrying, and producing an heir to the throne. That single act of terrorism made Charles realize how quickly death could strike. It also made him realize that it was his duty, first and foremost, to produce an heir for the future of the House of Windsor.

Whenever the name "Uncle Dickie" surfaces, or whenever she hears mention of Earl Mountbatten, Diana freezes. She has nothing against him; in fact, everything she ever heard of Mountbatten from Charles reinforced the idea that he would have been a wonderful man for her to know. He seemed so wise, so sensible. It's not his name she can't bear, it's the memories that flow from it, for Diana realized some years after her marriage that Charles would never have asked her to marry him if Uncle Dickie had not been assassinated. Thus she would not have had to go through years of misery and loneliness. And she would hardly have known Camilla Parker Bowles, the woman she still holds responsible for the breakdown of her marriage.

Diana, of course, knew nothing of the extraordinary, intense relationship that developed after Mountbatten's assassination. Diana did not realize how Camilla had saved Charles's sanity at that time when he was so full of hatred and anger, desolated by the fact that the Irish question, as he called it, would end in the murder of his beloved Uncle Dickie, the only man in the world whom he truly worshiped.

To Charles, Uncle Dickie would be the father he never had, the man he looked up to throughout his life, the man he turned to for advice and friendship, the man whom Charles wanted to emulate. His father, Prince Philip, never understood that, for Philip was far too cold, too severe, too offhand with his children, behaving more like a Victorian father with little time for his offspring. That was why Charles grew apart from his father from a young age and why the two men have hardly spoken to each other for the past fifteen years.

Now, Charles knows the principal reason. His father has always been absurdly jealous of him for Philip has never achieved anything in his life, could never do so, always made to walk two paces behind his wife, Elizabeth; with never a chance of being anyone of importance in the House of Windsor except a good father figure. And his character wouldn't permit that. The arrival of Charles, the male heir and someone instantly more important in royal terms than Philip could be, consumed him to such a degree he could never hide his deep-seated envy.

Charles turned to Camilla for comfort and reassurance after Mountbatten's murder. For the first few days Charles acted with remarkable sangfroid, for he had been trained as a Royal never to show emotion in public. In private, however, he would throw himself on his bed and weep for hours.

In his agony Charles phoned Camilla, someone he had always remembered with deep affection and with whom he had

kept in touch by letter and the odd phone call during the years
of her marriage to Andrew Parker Bowles, the Army officer
she wed in 1974.

Charles had met Camilla in 1973 before going away to sea
with the Royal Navy. They had been instantly attracted and
Charles found Camilla wonderful, convivial company. They
became lovers for a brief period and Charles would take
Camilla for weekends to Broadlands, the country home of Earl
Mountbatten. For Charles, then in his mid-twenties, marriage
was a distant prospect. He had to go to sea to prove himself a
competent naval officer. Within a year of his departure Camilla
had married her Guards officer, Andrew, a thoroughly likable
man some ten years older than Camilla and Charles, who were
of a similar age. Charles, however, would become godfather to
their eldest child, Tom.

After Mountbatten's murder Camilla recognized a cri de
coeur in Charles's voice, and she immediately invited him to
stay at her country home in Wiltshire for as long as he needed.
During September 1979, Charles and Camilla would talk for
hours, take long walks with her dogs through the woods and
countryside, go for the occasional ride, and chat into the early
hours of the morning in the drawing room of her home.

Her husband, Andrew, then a major, would be asked to go
to Rhodesia for six months as a military aide to Lord Soames
while the former British colony introduced black majority rule
and the country became Zimbabwe.

Charles would spend most of that six months with Camilla,
trying to come to terms with the trauma that had made him feel
physically sick, angry, and desolate. Camilla offered him love
and affection, and within a matter of weeks they became lovers
again. In those months Charles discovered a sexual passion he
had never found with any other woman. He found he needed
Camilla completely and absolutely and would spend hours in
her arms, sometimes in tears, at other times making love with a
frenzy he never knew he possessed.

Charles pleaded with Camilla to divorce her husband and
marry him. He told her that he didn't care if that meant he

would have to give up the throne, as his great-uncle the Duke of Windsor had done, forced to abdicate in 1937 when he decided to marry the woman he loved, the American divorceé Mrs. Wallis Simpson. But the sensible Camilla would over the weeks persuade Charles that his first duty could not be to her or to his selfish needs, but to the nation, the crown, and the House of Windsor. Camilla offered to help find Charles a suitable young woman who would become the next queen of England, sitting on the throne beside Charles.

"I will never find anyone like you," he would tell her time and again.

Camilla would be adamant. "You must," she would say, brooking no argument.

During the early summer of 1980, Charles met Diana at a party and for the first time found himself attracted to someone other than Camilla. Eighteen months later they were married in a ceremony watched on television around the world. Charles had followed the advice of Uncle Dickie, who had told him, "What you must do is to go out and sow your wild oats for a while. Then find some suitable young virgin, marry her, educate her to be the next queen of England, and have some children."

Before marrying Diana, Charles needed the approval of Camilla, the only person he had ever trusted save for Uncle Dickie. Camilla and Diana met on a number of occasions before her engagement, and Camilla thought Diana would make Charles a good wife, a good mother to his children, and eventually a good queen. She persuaded him to go ahead. Diana had no idea that Charles asked Camilla for her seal of approval.

To Diana, Camilla had seemed the perfect older woman, a friend who had known Charles for many years and who was happy to advise and befriend Diana. She had no idea that Camilla and Charles had been lovers.

Even today Diana has been unable to forgive Charles for not telling her the truth of his relationship with Camilla at the very beginning. But she reserves her anger and hatred for "the bitch." She is convinced that when her marriage to Charles was going through a rough patch after the birth of Harry in 1984, Camilla happily provided Charles with not only advice and her shoulder to comfort him, but more importantly, her bed and her body.

On one occasion Diana went further and described Camilla as a rottweiler, suggesting that the woman she had come to loathe was more akin to a highly dangerous dog, capable of causing considerable injury to people. Diana had been greatly hurt by Camilla, and she would find other nasty, brutish words to describe Charles's mistress. On most occasions, whenever such phrases were splashed across the lurid tabloids, Camilla would simply shake her head, hoping that Diana would become more rational and understanding rather than blaming Camilla for everything that had happened to her marriage.

Diana would scour the newspapers for any reference about Camilla, reading whatever was written with the closest interest. In 1994 a book, *Camilla: The King's Mistress* by Caroline Graham, was published in London and serialized in two tabloids. As soon as Diana read of the book, she sent one of her staff to buy a copy. She would have gone herself but felt a bright shop assistant might have telephoned a newspaper with news of her purchase.

Diana devoured every word. The book included some colorful stories suggesting that Camilla and Charles regularly had sex outside on the grounds of Highgrove House; that when still married to Diana, Charles would spend four nights a week drinking wine and "romping" in Camilla's four-poster bed; and that Charles and Camilla would phone each other up to six or eight times a day.

Despite such evidence Diana had always, innocently, hoped that the relationship between Charles and Camilla had been platonic. She knew they had known each other for many years; she understood that Charles, Camilla, and Andrew Parker Bowles would frequently meet or have lunch or dinner. Diana remembered having had lunch at Middlewick, the beautiful

Parker Bowles home at Corsham in Wiltshire, not more than ten miles from Charles's country home, Highgrove.

On such occasions Diana had never noticed any particular intimacy between Camilla and Charles and never, for one moment, suspected anything untoward. When she did begin to suspect an affair, Diana challenged Charles repeatedly, but he would either deny the affair or simply not answer her questions directly.

Even this year Diana protested, "It was not until Charles told the world during that television interview in June 1994 that I knew for the first time, definitely, that Charles had been having an affair. I know it might sound extraordinary, but it hit me very hard."

# 8

## *Diana and Camilla*

———❧———

THE NIGHT OF Wednesday, June 29, 1994, will forever be forged on Diana's mind. For that was the night at around ten-thirty that Diana for the first time in her life heard Charles confess that he had been unfaithful while married to her. He had never admitted that to her before, not even during their violent, and frequent arguments.

The whole of Britain knew that Charles would be interviewed on television that evening by the author and broadcaster Jonathan Dimbleby, who had been provided extraordinary access by Charles over an eighteen-month period to write a definitive biography of him. The Prince of Wales gave permission to his aides, friends, and staff to talk unreservedly to Dimbleby about Charles's life and his work.

An estimated 15 million people tuned in that night, but Diana would not be one of them. She had read leaked reports that Charles would confess to adultery at some point during the two-hour-long interview. Rather than stay at home alone to watch the spectacular, Diana accepted an invitation to a gala banquet at the Serpentine Gallery in Kensington Gardens, only a few hundred yards from her home. Dressed in a breathtaking off-the-shoulder, above-the-knee, black chiffon Valentino dress, she dazzled the assembled 250 guests, who had paid $250 a head toward the $2.5-million gallery renovation. In its twenty-five-year history the gallery had been a home for the sort of avant-garde art that Charles would find distinctly unpalatable. Diana's photograph, showing her smilng, relaxed, and confident, appeared in every newspaper the following morning, challenging Charles's TV confession for space.

The following morning Diana read every paper and felt a surge of pleasure that she had stolen much of the limelight. "You see," she quipped to her staff, smiling broadly, "I left Charles some space in the papers today."

She would not tell anyone until much later that she had secretly videotaped Charles's interview and watched every minute as soon as she returned to the palace that night. "I kicked off my shoes and sat down in front of the TV with a hot drink. I didn't want to miss a thing, I had to hear what he had to say. His confession of adultery surprised me, the fact that he admitted it publicly. But what hurt deeply was his statement that he had never loved me. I couldn't believe he said that, not when he knew the papers would be full of the story and Wills and Harry would read what he had said. That's what angered me so much. He had no reason to say that. It is awful for two boys to hear their father say that he never loved their mother. It's brutish, despicable behavior. I kept asking myself how could he do that to them."

Charles bared his soul that night in the most revealing documentary ever made about a member of the Royal Family. During the long and extraordinary candid interview Charles confirmed that he had not been unfaithful to the Princess of Wales until their marriage had "irretrievably" broken down after many attempts to save it.

Diana would later say, "At the moment he confessed, I was shaking with nerves, the palms of my hands sweating, not knowing exactly what Charles would say. I felt nauseous wanting him to tell the truth but not wanting to hear the truth. Part of me wanted him to say he had committed adultery, but the other half wanted him to deny it."

She went on, "If he had denied it, if he could have given me some hope, I would have probably cried with the sheer emotion of the moment, elated that there had been no one else despite everything my heart and mind had told me about Camilla."

Diana continued, "When Charles issued that word 'until' I
had hope. Afterwards I felt so sad, so terribly sad, and so alone
that he had been having an affair. I bit my lip but that didn't
help. The tears came. There was nothing I could do to stop
them. I knew I had been right to watch the TV interview on my
own."

Later, Diana revealed that after the questions relating to
Charles's adultery she had hardly listened to the rest of the
interview for she had felt dead inside, as though a part of her
had been opened up for the world to see that she had been cast
aside like some piece of old clothing. That night she had hardly
been able to sleep, her mind going over and over the words
Charles had used to tell the world she meant nothing to him.

During the interview Charles would be shown at home and
on royal tours abroad, chairing meetings, on public platforms,
meeting dignitaries, making speeches, inspecting buildings and
factories, and sharing intimate moments with his two children.

To the British people, however, those few seconds of his
confession were all that mattered. His remarkable, unprece-
dented openness started a debate in political, church, and media
circles over the wisdom of allowing the documentary to be
made. The great majority of the media believed Charles had
been foolish and reckless to agree to the interview and had made
a blunder in confessing his adultery. One cartoon showed a
scaffold with a huge ax resting against a TV set with the title of
the program, *Charles: The Private Man, the Public Role,* on the
screen. Overhead were black clouds, and a shocked crowd was
watching. The cartoon was meant to resemble the execution of
King Charles I in 1649.

Many debated that his extraordinary admission might well
stop him from ever becoming king, asking whether Charles
had embarked on constitutional suicide. Some wondered
whether Charles had confessed all to test the water, to see
whether his confession of adultery would so shock the nation
that he might have to stand down in favor of his son William,
leaving him free to leave public life and marry the woman he
loved.

Many considered Charles may have found baring his soul in such a public manner a purifying experience, but others considered that his self-indulgence would inflict further damage on the monarchy and his relationship with it. Charles had gambled that laying bare his life would end the criticism that had surrounded him since his separation from Diana, for the nation had always blamed Charles for the marriage breakdown.

One or two media pundits suggested, with venom, that Charles had descended "into the gutter," along with pop singers and sports personalities, low-grade politicians, and TV soap stars, by trying to work on the public's affections through the television interview.

Within seven days, however, the pundits and politicians who had castigated Charles were made to eat their words. Charles had touched the heart of the nation. The people on whose behalf those papers claimed to speak so avidly had the temerity to disagree. In every form of phone-in, correspondence column, and opinion poll the people showed that they thought better of the Prince as a result of the TV interview. The constitutional crisis manufactured by Fleet Street and supported by some members of Parliament and the Established Church of England collapsed.

The nation had shown they were more fair-minded than their self-appointed tribunes. They recognized the film as a balanced portrait rather than a whitewash and were ready to accept the central theme, which was that Charles tries to live up to his motto that adorns his coat of arms: *Ich Dien*—I serve.

Many Brits feel Charles is odd, that some of his views are wrong or plain silly, his mannerisms maddening, his speech stilted, that he was the villain of his failed marriage. And yet the nation showed they could forget all those things because what shone through that night was that Charles devoutly wants the best for his country and works devotedly to achieve that aim. They felt sympathy for someone, however privileged, working relentlessly under permanent scrutiny.

Every poll taken immediately after his confession indicated

Charles's decision to bare his soul had gone down quite well. The nation still favored a monarchy and did not unduly worry about having an adulterer on the throne. One-third of voters in one poll believed Charles should be denied the crown, that he was not fit to reign. Two-thirds, however, said he should be king.

The TV interview stirred a host of related topics, some believing Charles's interview was but a sideshow to the need for a real agenda for change in Britain. Some argued that the prince's behavior was no problem; that, far more importantly, Britain faced a crisis that was not institutional but lay in the nation's failure to maintain consistent economic development. The monarchy in Britain used to be the authentic representative of a successful political, social, and economic order. Some argued that what remained of it was only a symbol of a decayed constitutional order.

Some pundits suggested that Charles's honesty, though admired by the nation, threatened in the long run to weaken him. For the rest of time he had risked his enemies speaking of "that self-confessed adulterer."

By the end of the interview Diana hoped that Dimbleby would have become more inquisitive. Like most of those watching, Diana found herself wanting to know the answers to numerous other questions that crowded her mind. He had admitted being unfaithful only after the marriage had "irretrievably broken down." When was that? Diana wanted to know. When did you see Camilla? How often did you see her? What did you do? How often did you make love? Where? And when? And why?

Charles had never realized Diana's abject feeling of personal failure when she finally realized that Charles had quit the marriage. All her life Diana had been a failure: at school, at music, at horse riding, at any exams she had ever taken. Charles had not understood how inadequate Diana had always felt, never comprehended that her feeling of inferiority had begun in her childhood when she tried to save her parents' marriage. She had constantly blamed herself for her parents' parting.

From her first meeting with Charles, Diana had always compared herself unfavorably to him and realized how unfit and mentally lacking she was to be the wife to the heir to the throne. Diana would try to understand the discussions with his intellectual friends, but would lose the thread of their arguments and give up, exacerbating her feeling of inferiority. She barely understood his work, his royal duties, or his responsibilities but would sit mesmerized by the brilliance of Charles's speeches, some of which she couldn't and, later, didn't bother to follow.

Diana wanted Dimbleby to ask questions about her so that she could understand where she had gone wrong, for in her heart Diana blamed herself and her lack of intelligence for the marriage collapse, just as much as she blamed Charles for turning his back on her and going off with his old mistress. She wanted to know why Charles no longer loved her. Was she a lousy wife? Was she hopeless in bed? Was she poor company? Was she boring? Was it the fact that she had no brains? Was she never fun?

She would recall the times she had spent hours alone agonizing over her marriage, and her approach to Charles. She would always wear the clothes he liked; always do her hair the way he liked it done; had lost weight to make herself more attractive; had been as seductive as possible, always showing her love in the way she thought he liked; tried to read intelligent books; tried to enjoy classical music and opera, but found them all boring and impossible. God how she had tried.

She would say to one of Charles's close confidants, "Doesn't he realize what he does to me when he leaves me on my own in this godforsaken hole? I tell him how terrible I feel when he leaves me, but he refuses to take any notice. I have told him that I cry on the bed waiting for him to come back, sometimes waiting three or more hours before he returns. "Then he walks in, sees I've been crying, and his voice heavy with sarcasm, says, 'What's the matter this time?'"

Diana would beg Charles's close advisers to explain to him the traumas she was going through every time he left her on her own. That message would be passed on to Charles, and he would nod in acknowledgment. But he had no idea how to placate Diana.

Those same advisers also knew that Diana would scream and plead with Charles when he had no choice but to attend meetings, consult staff, make speeches. For a while Charles had tried to placate his wife. He understood she was young and lonely, with few friends and fewer interests. He knew she would wander around Buckingham Palace listening to her Sony Walkman, spending afternoons and evenings lying on a sofa watching her favorite TV soaps. But the protests continued despite his attempts to calm his distressed young wife. He was at a loss at what to do.

He would ask Diana's adviser Michael Colborne, and her personal secretary, Oliver Everett, and others to make her understand that it was his duty to carry out royal functions and there could be no argument or debate about that. They tried, but it seemed Diana couldn't or wouldn't understand. Finally, he turned to the one person he believed might be able to help: an older woman, a friend of many years who knew Diana and who understood the pressures and the loneliness of the life she was leading with him. That woman was Camilla Parker Bowles.

At the time, Diana had no idea that Charles had turned to Camilla for help and advice. She accepted that they had been friends for many years, and on occasion, Charles and Diana would have dinner with the Parker Bowleses. She had never been aware of any frisson between Charles and Camilla. When they said goodbye, they would kiss each other on the cheek, but nothing more.

As she watched the interview, Diana wondered why Charles had ever married her, for she believed in her heart that he must always have been in love with Camilla. She also wondered whether Charles would apologize to her, to the boys, to the nation—for he would be their king—for his actions in marrying someone he didn't really love and then walking out on the marriage. She thought he wouldn't apologize because she believed him to be too arrogant, and as he often told her, she, too, was partly to blame for the breakdown because of her impossible behavior. She was right; there was no apology, to anyone.

And Dimbleby asked no more questions on that most private of matters, his adultery. Some viewers felt cheated; Diana certainly did. Many women viewers were sad and deeply sorry for Diana because she had to face such public humiliation, her husband confessing to adultery in front of the entire nation. But none of them knew of Diana's secret that Charles was not alone in his adultery. Diana's passionate affair with James Hewitt had started at about the time her marriage was falling apart around 1986.

Today Diana understands that Charles and Camilla are an item, that they live together most of the time, enjoying a quiet life, much like any other wealthy, upper-crust English couple fast approaching their fiftieth birthdays. She sees both Charles and Camilla as nearly middle-aged and believes they may be ideal for each other, listening to classical music and opera, reading serious books, and taking gentle exercise in long country walks and occasional days of riding to hounds.

At one time Diana wanted to show the world how stupid Charles had been when he dumped her for the rather frumpy-looking Camilla with the out-of-date hairstyle and the country-dress sense. The newspapers happily carried out that task for her by constantly printing pictures of Diana on one page and Camilla on the opposite page. The comparison may have been unfair, some would suggest cruel. Diana loved it.

Diana had often considered phoning Camilla's husband, Brig. Andrew Parker Bowles, thinking it might be sensible to chat and compare notes with the wronged husband, the fourth member of the quartet. She wondered how difficult, almost impossible, it must have been for him, having to make way for his former friend, his fellow officer, former polo-team player, and the heir to the throne.

Diana, however, never phoned because she felt it would be grossly unfair to embarrass him. "What would I say? What could I say?" she mused when discussing the idea with a friend.

She knew that Andrew had to call Charles "sir" on all occasions, even when having a drink together at a party. Since Camilla and Charles had begun their serious affair sometime in the late 1980s, Andrew had tried to avoid meeting Charles for fear of any paparazzi photograph that could cause Charles possible embarrassment.

Diana was surprised that Andrew never spoke a single word about his wife's adultery in public. I had known Andrew Parker Bowles during his tour of duty in Rhodesia in 1979–80, and we would sometimes chat, often about polo. In those days I remember Andrew to be a man who loved a party and a drink and who enjoyed the company of attractive, intelligent young women. He was also most conscientious, putting in long hours every week during that delicate transition from white government to black majority rule after a hard-fought, fifteen-year guerrilla war.

At that time he must have known that his wife was "taking care" of the traumatized Prince Charles, yet he did not show the least concern, proving most popular with a number of young ladies, and indeed, he struck up a strong relationship with a young woman photographer. By the end of his six-month tour of duty some people suggested the two had become an item, always attending parties together and seeing much of each other.

From the mid-1980s, Andrew Parker Bowles and Camilla were still man and wife but, according to friends, in name only. They remained friends, talked regularly on the phone, still enjoyed a good relationship with their two teenage children, but to all intents and purposes lived separate lives.

Andrew "understood" a "relationship" existed between Charles and Camilla, but he felt that since his marriage had in effect ended, it was no concern of his how close his wife was to the Prince of Wales. Most of the time he stayed in London while Camilla lived in their beautiful home at Corsham in Wiltshire, a short drive from Highgrove.

And yet Andrew had to show extraordinary restraint for more than seven years, dubbed the most selfless man in Britain, prepared to "lay down his wife for his kingdom!" Occasionally the odd rude comment would be made by someone in Andrew's presence. Most of the time Parker Bowles would simply ignore the remark. At other times he would fix the person with a hard stare and say nothing.

On one occasion a young toff, wearing a brown trilby, a green Harris-tweed suit, and brown brogues, appeared in the members bar at a race meeting at Newbury, Berkshire. In front of friends, he showed off by making a disparaging remark about Camilla. The comment was made only a few feet away from Andrew and in a deliberately loud voice. Andrew remained calm but flushed visibly. He turned, walked over to the young man, and looked him straight in the eye. "Is there anything you wish to say?" he inquired menacingly. "For if there is, then you had better say it to me outside."

For a moment the man, a little taller and heavier than Andrew but not nearly as fit, looked him in the eye. Andrew didn't move a muscle but continued to stare at him. He was determined the man should apologize or be humiliated in front of his friends.

One of the younger man's friends tried to intervene. "Who asked you to comment?" said Andrew harshly. "I'm talking to your rude friend."

The man looked at the ground, then back at Andrew, who stood stock-still. "I've got nothing to say," the man said.

"I think you have," Andrew said bitterly.

"What are you talking about?"

"I think you have an apology to make. To me."

"Oh, that," said the man, trying to laugh it off.

"Yes, that," Andrew said, unsmiling.

"I was only joking. Sorry if I offended."

"Yes," Andrew replied, relaxing, "you did offend. Thank you for the apology."

The man immediately offered to buy Andrew a drink, but Andrew told him, "No, thank you very much, I prefer to drink with my own friends." He turned and walked away.

The incident highlighted Andrew Parker Bowles's extraordinary predicament. To many, Andrew was the cuckold who should have protested about his wife's behavior. As it turned out, Camilla wasn't having an affair behind her husband's back for she had told him about herself and Charles. In private, Andrew was perfectly at ease with the situation despite the fact that Charles's emotional relationship with Camilla had started years before it became public knowledge. And Andrew enjoyed a discreet bachelor life of his own in London. Occasionally, like the incident at Newbury races, the odd remark would hurt, primarily because Andrew didn't want his wife's name dragged through the mud by people who received their information only through the tabloid press.

Only one point rankled with Andrew Parker Bowles. He believes that Charles, or most certainly Camilla, should have "done the decent thing" and warned him that Charles was to admit his adultery in the TV interview with Dimbleby. He had no idea that Charles would confess to such an indiscretion. Everyone knew the woman he referred to was his wife, Camilla.

Three months later Camilla and Andrew made it clear they were no longer together when they attended a memorial service for Camilla's mother, Rosalind Maud Shand. Camilla and Andrew arrived at and left St. Paul's Church, Knightsbridge, in separate cars. In that inimitable understated tradition of the English upper class, Camilla and Andrew had, without making any public statement about the matter, revealed their intention to live apart.

The signal inherent in the separate cars was timed to perfection. Three weeks later, in October 1994, Jonathan Dimbleby's biography of Prince Charles would appear revealing more of his relationship with Camilla. Their close friendship had developed from sharing a zany sense of humor, both laughing at jokes from the *Goon Show*, a highly popular cult radio show in Britain in the 1960s. They enjoyed a whirlwind romance around London in the summer of 1973, just weeks before Charles would leave for a nine-month tour of duty at sea with the Royal Navy. A year later Camilla had married Andrew.

In December 1994, Diana was told by one of her few

remaining friends within the senior ranks of the Queen's courtiers to prepare herself for a statement to be made about her marriage to Charles. She was informed one morning, privately by word of mouth, for her confidant believed the information to be too sensitive to risk telling in a phone call. They were drinking coffee at Kensington Palace at the time. Diana felt herself shaking, fearing the worst. She said later, "I tried to put the cup down quietly in the saucer but I found it rattling for I had suddenly suffered an attack of nerves."

She asked her confidant, "What statement? I don't know anything about any statement. Do you mean he's going to divorce me? I don't know anything about this, nothing. Charles and I have never even discussed divorce."

"No, no," said the confidant, "I don't know the details but apparently someone will be suggesting that divorce could take place at some future date."

Diana would not be so easily placated. Worried that she would be faced with the ultimatum of her own divorce without even being informed had been one of her worst fears since the separation. She knew only too well the power of the monarchy and the lengths to which the Buckingham Palace hierarchy would go if it suited their cause.

Before leaving, her confidant tried to reassure her, "If I learn anything definite, I'll let you know immediately."

Diana knew little of the divorce laws but suspected that Charles could, legally, file for divorce without informing her because they had been separated for two years. She decided to seek advice and contacted Lord Mischon, her lawyer. He reassured her that he was convinced nothing would occur. Diana was somewhat placated, but she didn't sleep peacefully that night.

Days later one of the Queen's most trusted and senior advisers, Lord Charteris of Amisfield, aged eighty-one, the man who had served Elizabeth for twenty years as her personal secretary from 1952, issued a statement making it plain that at some future date the "Prince and Princess of Wales would certainly divorce."

Diana would later say, "Those words hit me like hammer
blows. I read and reread the statement to make sure I understood. I knew then that the Royal Family and their most senior
advisers had decided my fate. I felt empty and defeated, as
though my life's blood had drained from me. No one had said a
word to me. No one had discussed anything. No warning had
been given to me or my secretary."

Suddenly Diana exploded. A rage took hold of her. "Those
fucking, fucking bastards," she screamed out loud. "Those
shits," she screamed while her staff outside in the office
pretended not to hear.

Diana would rage for about thirty seconds, yelling
obscenities at the top of her voice, then be silent for a minute or
more before another outburst took hold of her and the screams
of anger swept through the apartment. Her staff heard her
thump tables with her fists and wondered when the storm
would subside. Those listening looked at each other, wondering whether to intervene. No one moved.

Her rage would end in tears of anger and frustration that she
had been treated in such an offhand manner. Those who didn't
understand the machinations of the palace would have thought
little of Lord Charteris's statement. But Diana was nobody's
fool. She knew what it meant. She understood the oblique
statement by Lord Charteris only too well. Those few words
from that man spoke volumes to her. A decision had been taken
and this was the first shot to be fired in the crown's campaign
to slowly educate and prepare the nation for the forthcoming
divorce of Charles and Diana.

That night Diana felt lost and alone, not knowing what the
future would hold for her. She had no man for whom she cared
and no man who cared for her. It seemed that whomever she
found attractive and warm, considerate and kind, was either
married or found wanting.

Also, that night Diana thought of the only people in the
world whom she genuinely loved, her boys. And they weren't
with her either but away at boarding school, exiled for most of
the year. That night she would feel more alone than ever,

believing even her sons were growing apart from her, her influence becoming less as they became teenagers and more independent of her. Soon they would no longer need her. Then she would have nobody to care for, to worry about, to fuss over. She shivered at the thought.

Diana confessed all these thoughts to her newfound friend, a wealthy man in his fifties who worked in the City of London but whom she had met through her charity work. He would treat Diana more as a kid sister, but she believed that she had discovered someone whose advice she could trust. There was no sexual attraction between them, but Diana could tell him all her secrets with no feeling that he would betray her. She began turning to him more and more for advice. She felt at the end of her tether.

The next morning, after only a few hours' sleep, Diana would be at the Harbour Club by eight o'clock and would swim until physically exhausted. Yet, as she swam, she found new inner strength and greater determination.

Later she would say, "If they think I'm going to give in without a fight, then they have another think coming. I am going to tell Lord Mischon to fight them all the way until I get everything I want for myself and for the boys."

The New Year would be only a few days old when Diana would be surprised once more. Gossip columnists, and friends within the royal circle who had discussed the bizarre royal triangle over dinner and teatime for a number of years, finally learned of the outcome when solicitors representing Camilla and Andrew Parker Bowles issued a joint statement on behalf of the couple revealing that they had secretly been living apart for two years. It read: "Brigadier and Mrs. Parker Bowles have asked that it be known that they have instructed us to seek on their behalf a termination of their marriage, and that divorce papers have been filed. The divorce is by mutual consent, the ground being that they have lived apart for more than two years."

They also issued another, more illuminating statement, saying the real reason for the announcement was to ensure that their family and friends should be saved from harassment, especially their two children. In an effort to answer their critics and to overcome the general acceptance that Andrew had been a cuckold for many years, their statement went on, "Throughout our marriage we have always tended to follow rather different interests, but in recent years we have led completely separate lives. We have grown apart to such an extent that, with the exception of our children and a lasting friendship, there is little of common interest between us, and we have therefore decided to seek divorce."

Later that day Diana was brought a copy of the *London Evening Standard*. "Camilla Free to Remarry" was the headline. A subhead read, "Official: Divorce for Parker Bowles and Charles's Great Love."

Diana retired to her drawing room and read the five pages devoted to the sensational story. All that interested her, and most of the country, was the question of remarriage. Later she told her City friend that she burned with jealousy and anger at the thought that within perhaps a year or more the nation would accept both her divorce from Charles and, maybe, his marriage to the bitch.

Diana, however, had no idea that one of the primary reasons for the divorce announcement was that Andrew Parker Bowles had become involved with an old friend of the family, Mrs. Rosemary Pitman, whom Camilla also knew very well. Indeed, Camilla and Rosemary had in the past organized clothes sales together, and both were members of the elite West County social set, attending dinner parties at each other's homes over many years.

Mrs. Pitman, fifty-five, the mother of three grown children, comes from a wealthy family of solicitors. She divorced her husband, Col. Hugh Pitman, in 1991. Like Andrew, he was an ex-Army man who quit to establish a successful recruitment agency.

Both Camilla and Charles knew that Andrew Parker Bowles had become romantically involved with Mrs. Pitman. But the secret had not been shared with Diana. In February

1996, Andrew surprised all his friends, as well as Diana and Charles, by marrying Rosemary within twenty-four hours of anouncing their engagement. At Brigadier Parker Bowles's wedding to Camilla in 1973, several members of the Royal Family and a guard of honor were in attendance at the Guards Chapel. This time, Andrew married Rosemary in a quiet ten-minute civil ceremony at the Chelsea Register Office. The only people present were the five children from their first marriages.

Diana would discuss the surprise marriage with friends, wondering whether Camilla would ever remarry. Diana commented, "Camilla won't make the same mistake twice. She married the wrong person the first time round. There is still only one man in her life. And we know who he is."

# 9

# *A Princess Goes Cruising*

——— ❧ ———

AT THE FIRST OPPORTUNITY, Camilla and Charles opened a bottle of Dom Pérignon pink champagne in the seclusion of Highgrove, the country house that had been their sanctuary and their home. "To *our* future," Charles said, proposing a toast. They clinked glasses and Camilla felt that the trauma she had been through over so many years was finally ending.

"To us," she replied in her husky voice, taking a sip of champagne.

Charles would suggest to Camilla that nothing should now stop them from leading a normal life like any other couple in the same situation. Camilla, however, is understood to have proposed caution, reminding Charles that they had never been an ordinary couple and never could be. As usual Charles would agree that perhaps he was being a little hasty, that they might have to wait a short while before appearing together in public. Camilla was heartened by Charles's agreement because she knew he tended to be impatient.

Charles and Camilla would continue to be invited to lunch and dinner at friends' country houses where the hosts would seek out only those close friends who could be trusted to remain silent, and who would treat the Prince and Camilla as an ordinary couple. They would dine and sometimes stay at Anmer Hall, the Sandringham home of Hugh van Cutsem, fifty-three, the millionaire farmer and pedigree stud breeder and his wife, Dutch-born Emilie van Cutsem, forty-eight. Ever since Charles had decided to live apart from Diana, he had frequently stayed with the van Cutsems with both Wills and Harry during school holidays. The young princes established a close friendship with the van Cutsems' sons, Edward and Hugh, both of whom are several years older than William.

So happy were Wills and Harry with the motherly Emilie that she became another surrogate mother to the boys. Emilie relished the idea of helping Charles in whatever way she could in bringing up his sons. The boys enjoyed the lively, happy, convivial atmosphere of Anmer Hall, which buzzed with noise and activity, so unlike the somber mood that prevailed at nearby Sandringham when the Queen and Prince Philip were in residence.

Diana discovered that when the boys were purported to be staying at Sandringham with Charles, she would sometimes telephone to find they were, in fact, all staying at the van Cutsems' home. Diana talked to the boys about their visits there and, on occasion, found that while Charles was absent, the boys would be left to enjoy life with the van Cutsems on their own.

Whenever Diana found that Charles had left Wills and Harry, she would immediately try to contact Charles to remonstrate with him, often in a string of four-letter words, telling him that if he was having the boys for a weekend or a few days, then he should be staying with them, not handing them over to strangers. She would also tell him that if he couldn't for any reason care for them personally over a weekend, then she would be only too happy to have them stay with her at Kensington Palace.

Diana would tell Charles he was being "beastly" and "unfair" for he knew that she longed to see her sons anytime, anywhere. "I am their mother for Christ sake," Diana would yell at Charles. "How dare you bundle them off to some fucking stranger without my permission."

In fact, both Emilie and Hugh van Cutsem were no strangers to Diana. Before her wedding, Diana would become very friendly with Emilie, whose son Edward, then eight, would serve as a page at Diana's wedding in St. Paul's Cathedral. Diana and Emilie would attend the Wimbledon tennis championships and sometimes dine together.

But Wills and Harry also informed Diana that Emilie had told them to treat her "like another mother," contacting her if they were ever in any trouble or wanted to come and stay or simply have a chat on the phone. Both Wills and Harry enjoyed playing with their new friends, Edward and Hugh, whom Emilie suggested they should treat like older brothers.

And there was more. Diana learned that both Camilla and Charles would stay at the van Cutsems, and so close was the friendship between Emilie and Camilla that, in 1993, the two of them went on holiday together to India, visiting historic palaces. They toured the Taj Mahal, on the banks of the sacred river in Agra, where Diana, by posing alone in front of the famous monument to love in 1992, deliberately gave credence to the rumors that her marriage to Charles was in serious trouble.

Diana believed that Emilie van Cutsem had betrayed her friendship. She felt that Emilie had gone out of her way to nurture a relationship during the early years of her marriage, always offering help and advice and, later, by offering her services as an independent go-between if there was any chance of a reconciliation with Charles. Emilie would phone asking whether she could help, and Diana would pour out her heart to the woman who seemed to have taken her side in the arguments and rows she had with Charles. Since that time Diana felt deceived by her actions, wondering how much of their conversations Emilie had passed on to Charles.

She would accuse Emilie van Cutsem of being a false friend, giving comfort to her while entertaining her husband's mistress under her own roof. Later Emilie would compound that betrayal by befriending Camilla. In Diana's eyes worse would follow in her attempt to usurp her role as the princes' mother.

"I will never speak another word to that woman as long as I live," Diana has said, and few believe she will ever do so.

There were other friends who Diana believed had betrayed her friendship and hospitality among them. Lord Charles Shelburne, fifty-four, and Lady Fiona, forty-five, who had been close friends with Camilla and Andrew Parker Bowles for a number of years. They lived at Bowood House, Calne, in Wiltshire, not far from the Parker Bowles country home, and through them they met both Charles and Diana. The Shelburnes were at the heart of what became known as "the Highgrove set," that group of wealthy country families who lived within a twenty-mile radius of Highgrove whom Charles and Diana came to know well, entertaining them on occasion and accepting invitations to visit some of their homes.

The atmosphere at those get-togethers would be far more relaxed and friendly than at similar get-togethers in London homes, where many would behave in such a formal manner simply because the Prince and Princess of Wales were in attendance. In the country, however, people were far less stuffy, and Diana would enjoy the relaxed atmosphere where their friends would happily chat about any number of subjects, whether it was babies or the local hunt, educating children or disciplining dogs. And people dressed in a far less formal fashion, which, to the surprise of many, Diana does thoroughly enjoy. Brought up on her father's Norfolk estate, Diana's wardrobe throughout her teenage years consisted mostly of jeans and sweaters with casual cotton skirts and shirts in the summer. Only since Diana became Princess of Wales and the fashion gurus of *Vogue* educated her had she become one of the foremost exponents of fashion and style.

Diana felt at home visiting the mansions of the Highgrove set. She was among trustworthy friends, many miles from the hard-nosed ladies of fashion and wealth who, she believed, more often than not, treated her with contempt, accepting her only because she was married to the Prince of Wales and not because they wanted her to be part of their snobby, elite set.

As Charles came to spend more time at Highgrove in the late eighties, Diana had noted a cooling off in her relationship with those friends she had felt had been genuine in their warmth and hospitality. Later she realized how much socializing Charles had done during those years with Camilla among the Highgrove set.

Ever since Charles had demanded a formal separation in the autumn of 1992, Diana had wondered when he would seek a divorce. And yet he had not raised the matter and she had never wanted to know what was in his mind for she was happy to remain the Princess of Wales, mother to the heirs to the throne.

Diana recognized that she owed her position totally to the fact she had married the Prince of Wales. She had said, "If I hadn't married Charles, I would probably never have had my picture in the newspapers throughout my entire life. No one would ever have heard of me and I would have led a quiet, unassuming life. I suppose I would have married, waited for someone to come along, because my sisters and most of my friends have married. But it would have been a quiet wedding with, at the most, a line or two in the *Times*."

Following the separation, Diana found herself trusting fewer and fewer people, whether girlfriends or men friends, her police bodyguards, members of her own staff, her chauffeur, or anyone with whom she came in close contact. She would go further, refusing to permit armed police bodyguards to accompany her as before they had shadowed the Princess of Wales's every move whether on an overseas tour, on a charity visit in Britain, to her gymnasium, or even to Harrods. Shortly after announcing her decision in December 1993 to retire from royal duties and lead a more private life, Diana informed the chief of the Royal Protection Squad that she would no longer be requiring the services of any of his officers.

Senior officers remonstrated with her, detailing the sort of attacks she could expect from terrorist squads or hard-line political activists capable of kidnapping or killing the Princess of Wales as worldwide publicity for their cause. There were also screwballs, "nutters," drunks, or hangers-on who might try to take advantage of her if she traveled around the country or around London unescorted.

Diana would patiently listen to all arguments. "Thank you very much, but I have made up my mind," she would say. "I don't want any escorts whatsoever. Nor do I want police tailing me in their vehicles either. Is that understood?"

"Yes, ma'am" would be the reply. The only response police could give.

But Diana's bid for freedom courted disaster, encouraging some to take advantage of her trust in the public. In November 1995, a twenty-seven-year-old mental patient cycled up to Diana while she was out enjoying a walkabout, pressing the flesh, chatting to housewives in Liverpool. The patient had made a bet with colleagues at the Broad Oak psychiatric unit that he could get a kiss from the Princess of Wales. He rode his bicycle along the street, where hundreds of people were standing behind barriers waving and calling to Diana, and stopped next to her.

The crew-cut young man, dressed in jeans, leather jacket, and trainers said, "Would you like a roll-up fag?" (a cigarette), which Diana refused with a laugh. "Can I have a kiss then?" he asked, and Diana leaned forward and the man kissed her on the cheek, before riding off to cheers.

Diana, of course, had no idea that the young man was a mental patient, named Paul Fahy, who once threatened to shoot the mother of his two children and who calls himself Damien—from the horror movie *The Omen*—claiming he is the son of the devil. The ex-con has more than twenty convictions, one for assaulting a cop.

After his kiss, Paul Fahy told reporters that, before dying, his father had told him that he was a distant relation to John F. Kennedy. "For some time after that I would get into a panic believing I might be the next president of the United States." But he also reassured Diana, saying, "No one need worry. The Princess was never in danger from me. I love her with all my heart. I think she's the most beautiful woman in the world."

Police chiefs of the Royal Protection Squad would use that example to try to persuade Diana to relent and agree to officers accompanying her whenever she leaves the security of Kensington Palace. She refused point-blank. However, unbeknown to Diana, armed officers do, on many occasions, follow the Princess from a distance, particularly when she is walking around London shopping. They will also try to follow her when she is driving recklessly around London and on the motorways. Though they will often lose her, they can always trace her. The police have concealed an automatic bleep signal under her car that pinpoints the precise position of the vehicle anywhere in Britain.

There had been a number of other scares since Diana had refused police protection. In September 1994, another mental patient, Ricky Cotlarz, a twenty-nine-year-old born-again Christian, pushed his way through a crowd and came face-to-face with Diana when she was walking to her car after attending a charity function in London. There was no police presence as Cotlarz, a married man with one child, shoved through the throng and raised his fist at her, shouting and gesticulating. Only quick action by a security guard saved her, for Diana was trapped, the man standing between her and her waiting car. The guard managed to open the car door and push Diana in as the man continued to shout at her. On that occasion members of Parliament demanded that Diana be given police protection whether she wanted it or not, angry that she should put herself in such danger.

Diana has also received two death threats, both delivered by phone to Buckingham Palace. Neither British Telecom or the police were able to trace the calls; as a result, Diana was persuaded that she should be accompanied by armed police when attending official functions where her presence would be well-publicized beforehand. Police armed with either a Smith and Wesson handgun or a semiautomatic Glock machine pistol accompany her but stay in the background. Even after the death threats Diana was far from keen on being escorted anywhere at any time by any officers.

Diana didn't tell the senior police officers the reason behind her decision. She believed she could not trust the men who, ironically, had been entrusted with her safety. She believed they were under orders to reveal everything about the Princess of Wales to their superiors: about her trips, her visits, her lunch dates, her private visits, and always the names and full information on the men she might meet at any time, day or night.

Diana knew that there would be a computer record of everyone she met and exactly what had gone on between them, whether they had just shaken hands or said "Good morning" after having spent the night.

Diana would tell friends of this author, "I had become fed up knowing that every aspect of my life was known not just to the police, but any senior palace courtier who decided, allegedly for security reasons, to spy on me and find out what I was doing twenty-four hours around the clock. I wanted once more to enjoy some privacy, and the only way I could achieve that would be to get rid of those bodyguards."

And Diana certainly had no faith whatsoever in those aides of the Queen, not even her brother-in-law Sir Robert Fellowes, who Diana felt had turned against her over the collapse of her marriage to Charles. She knew her brother-in-law's job was to preserve the authority of the crown, above all other considerations, even the future happiness of his sister-in-law.

Diana came to believe that her telephones and her magnificent royal apartment in Kensington Palace were constantly bugged. She would deliberately carry out searches in her bedroom and study, checking under the beds, tables, and other furniture to see if she could find a bug. She became convinced her conversations were taped, so that the authorities would know precisely her whereabouts, though ostensibly having no idea where she went or whom she visited.

No one could convince Diana the police were not spying on her. "I know they're bugging me," she would protest. "I just know they are. They want to know everything about me and I'm not prepared to let them. It's my life, for God's sake."

On occasion, Diana would test the Royal Protection Squad by leaving the palace around midnight, getting in her Audi sports coupe, and taking off around London, sometimes driving at 90 mph, always searching her rearview mirror to check whether she was being followed. She would stop in side streets, then turn her car around after a few minutes and race off in the direction from which she had come. Sometimes she would zoom off down the M4, a motorway she knows well, past

Heathrow Airport, and drive for maybe fifty miles before leaving the highway and returning to London.

Sometimes, she would deliberately tease other drivers who recognized her, especially if it was a young man driving alone. She would drive up close behind him, flash her lights, slowly overtake him, making sure the man had a chance to recognize her. Then she would pull over in front of the man's car and slow down, making the other driver slow down, too. He might then overtake and carry out the same maneuver and Diana would repeat it, laughing and waving to the man. It was a dangerous game but it gave her a buzz.

And she would take greater risks. On occasion she would leave the palace and drive into Soho, London's notorious red-light district, to cruise the streets around midnight watching the girls parading the streets, the drunks and the drug addicts looking for kicks, the late-night revelers enjoying themselves, and the young people out to enjoy a night in Soho clubs. The traffic at midnight can only crawl along. Diana would wear one of her favorite baseball caps but would wind down the window of her car, chat to people on the sidewalk, some of whom would recognize the Princess of Wales.

She would talk to these people as though she knew them when, in fact, she had no idea who they were. She would be extremely lucky for most would laugh and joke with her. If any of them had tried to get into the car or make a grab for her through the open window, Diana would have been in some trouble for the cars, nose to tail, were traveling at a snail's pace with no exit she could take.

Diana really enjoyed taking those risks. She loved proving she was no longer the prisoner in the palace but able to get out and enjoy herself, whether cruising the streets, swimming in a pool, or keeping fit in a gym. It would become one of her favorite ways of challenging the system, showing she could and would rebel whenever she wished. But Diana would go no further. As far as is known, she would never leave the security of her car, never park and walk to a bar or a club. She would get the thrill of momentarily living on the edge, passing through the hard street life of a red-light district.

Diana had also enjoyed the excitement of her three secret years with James Hewitt, dodging the paparazzi, telling white lies to her staff and the Royal Protection Squad, and feeling the thrill of an illict affair. She felt no guilt for the affair with Hewitt that began in 1987 when, to all intents and purposes, her marriage was over. By the end of 1986, Charles and Diana had stopped sharing the marital bed, but at that time there was no talk of separation or divorce.

When, later, the question of divorce arose, they both said divorce would be an unfair burden for Wills and Harry to endure. Apparently, the two boys had accepted the separation, which had taken place slowly over months, even years, with Charles telling them of his decision to move to Highgrove where he could work better. Later, he would move his office there and a number of his staff would move from London to the country.

The boys continued to see their parents at school functions, and they would still tour overseas together and sometimes attend royal duties together in Britain. Their dual appearance, however, would occur less often, mainly because Diana had decided to take on more charities of her own.

As events moved faster, Charles and Diana explained to their sons that they would be leading separate lives and living in different places, Diana remaining in London at the palace and Charles spending most of his time at Highgrove. Both Wills and Harry knew Camilla Parker Bowles for they had met her occasionally at Highgrove. But they didn't know her very well.

Occasionally, William would ask both his parents if they were planning to divorce and seemed greatly relieved when they told him that they had no plans to do so. Only later would the boys be made aware of their father's real relationship with Camilla Parker Bowles, but they would never learn of their mother's relationship with Hewitt, despite the tremendous furor that occurred following the revelations of the book Hewitt cooperated in writing.

Diana would tell her sons that Hewitt had been a dear friend, that he had taught her to ride in the same way that he had given the princes riding lessons, and that the revelations in the book *Princess in Love* had been grossly exaggerated. The boys were not surprised, for whenever they had seen tabloid newspaper stories about themselves or their parents, they knew much of what was written proved to be pure speculation or totally inaccurate.

Wills was only twelve, Harry barely ten, when the truly embarrassing revelations of their parents' affairs were splashed over the newspapers and the television news programs. Charles would confess on TV to adultery, and a year after *Princess in Love* appeared, Diana would reveal her three-year-long affair with Hewitt in her TV interview. Now there was no hiding place for the boys and they had to face the fact that both their parents had had lovers while they were married.

After the official announcement of Camilla and Andrew's divorce, Charles was happy with the arrangement. He had no wish to further upset his sons or risk alienating any lingering support that he still enjoyed with the public. He understood full well that the nation still loved Diana, far more than any other member of the Royal Family. They still wanted to hear nothing untoward said about her, nor see anything done to humiliate her or remove her from the forefront of the Royal Family.

When Charles publicly confessed to adultery, he felt a tremendous release from a burden he had been carrying far too long. And now since Camilla's separation he felt that he could begin to enjoy life with the woman he loved, without the appalling shame of resorting to the most embarrassing subterfuges. On occasion, both Charles and Camilla would hide in the trunks of cars to escape the paparazzi and be smuggled into each other's home. On other occasions Charles would change cars, pretend to drive in one direction, and then return via back lanes, and sometimes across ploughed fields, to be with Camilla. He deeply resented having to live that sort of life.

Charles and Camilla had telephoned each other constantly, often talking five times a day, always trying to say good night and wish each other a peaceful sleep as their last act of the day. Charles would come to rely more and more on Camilla, not simply for her love and strength but for her common sense and surprising sense of humor in the most trying circumstances. On occasion Charles wondered how he managed to stay sane when the papers were full of the bizarre triangle, which the public seemed to savor with every new prurient revelation.

From time to time, Charles discussed the question of divorce with his mother, though he never wanted to have such conversations with his father because he knew that Prince Philip would begin to hector him, as he had done all his life. The Queen would tell Charles that one day the question of divorce would have to be faced, but Charles would argue that neither he nor Diana wished to divorce yet, preferring to allow their children to slowly get used to the possibility. In conversations with his mother Charles put no time limit on their marriage. And his mother accepted that situation though she wished that Diana would melt into the background forever.

It wasn't that the Queen disliked Diana, for she hardly knew her. Whenever they spoke, Diana appeared shy and embarrassed and conversation was awkward and stilted. Elizabeth simply realized that Diana was a strong-willed young woman who demanded her freedom and was not prepared to accept the strict rules of being a member of the Royal Family. Elizabeth feared that Diana, with her sharp swings of mood, could cause severe embarrassment to the monarchy, and she wished to avoid such unwelcome occurrences at any cost.

Elizabeth would discuss Diana with her mother, the Queen Mother, who was in her nineties. Much loved and respected in Britain, the Queen Mother had led an exemplary life and had endeared herself to the British people during World War II, refusing to leave Buckingham Palace at the height of the blitz because she wanted to stay with her people. The Queen Mother simply did not trust Diana and gave her daughter and Charles, her favorite grandson, the same message. She would tell them, "You must be able to trust anyone who becomes a part of our family. But that is a young woman you cannot totally trust."

The Queen Mother would never give any reason for what seemed a totally unreasonable comment to make of a young woman destined to be the next queen of England. "I have my reasons" was the only comment she would make.

In conversations with her senior advisers Elizabeth was believed to have agreed with her son's interpretation of the mood of the nation. There was no need to rush the divorce for many reasons other than those stated by Charles. During the past few years the Royal Family and the institution of the monarchy had taken an awful battering in the press and, according to polls, by the nation. Newspapers and commentators were critical of the amount of money the monarchy spent each year for what they perceived were dubious rewards for the nation. The behavior of the younger Royals had revealed a growing public cynicism toward the monarchy. The fire that destroyed part of historic Windsor Castle in November 1992 also unleashed a pent-up resentment toward the Royal Family that had been simmering for some years.

The fire had destroyed the magnificent St. George's Hall, the adjacent Waterloo Chambers, and treasures that experts suggested were, literally, priceless; it also destroyed the unique relationship between the Queen and her people. The government immediately announced that the nation would happily pay for the full cost of repairs to the castle, estimated at about $75,000,000, since the castle was not insured. It had been accepted practice for decades that any such tragedy would be paid for by the nation, for the British taxpayer was responsible for sustaining their monarch in luxury and splendor. On this occasion the nation's taxpayers disagreed.

The British people demanded that the Queen herself pay for the repairs, complaining that the Queen, who paid no taxes, would make no contribution to the cost of the castle repairs while her people, who were heavily taxed, would pay the entire bill. The Royals were accused of meanness, greed, and blinkered disregard for the feelings of the people, a mark of a dying, not a lasting dynasty. Such a reaction of anger and hostility had never before occurred in this century.

Elizabeth was unable to comprehend such a dramatic sea change in the people's affection for the Royal Family and respect for the monarchy. The press turned its attention to the Queen's wealth, and a crescendo of criticism ended with renewed demands that she pay tax, like the rest of the nation. Intensive behind-the-scenes arguments took place at the political level and among senior Buckingham Palace aides because Elizabeth didn't want to pay any tax, arguing that as sovereign, she should be above such matters. However, common sense, and a strong case made by Prince Charles for paying taxes, finally prevailed. In February 1993, Prime Minister John Major gave details to the House of Commons about taxes the Queen would pay. Tax experts believed her main liability would be on dividends from the $100-million stock portfolio she is believed to own. The vast majority of the tax would be levied at 40 percent. She would also have to pay capital gains tax on any stock sales.

Taken aback by the strength of the feeling running against the monarchy, Elizabeth decided to cut back on crown expenditures, taking the minor royals out of the limelight. Throughout 1993 and 1994, the Royal Family faded into the background. She ordered Royals who were not members of Elizabeth's immediate family to stay away from the annual spectacular gatherings, such as Trooping the Colour, celebrating the Queen's official birthday.

The latest polls indicated the nation wanted a change from the distant, aloof, old-fashioned monarchy Elizabeth had epitomized throughout her forty-year reign. They preferred a slim-line Scandanavian-style monarchy with fewer Royals involved, less ceremony, less grand living, and less ostentation. They also wanted all the lesser Royals to get proper, worthwhile jobs, rather than just opening the occasional hospital wing or fete, presiding over a charity meeting, or representing the Queen on official occasions. And they insisted on a significant cut in the cost of the Royals' upkeep.

Elizabeth feared the furor Diana's divorce might create. She and her advisers believed the nation would interpret the divorce as an act by the Royal Family to remove the people's favorite

Royal. However, powerful voices among the Establishment and the grandees of Buckingham Palace were advocating that the sooner a divorce took place, the better it would be for the future prestige of the Royal Family and, ultimately, of the monarchy itself.

Those pushing for a quick divorce would point to Diana's behavior and successive revelations about her life that still dominated the British press. Her three-year affair with James Hewitt had caused people to raise eyebrows; her relationships with a number of married men caused more serious disquiet; and her single-minded approach to her future, independent of the Royal Family, worried those responsible for advising the Queen. They could see Diana, young, attractive, royal, and a princess, creating untold problems for the dignity of the crown in her ambition to become the focus of attention, outshining all the other Royals, and in particular Elizabeth and Prince Charles.

Two years after their separation, the pressure mounted, for the divorce laws of Britain stated a couple could then automatically divorce on the grounds of an irretrievable breakdown of marriage. The nation waited for a statement from Buckingham Palace announcing the divorce. But none would be forthcoming. Commentators and newspapers demanded that they divorce "in the couple's best interests." In the autumn of 1995, after so many revelations of Diana's private life had been leaked, further demands for a divorce were made.

The conservative *Daily Telegraph* commented, "It is true that Diana has suffered a good deal, and that her situation, though privileged, is not enviable. But it is also true that what she is doing is not good for this country. The Princess melodramatically 'retired from public life' but now she seems to have returned to it, with equal melodrama. She remains royal, in title, in prestige, in her residence and paid for by royal money. Yet she is royal only when she chooses, not allowing her engagements to be run by Buckingham Palace and avoiding the full, irksome round of duties. She remains married, but to a man she is known to dislike, and with a rather too obvious interest in attracting his successor."

The highly critical article seemed to echo the views of the Establishment. It continued with even greater vitriol, "Even her undoubted brilliance as a public performer has more of a filmic quality about it than that of restrained, formal, self-effacing altruism which best suits British royalty. Her style is more Monaco than monarchy. She is damaging herself, and the public interest. Since she cannot be reconciled with her husband, she should divorce, and learn to hide her dazzling light under the bushel of motherhood."

Marital advisers sensed there was so much hostility between Charles and Diana it would be preferable for Wills and Harry for their parents to divorce. They argued a divorce would at least put an end to all the harmful stories of their parents' respective love lives. It might also help Wills and Harry heal the scars they must both carry and help them forget the awful scenes they had both witnessed. It would also end any lingering hopes the boys might still harbor of bringing their parents together again.

# 10

# *A Princely Dilemma:*
# *A Kingdom for a Wife*

———— ❧❧❧ ————

IT IS DOUBTFUL WHETHER Charles will ever marry Camilla, the woman he has loved all his life. When news of the impending divorce was announced from Buckingham Palace in December 1995, Charles declared that he had "no intention of remarrying."

Many took that remark as an unequivocal statement that he would never marry Camilla, but that is not necessarily the case. Charles has found himself in a most difficult situation, for when he becomes king he will also automatically become head of the Church of England. The regulations under which the Church currently operates were passed in 1938, partly in response to the abdication crisis. Those regulations state unequivocally that the marriage service should not be used a second time for anyone who has a former partner still living.

Individual clergy are free, as legal registrars, to marry divorced people in church, and an increasing number of them do so. But they act with what is called freelance compassion. The primary regulations of the Church, however, forbid such freelance compassion. Prince Charles, as heir to the throne, cannot act as a private individual and quietly visit a registry office, the places in Britain where marriages are conducted without religious ceremony. He can only marry with the sovereign's permission, and the Queen, as supreme governor of the Church of England, could not give permission for him to marry in England because Diana, his first marriage partner, is still living.

To marry, Charles requires a special license from the archbishop of Canterbury, and the archbishop will not issue his license to anyone who is divorced and has a former partner living. At the moment, therefore, Prince Charles could not marry anyone in the Church of England.

Even in the most unlikely event that Diana suffered a tragic and fatal accident, Charles could still not marry Camilla without jeopardizing his right to succeed to the throne, not even if the Church did change its rules. There is wide agreement in the Church of England that there is one circumstance in which divorced people cannot be married in church: that is, if the relationship of the two people wanting to get married was a significant factor in the breakup of the previous marriage. For the Church to marry divorced people in such circumstances would mean condoning adultery. So if Charles wanted to marry Camilla, the archbishop of Canterbury would have no alternative but to refuse permission.

If, however, Charles went ahead and married Camilla outside England, for example in Scotland, the archbishop would then have to raise serious questions about his coronation. With the monarchy in its present fragile state, no heir to the throne could afford to take that risk. And Charles has been drilled with one fact all his life: his principal objective must be to uphold the monarchy and the House of Windsor. Hence the categorical statement that Charles, under any circumstances, cannot marry Camilla and remain heir to the throne.

However, the prohibition against marrying Camilla will not alter their relationship. Charles and Camilla will continue to be a couple, Camilla caring for Charles and loving him but remaining forever in the background, even when he becomes king. That fact brings a wicked smile to Diana's lips.

Charles himself was never that keen on marriage. He loved the bachelor life of polo and shooting, stalking and skiing, opera and music and books, while satisfying his interests in architecture, ecology, and gardening. He thoroughly enjoyed having his crew about him, his band of former armed service personnel, loyal and keen; and he rather liked inviting his male friends to the palace for lunch or dinner for discussion and intelligent debates on any number of subjects. All that had come to an end shortly after he married Diana, and he hated those changes to his life.

As previously mentioned, Chief Petty Officer Michael Colborne met Prince Charles during his years with the Royal Navy and served with him on several ships during the 1970s. Such was the empathy between the two men that when Charles quit the Navy, he asked Colborne to become his secretary, and a firm friendship developed. After his marriage, Charles asked Colborne to become Diana's secretary to guide and advise her. After three years with Diana, Michael Colborne left royal service but has since remained friends with both Charles and Diana and still sees them.

Colborne understands Charles very well. He commented, "In many respects Charles was a born bachelor. He enjoyed a wonderful life as a single man and he never wanted it to change. He only married because he knew that it was his duty to provide an heir to the throne. It was the dramatic, sudden death of Uncle Dickie that persuaded him that he had to marry, and quickly. For suddenly, he had realized that his life, too, could be snuffed out like a candle at any moment.

"It was Camilla who persuaded Charles that he must find a suitable bride who would make him a good wife and have the aristocratic background to become a first-rate queen and consort. Camilla had refused his incessant pleas to divorce her husband and marry him because she realized only too well the enormous constitutional crisis that situation would create. Diana came along at exactly the right moment and Charles was hooked. She was young, beautiful, and vivacious. She was also from an impeccable aristocratic background and she absolutely worshiped Charles."

Colborne continued, "I also know that Charles did love Diana. Any suggestion that he never loved her is hogwash. I saw them together in the good times when they were wrapped in each other. They loved each other, pure and simple. It was a tragedy when it all went wrong. I now believe that having regained his independence, he is, once again, a happy man. I believe he will probably remain single even after his divorce from Diana, whenever that comes about. There is obviously a deep love and affection between Charles and Camilla, but they are both adults. They know they have the rest of their lives to be together, and the strength of their relationship won't be dimmed just because they don't live together as man and wife."

According to friends who have known Charles for some years, he is, once again, happy living a bachelor life with his mistress ensconced in a beautiful house not far from Highgrove. His sense of humor has returned and he has become more patient with his staff. And he no longer feels embarrassed because until 1995 he could only visit Camilla in her marital home or invite her over to Highgrove.

In the summer of 1995, Camilla bought Ray Mill House, a twenty-minute drive from Highgrove. A delightful Bath-stone, late-Regency villa, it is located near the picturesque National Trust village of Lacock, Wiltshire, and cost $1.2 million. She purchased it after selling the former marital home Middlewick House, her seven-bedroom, eighteenth century home in Corsham, to Pink Floyd drummer Nick Mason for $1.8 million.

Some work had to be done to make the six-bedroomed house into the home Camilla wanted, a bijou residence set in seventeen acres of beautiful Wiltshire countyside. The house is not too large, but comfortable enough for her children Tom, twenty-one, and Laura, eighteen, to stay in when they are down from university. And Ray Mill House makes a cozy home for a couple entering middle age.

Before buying the estate, which borders the banks of the river Avon, Charles went over the property with Camilla several times and both agreed it had great potential, with the a house well-hidden from prying eyes and long-range camera lenses. Charles went further and happily provided Camilla with a handsome check, estimated at more than $100,000, toward the renovations and interior decorations they both felt necessary to stamp their characters and personalities on the beautiful house they want to make their home.

Having spent two months refurnishing and decorating the main house, Camilla will now concentrate on converting the large stone barn into a luxurious four-bedroom retreat on the estate, two hundred yards from the main house, but first she must secure permission from the local planing authority. That might not be automatic because the authority has a reputation for not wanting the village spoiled or changed in any way. Camilla intends to invite her widowed father to move into the refurbished barn so he can be near his beloved daughter.

Charles and Camilla intend to make Ray Mill House their hideaway home where they can be totally on their own, whenever they want seclusion and intimacy. To Charles, High-grove has few happy memories. They are mostly awful recollections of his disastrous marriage and the appalling battles that went on there between Diana and himself. After 1987, Charles carried on much of his work from Highgrove, moving his office from London to his country estate. Since the official separation in 1992, Charles has moved most of his business affairs and his staff back to London, taking a suite of offices in St. James's Palace, two hundred yards from Buckingham Palace. He also has a small apartment in St. James's Palace where he stays when remaining overnight in London.

Having recovered from the marriage he once described as "a life of absolute mayhem," Charles believes he is fortunate to have been reunited with the woman he loves and respects, and who makes him laugh and relax. Camilla is also in no hurry to urge Charles to marry her. She, too, believes Charles should remain a bachelor when he finally divorces Diana, for then there would be no constitutional problems for him to face when the time comes to ascend the throne.

Camilla believes the passage of time might alter his outlook on marriage. But that raises another consideration, which she has discussed with Charles, his all-important relationship with the two most important people in his life, Wills and Harry. For their sake Camilla feels it would be a major error if they thought, for one moment, that their father was eager to divorce their mother so that he could immediately marry the woman whom Diana, and much of the nation, blames for the marriage breakup. She also believes Charles should retain his independence for as long as he wants, perhaps as much as fifteen years. Charles would then be over sixty, Wills would be nearly thirty and Harry twenty-seven.

Camilla has great trust in her relationship with Charles, and she does not believe the passage of time will harm their deep feelings for each other. Ever since the dark days of 1979, following the assassination of Uncle Dickie, she has known that Charles needs her. She understands his strengths and his weaknesses. She is probably the only woman in the world who has held Charles in her arms while he openly sobbed, unable to control his tears after Mountbatten's senseless murder. She believes she knows his heart and his soul better than anyone else. She also understands that he needs time alone fishing and reading and listening to music. And she is all too happy to give him the freedom he must have.

In the unlikely event that Elizabeth, who turned seventy in 1996, should die in the near future, Charles would automatically become king. And, if still married, Diana would have been crowned queen. Charles, however, would not have been able to bear the sight of Diana sitting beside him in Westminster Abbey being crowned queen consort.

If Charles and Diana had not divorced before that time, Britain would have faced the unseemly prospect of King Charles III, supreme governor of the Church of England, divorcing his wife, the most popular member of the Royal Family, between the time of his mother's death and his coronation, a matter of perhaps six months. Such a quickie divorce would have proved a disastrous start to a new king's reign, and his advisers would never have permitted him to take such a step.

For these reasons the Establishment, the politicians, and

Church of England leaders advised Charles and Diana to divorce sooner rather than later, despite the fact that neither Charles nor Diana wanted to take such action until Wills and Harry were some years older.

# 11

## *A Nanny Named Tiggy*

———— ❧❧❧ ————

DIANA HAS ALWAYS BELIEVED that despite all his faults and lack of warmth toward her, Charles truly loves both William and Harry and throughout their lives has proved his love in his treatment of them. On many occasions during their early years together Charles had told her he would try his damnedest to be a good, natural, loving father to his boys, the exact opposite of the way he remembered only too starkly how his father, Prince Philip, had behaved toward him.

Prince Philip would treat his eldest son as though he were a junior naval rating rather than a beloved firstborn. Philip's attitudes toward child rearing verged on the Victorian: Charles was to remain quiet at all times, unless invited to speak; be sent to his room as a punishment for the least misdemeanor, even something accidental; and be threatened with a good thrashing for the faintest sign of naughtiness.

The German-born Philip frequently administered corporal punishment to his young son, usually his hand, giving four or six hard slaps on Charles's backside. Later, Philip would use a slipper or a tennis shoe to beat Charles. Philip once gave Charles a spanking for sticking out his tongue in public, another time for slipping an ice cube down a servant's neck, and in yet another instance for being rude to guests. And Charles would always be beaten for not immediately obeying his father. All these beatings took place before Charles was six.

Miss Catherine Peebles (nicknamed Mipsy), Charles's first

governess, believed that Prince Philip was partly responsible for the boy's nervous, oversensitive personality. Mipsy recalled, "If you raised your voice to him, he would draw back into his shell, and for a time you would be able to do nothing with him."

At first, Elizabeth tried to intervene to protect her firstborn from Philip's strict discipline, but he would say, "The child must learn to obey, and I intend to teach him."

Charles would tell Diana of all his childhood experiences at the hands of his father, but he would examine how his relationship had changed toward him over the years. Despite the beatings and the discipline, he loved his father, believing him to be brave, good, and invincible. He copied his every mannerism, the way he spoke, the way he walked, and above all, he absorbed his passion for sailing and polo. Charles desperately wanted his father's confidence, his love, and his acclaim. But they would not be forthcoming no matter how hard Charles tried. Years later Charles would realize that his father had resented the life Charles would lead as heir to the throne. Instead of encouraging him, Philip subjected his son to a regime of obedience, trials, and punishment. The man who should have been proud of Charles's achievements hardly ever praised him, and whenever he failed at anything, Philip was quick to condemn.

Philip's harsh approach to his son's development made Charles stand on his own two feet, but at a great price. Mistakenly, Philip would even refuse to help Charles when he needed it, nor give Charles advice when he sought it, and more important, turned his back when Charles yearned for affection and parental love. The adoration and love Charles bore his father gradually turned to estrangement and fear in the face of icy behavior. Charles had always respected his mother for her diligence and sense of duty and the way she had coped with her difficult, truculent husband for so many years.

Diana would tell her girlfriends who were mothers of young children, "Charles is wonderful with the boys. He may be a little naive about babies, not having any idea what to do, but he loves being with them, holding them, feeding them, playing with them, and enjoying their company. He gives them so much love because he realizes how little love he received from his parents. And thank goodness he realizes how important love is to a child's emotional development."

That simple but vital attachment between Charles and his sons is something that has always confused Diana. She would see the way he behaved with both Wills and Harry, observe the joy in his eyes when he picked them up, cuddled them, or later when he would take their hand while they walked beside him. She has not yet been able to understand how he found it possible to turn his back on them simply to spend more time with another woman.

When those thoughts flashed through Diana's mind, her mood would immediately change and anger would overcome her. "The stupid, fucking bastard," she would scream. "How could he leave us for that bloody woman? God, he infuriates me. How could he walk out on them if he really loved them? How could he?"

More often than not, her anger would end in a flood of tears, which she didn't want to shed but which simply welled up in her eyes.

Even ten years after the breakup Diana finds herself becoming overwrought whenever she thinks deeply about Charles and his relationship with their sons. She has to tell herself that Charles does still love them and he wants them to grow up with far fewer emotional hang-ups than he has.

In his famous 1994 TV interview Charles told Dimbleby that he wanted to mention his sons, and he did. He wanted to explain his relationship with them in an ordinary way so that everyone would understand the bond between them. "I have always mucked around with them a great deal. When William was tiny, I used to muck around with him as much as possible." The film footage showed Charles with Wills and Harry in the open air in Scotland, smiling, laughing, and joking together. The boys seemed happy and natural.

Diana has always disliked and has often violently objected to Wills and Harry being taught to shoot and to hunt, but she didn't mind their father teaching them to fish. She was concerned from the very beginning that simply being with the Royal Family in Scotland would influence them to such an extent that shooting and hunting would become natural sports to them. That was why she wanted to dissuade them from engaging in such sports from an early age.

She hated family holidays at Balmoral because Wills and Harry were so eager to accompany their father whenever he went out shooting, stalking, or riding. At first she tried to dissuade them by suggesting they stay inside with her, playing with their toy trains or cars, their board games, or reading or watching a children's video on TV. But the boys loved to emulate their father's sporting interests. They wanted to be like him, to be with him. And she had to confess they had that look of enchantment and excitement on their little faces whenever they put on their outdoor clothes to join their father in the cold and rain of the moors stalking, shooting, or simply walking the dogs.

Diana found she was losing the arguments over hunting and shooting, which continued for a number of years. By the time Wills was eight and Harry six, she knew there was no point in her objecting for they loved both those violent sports. Their decision upset Diana greatly for she felt powerless, unable to dissuade even her sons from indulging in what she believed to be "vile, disgusting sports" that she felt should be banned by law.

On one famous occasion at Balmoral, when the boys were very young, Diana had a ferocious argument over dinner with the whole family as she stridently explained in no uncertain terms that people who supported such cruel sports weren't fit to be parents.

"What?" interjected Philip. "What did you say?"

Diana would not be calmed. "I said," she repeated, blushing madly, "that parents who condone such cruelty aren't fit to be parents."

Elizabeth said nothing but looked angrily at Diana, then at Charles.

"I don't think Diana actually means that," Charles said, trying to diffuse the tension building up around the table.

"Yes, I did," Diana said, sticking to her guns. "I meant

every word. How can you call yourself responsible parents encouraging young boys like Wills and Harry to shoot birds and kill foxes. It's disgusting."

"I think you've said enough for one dinner," Philip commented, hoping to stop Diana from continuing her argument.

"Well, I don't think I have. I've only just started. I don't want my sons brought up enjoying such awful, cruel country activities. I don't want them to be taught to kill innocent animals and birds. They weren't brought into this world to kill."

Her voice rising higher, the tears began to well in her eyes as she looked at the family staring at her, unable to believe her blasphemy.

"I think that's enough," Elizabeth said quietly, and she began to eat again.

"Well, it isn't enough for me," yelled Diana, "not until I stop them practicing such cruelty. Only then will I have said enough. Good night."

With those words she picked up her napkin and all but threw it on the table before walking out of the room. No one is permitted to leave a royal table before the Queen departs without her express permission. And that applies to her own family in the confines of their own home.

Philip was about to leap to his feet to stop her, but Elizabeth raised her hand. The Queen wanted no more trouble, for Elizabeth cannot abide such scenes. The family, however, would never forget what they considered an extraordinary emotional outburst.

It was not surprising, with such scenes and with such an adverse view on the principal sporting pursuits everyone enjoyed at Balmoral, that Diana never liked visiting the castle and could never escape the place quickly enough. Charles loved Balmoral, situated in a desolate part of Scotland, devoid of paparazzi and journalists, a cold, windy place where the Royals could do whatever they liked with complete freedom.

"That godforsaken place" was Diana's description of Balmoral, where all she could remember was boredom, frustration, loneliness and unhappiness.

Diana would not admit this point to many, but she was annoyed that Charles had won the argument over blood sports, which made her feel useless and lonely. Often Diana would walk into a room to hear Charles and the boys deep in conversation about the events of that day, nearly always involving one or other of the field sports.

Though she knew her thoughts to be irrational, she would say, "Sometimes I feel the boys don't want me, don't need me, don't even love me."

Her dramatic mood swings would change everything. Wills and Harry would run into her bedroom and throw themselves on her bed, cuddle and kiss her, which happened after Charles had left London to move to the country. Thoughts of her unhappiness would dissolve in seconds, and she would hold the boys close. They would rush back to their bedrooms, dress, and go to breakfast, the noise of their laughter and shouts reverberating through the rooms as Diana, smiling broadly, pulled on a track suit to hurry to join them. At those times Diana was truly happy.

On many other occasions, however, when the children were away at boarding school or staying with Charles, Diana's moods turned black. Her thoughts would concentrate on Charles's "girl Friday," Tiggy Legge-Bourke, the thirty-year-old woman Charles employed in 1992, six months after the separation. Officially, Tiggy was hired as an assistant to Charles's private secretary, Comdr. Richard Aylard, but in reality she would become the boys' nanny whenever they stayed with their father or were with him in Scotland or on holiday abroad. She would be paid $30,000 a year.

Before employing her, Charles asked Diana to interview Tiggy to see whether she believed she would be suitable for the job. The interview took place in private at Kensington Palace with only the two women present. Diana posed all the pertinent questions, and although she had read her curriculum vitae, Diana asked her to recount her career so that Diana could interject an occasional question. They got on quite well.

One of the first questions Diana asked concerned Tiggy's unusual nickname. Her real name is Alexandra, but she so adored the character Mrs. Tiggiwinkle, Beatrix Potter's famous hedgehog, that her family called her Tiggy. The name stuck.

As Diana anticipated, Tiggy was the quintessential upper-class girl, raised in the Welsh countryside on her parents' family estate, Glanusk Park, which occupies six thousand acres around Crickhowell in Wales. She had first been educated at St. David's Convent in Brecon, south Wales, an independent Roman Catholic school of 150 pupils run by the Ursuline order of nuns. She then moved to the Manor House in Durnford, an elite preparatory school of only 50 girls owned by Lady Tryon, the mother-in-law of Charles's old friend Lady "Kanga" Tyron, with whom Charles once had a brief fling.

At age thirteen, Tiggy moved to Heathfield, in Ascot, Berkshire, one of Britain's top girls boarding schools, where she enjoyed herself immensely, excelling at tennis and netball.

Margaret Parry, then headmistress of Heathfield, remembers Tiggy as "one of the most agreeable people to have in the school; reliable, capable and very responsible, although not in the least academic." School records show Tiggy won her school colors at tennis, lacrosse, netball, and fencing, as well as being a member of the choir.

Academically, however, like Diana, Tiggy was below average, but she did manage to attain four O (ordinary) level examinations, four more than Diana achieved. Tiggy was then packed off to an exclusive finishing school, at Château d'Oex, near Gstaad, the Institut Alpin Videmanette, the same school where Diana had been sent to complete her education.

Diana, however, had only lasted six weeks, crying herself to sleep each night for the first week. At the end of six weeks Diana had returned home in tears. Tiggy was made of sterner stuff and lasted the course, brushing up her schoolgirl French, as well as her manners, deportment, and skiing technique.

At school, Tiggy earned a reputation for thoroughly enjoying life, keen to take part in all school activities, throwing herself into sport and social functions, remaining popular throughout her years there. After returning from Gstaad, she took a Montessori nursery-teaching course in London and in

1985 opened her own nursery, named Mrs. Tiggiwinkle's in the London suburb of Battersea. It would be hugely popular but she was forced to close the school three years later due to financial difficulties and staffing problems.

One problem had been that Tiggy was too kind, too generous, and too caring to the children, some of whose parents could ill afford the modest fees, so Tiggy would take them in for nothing. She had enjoyed the experience immensely and was sad for the children when forced to close.

When Charles was seeking a nanny, someone whom the growing boys could relate to and respect, Charles decided to search for a highly responsible young woman who could muck in with his sons, be almost an older sister, who could ride out with the boys, kick a soccerball, go swimming, and, if necessary, shoot rabbits! He was told that Tiggy would be ideal. Charles was told by his staff, "She likes the outdoors, she's not really bothered whether she's wearing up-to-the-minute fashions or jeans, Wellington boots, and an old sweater; most of the time she doesn't even wear makeup. Basically she seems straightforward and wonderfully uncomplicated. And there is another point: she has a reputation for being bighearted and generous."

Tiggy also had royal connections. Her aunt, Miss Victoria Legge-Bourke, had been an extra lady-in-waiting to Princess Anne for some years and happily talked about her niece, believing she would be most suitable for Charles and the boys. "Tiggy comes from a loving, happy family," she would say, "and you cannot help but warm to her. Charles couldn't have found a nicer person to take care of his children. And, what's more, she is absolutely discreet and loyal."

Charles was delighted with the young woman's no-non-sense approach to life, and her sense of fun and adventure. He believed she would get on well with the boys. Diana, too, approved, though in principle she hated the idea of another woman stepping into her shoes.

Tiggy was not a glamorous model. Overweight, with her long hair swept back with an Alice band to keep it in place, she would spend most of the time with Wills and Harry dressed in jeans and a shirt or sweater. She would, however, nearly always be seen with a smile on her face. There would be one drawback: Tiggy smoked cigarettes, something both Charles and Diana forbid in their homes. Tiggy agreed never to smoke indoors nor in the presence of the boys.

During the following few months a number of photographs would be seen of Wills and Harry, growing rapidly, enjoying a break from boarding school, and seemingly two happy youngsters. But now there would be no Diana in the picture. Instead, they would be seen walking along, linking arms or having fun with Tiggy, their new nanny, their big sister, favorite aunt, and stand-in mother, all rolled into one. All the photographs showed the boys to be happy and relaxed.

One day in October 1994 Diana saw a photograph of Wills and Harry with Tiggy in a newspaper. The caption read, "The royal princes enjoying life with their surrogate mother, Tiggy Legge-Bourke."

"No, no, no," screamed Diana, "They can't write that. It's not true." She jumped up and rushed into her bedroom in a flood of tears, crying out, "They're mine, they're mine, they're mine. How can they write that?"

On numerous other occasions during the following twelve months, Diana would become tearful and emotional, sometimes openly distraught, about her sons' relationship with Tiggy, fearful that they would become more fond of her than they were of their own mother.

When Diana collected them from school, knowing they would be spending a weekend or a number of weeks with her during school holidays, she would play one of her favorite tapes on the car radio and sing along to the music, so happy to be seeing and having them with her once again. When the boys are with her, Diana will unashamedly spoil them, permit them to choose what they want to do each day, and happily go along with their decision. She will give them whatever they want to eat at home, lashings of ice cream and lots of chips with home-made burgers.

"I know I shouldn't spoil them," she said, laughing, to

another young mother whose children attend Harry's school, "but they're mine and I love them and I don't see them nearly enough. In any case it will not be many years before they are leading their own lives. I don't think it harms to spoil them just a little bit." She adds, "In any case I can spoil them because I'm their mother."

Parting from the boys at the end of a weekend fills Diana's heart with gloom and makes her despondent. She would drive them back to school because it gave her more time with them, but for most of the journey Diana would find herself fighting back tears.

Diana found it almost unbearable if she was returning Wills and Harry to Tiggy's care. Diana and Tiggy would not meet frequently, but Diana would see occasional clips on television of Charles and the boys with Tiggy walking along together like a family. On those occasions Diana would need to bite her lip to stop the tears for she would feel despondent and lonely.

"They seem so happy with her around," she would complain to a close friend. "It's just not fair. I can't bear to see them being cared for by another woman. What hurts even more is when the boys tell me what they have been doing with Tiggy."

What irked Diana, and on occasion roused her to anger, would be Charles's habit of happily leaving the boys in the care of Tiggy when he could not for some reason be with them. In November 1994, both boys rode out with a special junior session of the Beaufort hunt near Highgrove. Charles could not be present so Tiggy rode along with them instead. Diana read about it in a newspaper, which showed the three of them together, without Charles. She read that they all had a marvelous time. That winter they would often go out riding with Tiggy from Highgrove while Charles stayed at home, working or reading.

After a matter of a few months Tiggy would accompany Charles and the children everywhere: to Balmoral for school holidays; to Sandringham for Christmas; to Klosters for skiing; to the Greek islands for sailing expeditions and Mediterranean beaches for summer sun. Charles would take all three of them fishing, usually in Scotland, stalking in the highlands; and sometimes rabbit shooting. Brought up in the country, Tiggy proved to be a good shot, and she happily taught the boys the skills of shooting. They would go out rabbiting together and return with braces of dead rabbits killed on the estate.

Diana would see a photograph of the boys in Scotland with their father and Tiggy out shooting and explode, "How could he? What the hell does he think he's doing bringing up the boys to kill innocent wild animals? Can't he ever use his head? Doesn't Charles realize the world has changed since his childhood? Shooting rabbits for fun is no longer a sport, it's a barbaric bloody crime!"

Charles would be oblivious to such anger and criticism, but Diana would later phone him and say whatever was on her mind. On such occasions Charles would usually answer, neither agreeing or disagreeing with his wife, "I hear what you say," infuriating Diana even more.

"Why won't he ever give me a straight bloody answer," she complained. "He never did and I suppose he never will, the little shit."

Diana would note that Tiggy was given her own bedroom at Highgrove. She heard that Tiggy would happily play with the boys while Charles would be busily tending his beloved garden or working in his study. As the boys grew older, the four would have dinner together. When the boys had gone to bed, Charles would invariably kiss them good night, then watch TV or a video with Tiggy; sometimes he would listen to music alone in his study, but not often.

Charles found Tiggy easy and enjoyable company and would at night often discuss the day's events or plan excursions for the boys. He liked that she never argued with him, for it made his life so much more pleasant. And he would compare their weekends at Highgrove to the maelstrom of screaming and violent arguments on weekends he and Diana had spent together in the country. Charles also came to value Tiggy's down-to-earth approach to Wills and Harry.

# 12

## The Duckling Becomes a Swan

———❧———

In the spring of 1995, Charles noted that the well-built Tiggy, weighing somewhere over 140 pounds, began to lose weight somewhat dramatically. He feared that she might be suffering from anorexia, the eating disorder Diana had fought against for some years, but Tiggy reassured him. "You see how much I eat," she told Charles laughingly. "I'm a glutton."

After blood tests and examinations, which Charles arranged, Tiggy was found to be suffering from celiac disease, caused by an intolerance to gluten. It meant a complete change of diet and she was forbidden to eat many of her favorite foods such as bread, cakes, biscuits, pasta, and porridge because they were causing her severe stomach upsets. Her new diet would be restricted to vegetables and fruit. The pounds rolled off. By the summer of 1995, Tiggy needed a complete new wardrobe for she had shed more than twenty pounds. With the disease under control Tiggy began to feel better, to enjoy life more. That she had lost so much weight delighted her, the pain and the discomfort worthwhile.

Initially, Tiggy would be given a small apartment in St. James's Palace, two hundred yards from Buckingham Palace, where Charles moved his London base after the final split from Diana. Most of the time, however, Tiggy preferred to stay in her luxurious $600,000 apartment in Belgravia, a home she had inherited as part of a family trust. However, her family decided to put the apartment on the market and she moved into a home of a relative who lived in West Kensington. After discussions with the executives who manage his Duchy of Cornwall's properties in London, Charles found a suitable house for Tiggy. Her family trust fund happily paid the $250,000 for the terraced house in Kennington, South London, though neither the address nor the neighborhood could compare to the exclusive surroundings of Belgravia.

Staff at Kensington Palace noted the deteriorating relationship between Diana and Tiggy after only a few months, and by the end of 1994 there was a distinct antipathy. Understandably, Tiggy would need to visit Kensington Palace on numerous occasions to pick up or drop off the boys. Diana, noting that the boys really seemed to enjoy having Tiggy around, would become somewhat jealous. Palace staff understood this was a natural maternal reaction.

When Tiggy entered the room where Diana was having a meal or simply chatting to people, Diana would seem to freeze. She would rarely look Tiggy in the eye when they held a conversation. She began treating Tiggy in an offhand manner as though she were a junior member of staff, not the woman responsible for the care of her sons.

In all royal households the nanny is treated with respect, held to be enjoying a position of privilege and trust, and therefore accorded more dignity than all the other personal staff. When Diana spoke to Tiggy, however, a frost would be in the air, and Diana would answer any questions curtly, without any of the usual gentle, flattering chitchat that she enjoys with most of her personal staff whether maids, hairdressers, or those who simply care for the hundreds of items in Diana's prodigious wardrobe.

An old friend of Diana's, a man of mature years who had advised her during the early years of her marriage, was enjoying a quiet lunch at Kensington Palace with Diana in early 1995 when he was somewhat taken aback by her attitude. He recalled, "We were enjoying a snack lunch at the dining room table with a few other people when we heard a great commotion as the boys arrived home. They rushed into the dining room, kissed their mother on the cheek, and then politely said hello to everyone. That part was fine.

"A couple of minutes later Tiggy walked into the room and said good afternoon to everyone, politely and pleasantly. She added, 'Good afternoon, ma'am,' to Diana, who totally ignored her. Those of us at the table looked at each other feeling the uneasy tension that had suddenly descended on the room, ruining the pleasant atmosphere and the lunch. When Tiggy asked a direct question, whether she should take the boys out of the room, Diana suggested she was being rather rude interrupting her lunch party. Tiggy apologized and walked out of the room, ushering the boys with her.

"Within seconds of Tiggy's departure Diana said, 'That's better, perhaps we can enjoy our lunch now.' And yet we all realized that it was the interruption of two young, happy boys that had caused the hiatus, not the behavior of Tiggy. It illustrated to us all the bitterness Diana felt towards the nanny. And the fact that Diana seemed incapable of hiding her feelings showed how near breaking point Diana had reached in her relationship with the new nanny."

Diana would read everything she could find in the newspapers about Tiggy's life. She would chat to staff at Highgrove and St. James's Palace to find out all that was happening. In the early summer of 1995, Diana sensed something was very wrong. She heard from staff at Highgrove that Tiggy and Charles were becoming closer. They had been seen kissing—at first just pecks on the cheek—whenever Tiggy came down to stay at Charles's country house. And they would kiss farewell if either of them left, leaving the other behind. Diana knew full well that Charles would never kiss members of staff. He hadn't in the past and she doubted whether he now greeted his secretaries, grooms, housemaids, and cooks with kisses.

Diana heard that Tiggy would stay at Highgrove some weekends when the boys were with Diana in London. By June 1995, staff at Highgrove, who happily kept in touch with Diana, were convinced that Charles and Tiggy were having an affair. Diana was told, "Staff saw Charles and Tiggy all but making love. They were kissing and petting one Saturday night. Later they went up to bed."

Of course, Diana asked her sources for any concrete evidence that Charles and Tiggy had become lovers, but they could add nothing more. She was told that the relationship between the two had changed, that Charles was warm and more considerate to her and that Tiggy would do anything and everything for him, looking at him "with the eyes of an adoring spaniel."

Diana winced. She realized that was exactly the way she had looked at Charles in their early married life together when she, too, was mesmerized and had been made to feel she was the most wonderful girl in the world.

The thought that Charles and Tiggy were having an affair infuriated Diana. She was now convinced that Tiggy had not only taken over her job, as mother to the princes, but had moved into her husband's bed. She would tell her trusted adviser, "I am still receiving reports that they sleep together on occasions, but I am informed that the children have no idea whatsoever that their father is screwing their nanny. And I hope for his sake that he keeps it that way; otherwise there will be trouble."

She went on, "I asked them if Camilla was still around, and they said that she still stayed frequently, but usually during the week when neither the children nor Tiggy were about. My friends tell me nothing seems to have changed between Charles and Camilla, still acting like a happy, contented middle-aged couple going for walks with the dogs and enjoying music and dinners together at Highgrove. They are still very much together."

Later, Diana would say, "I wonder what on earth has got into him. He must be enjoying a new lease on life, running two women at once. It's certainly not the Charles that I remember."

Several months later Charles and Tiggy were caught by photographers kissing in public when they met at Balmoral. Charles clambered out of a Land Rover on the Scottish estate and walked around to the back of the vehicle as Tiggy came running across. She put her arms around his shoulders, looked him square in the eye, and kissed him on the cheek. Not simply a peck but a definite kiss. For seconds they held the embrace. Nearby were other members of the shooting party including the Queen and Philip, but apparently no one saw them embrace.

The gossips began talking only after that first public kiss, noticing that Tiggy Legge-Bourke had changed beyond recognition. The Alice bands, the pearls, the frumpy frocks, and big sweaters had gone; so had the double chin. Instead, Diana and others saw a degree of elegance, though nothing to compete with the Princess of Wales. Tiggy would be seen wearing short skirts, silk shirts, high heels, and discreet gold jewelry, her hair cut and styled in a sophisticated manner. And there was now a touch of makeup and lipstick!

In some respects, believing that Tiggy was having an affair with Charles rather amused Diana. She wondered whether Camilla knew of the affair and smiled when she thought of what Camilla's reaction might be to the news. Camilla had given up her marriage for Charles, and Diana felt sure Camilla would be absolutely furious if she believed Charles was now two-timing her. Diana also worried that Wills or Harry might twig what was going on between their father and Tiggy, and she certainly didn't want them to suspect such goings-on. Diana believes her sons have already experienced enough ghastly traumas in their young lives without more being piled onto their shoulders.

Both Wills and Harry enjoyed having Tiggy around; they liked that she could ride, fish, shoot, ski, swim, and enjoy all the country activities they, too, have learned to love. And they enjoyed teasing her about her total inability to stop smoking. On holiday at Klosters they pretended to copy her, smoking a cigarette while racing fast downhill. She would chase them and roll them in the snow and they would pelt her with snowballs, reveling in the fun of it.

Back home in London, Diana would chat with the boys, asking them about their weekends and various holidays with their father and Tiggy. She would say, "I know I should laugh and relish their happiness and their fond memories of holidays abroad with Charles and the nanny, but I find it very difficult to hide my true emotions on those occasions."

She would explain all these thoughts in some remarkable detail, and great honesty, with Fergie as well as her close adviser: "While the boys are talking to me about their exploits, sometimes both chattering away at once, I just keep thinking of them being with Tiggy, enjoying life with that woman who seems to be taking over my role, my place, and even supplanting my love. I try not to think like that but I can't help it. They seem so happy with her, happier than when they're with me at the palace. They seem to have more fun with her."

On occasion Diana admits that she finds herself actually hating Tiggy, unable to think rationally of her with her boys, holding them, kissing them goodbye, teasing them, having adventures with them, imagining Wills and Harry laughing and joking with Tiggy rather than with her. She tries to control her feelings, to think rationally about the whole sorry separation, but on many occasions she feels a rage within her that she can barely control.

"I feel that the boys have been torn from me," she said during one of her moments of despair in the summer of 1995. "I feel they have been taken away to enjoy a better life with someone else, someone whose interests may equip her to bring up the boys as young Royals better than I ever could. I can't bear country pursuits, and Tiggy loves them, all of them. Now the children love all those sports as well, and I feel useless, cut off from my own children, my own family. It makes me feel so lonely."

Diana tries to tell herself she is being silly and paranoid, and more often than not, she manages to shake off her feeling of desperation, of guilt and jealousy toward Tiggy. Far better, she persuades herself, that the boys are happy with someone they seem to genuinely like rather than be unhappy with some harridan who might ruin their lives, or someone who might be too kind, spoiling them instead. Diana understands that either of those possibilities would be disastrous for the boys.

But Diana's paranoia over Tiggy does sometimes erupt. Both Wills and Harry were proud of their nanny when she showed them she had become proficient on rollerblades, usually wearing a crash helmet and knee pads, considered essential by safety experts. When Diana heard from her sons of Tiggy's exploits, she bought herself a pair of rollerblades and practiced in private. Four weeks later, in November 1995, she had become sufficiently confident and capable to venture into Kensington Gardens, next door to her palace, joining with many others who enjoy the sport. She could manage speeds of 20 mph but appeared a little shaky on spins and turns. But Diana wore neither a crash helmet nor knee pads, considered a great risk for beginners. When pictures appeared in newspapers of the Princess on rollerblades, she showed them to her sons when they next spent a weekend with their mother.

Diana would also come under fire from safety experts in October 1995 for permitting William to drive around a go-cart racetrack in London's Chelsea without wearing a safety helmet or any form of protective clothing. The thirteen-year-old prince clocked 19.66 seconds, the fastest lap time on record since the track opened in 1993. His time was even faster than that of Formula One drivers including former world champion Damon Hill and British go-cart champion David Coulthard. Both William and Harry enjoy the thrill of motor racing and have attended Formula One world championship races with Diana.

Diana would be under further censure for permitting William to attend a Fiesta Ball at London's Hammersmith Palais in October 1995 where a thousand teenage boys and miniskirted girls danced, kissed, and cuddled until 2 A.M. William begged his mother to permit him to go with others of his class at Eton. In the end she agreed. Alcohol was banned, but some of the teenagers managed to become sick and a little the worse for wear. Virtually all the teenagers spent most of the night on the dance floor, enjoying a wild time, sweating, shaking, shouting, and petting. When the precocious teenage girls realized the blonde-haired William was present, a considerable number approached him, asking for a dance and a kiss. His Eton pals, however, came to his rescue, pushing the girls away. William had a great time.

Diana argued that she was determined to allow her sons to enjoy the normal activities of adolescents. But outside the ballroom that night were empty vodka bottles and beer cans, and inside a number of the teenagers were petting heavily and more. Reading the criticism in some newspapers, Diana shrugged and commented, "They're just overreacting. Why shouldn't he enjoy himself?"

Diana is determined William and Harry will experience as much as possible while growing up and not simply the field sports their father enjoys. She knows that Charles had little of an ordinary, normal life when he was a teenager and neither did Diana. She firmly believes that the more ordinary teenage experiences Wills and Harry enjoy, the better they will cope with their privileged life later.

As a result, Prince William has already enjoyed a wealth of opportunities, pursuits, sports, and pastimes far in excess of almost any other teenager in Britain. All due to Diana's determination. He has gone white-water rafting on Colorado's Roaring Fork River; raced quad bikes along an American mountain track; enjoyed in the pits the thrill of Grand Prix motor racing; surfed off the Caribbean island of Nevis; and been on Jet Skis off the coast of Sardinia. He has his own pony, hunts, rides, shoots, stalks, and fishes and plays tennis and swims at the Chelsea Harbour Club.

But it hasn't all been fun. Diana has also taken William to hostels for the homeless and to visit terminally ill AIDS patients in hospitals. In early January 1996, Diana decided that after all the festivities of Christmas, Wills and Harry should see the harsh realities of life. So one evening she took them to a hostel for the homeless run by the charity Centrepoint in the heart of London's red-light district. Only three days before the boys had returned from a skiing holiday in Klosters, Switzerland, with their father and Tiggy. It was the boys' first joint visit to a hostel for the homeless.

Wills and Harry sat down in the canteen with Diana and chatted to twenty-five residents, all teenagers who had nowhere else to live. One asked Diana, "Why do you bother to come here?"

Diana looked at her sons and said, "Because we care."

Afterward, Gareth Jones, one of the volunteer workers, said, "Both William and Harry appeared bemused at first. Harry seemed tired and stuck close to his mother's side. William seemed genuinely concerned by their plight."

It was supposed to be a private visit, but within minutes of their arrival reporters and photographers arrived on the scene, tipped off by a phone call from Kensington Palace.

But Diana's decision to take the two princes to a hostel for the homeless did not receive unmitigated acclaim from the media, some commentators arguing that Diana had arranged the visit as a photo opportunity to show her caring image. One outspoken commentator, Richard Littlejohn, wrote, "There seems no stunt she is not prepared to pull in her campaign to become a state-registered Queen of Hearts. This week she stooped to a new low, dragging her sons round a doss house... visiting a few tramps and winos."

Despite the criticism Diana plans to continue her education of both boys. "They're mine and I will bring them up to be rational, sensible young men," Diana will say when chatting to mothers of other teenage sons. "Later on, they risk being cut off from normal life, so the more they can enjoy and experience the real world while they're still young, the better for them."

She understands that her boys need a woman's touch around them when they are with Charles, but she never wants Camilla to be involved in any way in their upbringing. She hopes that when the boys stay for a weekend at Highgrove that Camilla isn't around. And Diana has warned Charles that he must act responsibly and never permit the boys to see their father sharing a bed with Camilla.

During rational moments Diana tries to be positive in her attitude toward Camilla, but she finds that harder than facing up to Tiggy's presence and influence on the boys. She still believes that Camilla should never, under any circumstances, have restarted her affair with Charles, which she and Charles agreed to end after the murder of Earl Mountbatten. Diana believes that Camilla should have made Charles return to his wife and his children and make a go of his marriage rather than giving him advice, comfort, and finally her love and her body.

Diana will still discuss the matter with friends and those close to her because she finds it all but impossible to get Camilla out of her mind for she believes Camilla deliberately cheated her and Wills and Harry. Diana will say, "I believe that she did refuse Charles's request that she divorce her husband and live with him after Uncle Dickie's murder. At that time she showed great determination and wisdom. She showed me nothing but kindness, but then I didn't realize that she had just been having a raging affair with Charles.

"She should have sent Charles back home. She could have done so because Charles has always been in awe of Camilla, always rushing to her for sympathy and advice, for she bolsters his confidence. Charles needs a strong woman like Camilla. But Camilla didn't do that. She saw her chance and took it and ruined my life and the lives of Wills and Harry. That is why I can never forgive her."

Camilla has behaved with remarkable equilibrium throughout the dramatic saga that has been going on for ten long years. As a child she was more of a tomboy, preferring climbing trees and riding horses to party dresses and doll-houses. As a young woman she loved London's social whirl, dances and parties every night during the season, with a host of young men eager to impress the daughter of one of Britain's wealthy families.

Broderick Munro-Wilson grew up with Camilla in Sussex, and they attended their first dance together when both were twelve years old. They have known each other ever since. "Camilla," he says, "was much more self-assured than other teenage girls. She stood out as a confident young woman and at school became quite a rebel. Even today she is a woman who catches your eye when you walk into a room, because she exudes fun and warmth. She also knows how to talk to men, how to flatter them, and how to get them on her side. She has a slightly wicked twinkle, which is definitely enticing. I don't mean that she's a terrible flirt, just that she's comfortable with men and enjoys their company.

"She looks you straight in the eye when she speaks to you and always has a smile on her face. She is witty and intelligent, too. And she has a mellow, husky voice. She is undoubtedly a most capable and strong character, and that's how she has withstood all the pressure."

He recalled that on one occasion when Camilla's name was first linked with Charles, some women in her local supermarket in Wiltshire threw bread rolls at her because they held her responsible for ruining the marriage of the fairy-tale princess. Camilla simply turned on her heel and walked out of the store with her head held high as if nothing had occurred.

Munro-Wilson went on, "She does make the most perfect hostess for Charles. With Andrew she would be used to running a large house and entertaining parties of a dozen or more for dinner. The food would always be superb, and the evening a great success, though you would hardly notice Camilla's presence."

Those few people invited to dinner parties at Highgrove with Charles and Camilla believe that they would have made an admirable couple for some describe Camilla as the quintessential upper-class English lady, sensible, confident, and very capable, a near-perfect match for Charles. Throughout the epic drama Camilla has never spoken out or reportedly thrown a tantrum. She has always been the perfect lady. For that alone she has won admiration and respect from her peers, mostly wealthy aristocratic women who find such attributes of the utmost importance.

Munro-Wilson spoke for them all when he said, "It is really tough luck on both the Prince and Camilla that they fell in love, but her background would never allow her to marry him because she would not want to rock the monarchy. I do believe, however, from everything that has happened in the last ten years, that Charles will never renounce Camilla."

Increasingly, Diana's animosity toward Camilla has turned toward Tiggy. The more that Diana sees her sons enjoying life when they are with Tiggy, the more hatred she feels for the nanny she now sees as her rival for their affections. So consumed with jealousy had Diana become that she found it all but impossible to speak about Tiggy with equanimity. Diana's feelings of rancor had almost become a phobia since she had been led to believe Tiggy and Charles had become lovers. Since that time Diana had tried to avoid meeting Tiggy, but understandably, they did have to see each other on occasion, for example when Tiggy collected or dropped off Wills and Harry at Kensington Palace.

In early December 1995, Diana was informed that Tiggy had been admitted to a hospital during the summer and, allegedly, undergone an abortion. Diana knew no other details. She asked friends if they could find out the date, the hospital, and the surgeon, but she could find no confirmation.

The allegation came to haunt Diana. She wanted to know whether the story was true and, more importantly, whether Charles was the father. Some weeks later Diana found the opportunity to ask Tiggy. And took it.

In December 1995, Charles and Diana, as they had done throughout their marriage, threw a Christmas party for their respective staffs at the Lanesborough Hotel, Hyde Park Corner, a few hundred yards from Buckingham Palace.

During the party Diana went over to Tiggy and quietly said to her, "So sorry to hear about the baby!"

Devastated by the remark, Tiggy stared at Diana, then turned and fled, fighting back tears. She all but collapsed into the arms of Charles's valet, the tears streaming down her face. Later that evening Tiggy told Prince Charles what Diana had said, but not until the following day did Charles discuss the matter fully with his personal assistant.

After further consultations with Prince Charles, Tiggy

instructed Peter Carter-Ruck, one of Britain's foremost libel lawyers, to write to the Princess of Wales's lawyers, Mischon De Reya, demanding a retraction of "false allegations" she was said to have made toward his client. Carter-Ruck also issued a statement to newspapers about unfounded allegations being circulated that were, he said, a "gross reflection" on Tiggy's "moral character."

Diana treated the demand for a retraction with complete contempt, not even bothering to ask her lawyers to reply to the demand. To friends, Diana would say, "I know where the truth lies."

Tiggy had also instructed Carter-Ruck not to invoke formal legal action against the Princess of Wales because of the embarrassment it might cause Prince Charles. Tiggy also realized that such an action would make her position with William and Harry untenable.

Diana's remark about the baby and Tiggy's legal rebuttal meant that the two women were now at war, and Diana was determined that the nanny whom she referred to "as that trumped-up little tart" would soon be sent packing. "I will do everything in my power to remove William and Harry from that woman's care and influence," Diana told her City friend. "It is absolutely disgraceful that Charles should continue to employ her to care for the boys now that he is bedding her."

In anger, Diana would add, "But once again I suppose the Royals will take absolutely no action against her. They knew all about Charles and Camilla and did nothing. Now they all know about Charles and that tart Tiggy, but I expect they will do nothing about that either."

The fairy-tale wedding, July 29, 1981 (London News Service)

Off on their honeymoon through the streets of London. The world rejoiced.
(London News Service)

On honeymoon in Scotland.  Love and tenderness.
(London News Service)

The Queen with Princess Diana in a state carriage drawn by six white horses down the Mall, summer 1992 (London News Service)

Maj. James Hewitt pictured in Brigade of Guards mess kit, lying on the single bed in his mother's cottage where he used to make love to Diana (Express Newspapers)

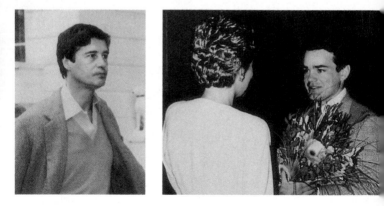

*Left, above:* Oliver Hoare, the handsome man who befriended both Charles and Diana as they battled to save their marriage. Later Diana would fall in love with the Islamic art dealer and bombard him and his wife, Diane, with annoying phone calls. (Express Newspapers)
*Right, above:* Diana with Will Carling, the England rugby captain, 1994 (London News Service)

Camilla Parker Bowles, Charles's mistress for the past ten years, pictured shopping, 1992 (London News Service)

The new, slim-line, fashionably dressed Tiggy Legge-Bourke leaving her London home in January 1996. Gossips inside royal palaces believed Tiggy and Charles were enjoying an affair. (London News Service)

Tiggy Legge-Bourke plays in the snow with Wills and Harry during a skiing holiday with Charles at Lech, Austria, in April 1992. (London News Service)

Diana attending a church service in summer 1994 dressed in a stunning but simple white dress and wide-brimmed hat (Express Newspapers)

*From left to right:* The Duke of Edinburgh, Prince William, Earl Spencer, Prince Harry, and Prince Charles in the procession before the funeral service for Diana, Princess of Wales, September 6, 1997 (Reuters/Jeff J. Mitchell/Archive Photos)

Prince William, Earl Spencer, Prince Harry, and Prince Charles follow Princess Diana's coffin into Westminster Abbey. (Reuters/Paul Hackett/Archive Photos)

Prince William bids farewell to his mother. Her coffin is draped with the Royal Standard. (Reuters/Ulli Michel/Archive Photos)

A little girl pays her respects at Buckingham Palace. (Express Newspapers/Archive Photos)

# 13

## Diana and the Rugby Hero

———— ❦ ————

Diana LOVES TO TURN HEADS. And the more she captivates the attention of both men and women, the more she boosts her self-confidence and self-esteem. Even today she smiles at the way she would behave in the past before she found the confidence to lift her head in public or the pride to look people in the eye.

It has taken Diana a long time to achieve such self-assurance. Throughout her teenage years she would walk through the streets head down, too shy to show her face. Then no one knew her identity, or even cared. At the age of nineteen, when she first dated Prince Charles, Diana realized how diffident she behaved, particularly when meeting strangers. She loved caring for young children partly because she didn't have to face the agony of meeting strange adults with whom she would become self-conscious, unable to contain her blushes. She would wear little or no makeup, or lipstick and only colorless nail varnish for she didn't want to attract attention. She didn't bother with her figure, keeping fit, or exercising. She would have her hair cut and styled every so often, but nothing more. The rest she would leave to nature.

When Fleet Street discovered the identity of the pretty, but painfully shy nanny the Prince of Wales had taken a fancy to, she didn't care what people thought of her appearance, her looks, her makeup, or her dress sense. The fashion editors, however, would make the young Diana realize that she had to shape up. Stung by their criticism, she worked hard at her grooming, employing a team of talented experts from *Vogue* to advise and instruct her on how to change her image, become fashionable, make the most of herself, and overnight, transform the country girl into a sophisticated bride fit for a prince. The most difficult part of the metamorphosis Diana had to carry out on her own, losing more than fourteen pounds over a four-month period. On the day of her wedding in July 1981 she was proud of her achievements. She had every right to be. The world hailed a beautiful fairy princess.

The births of both William and Harry, in 1982 and 1984, caused Diana far more anguish and worry than she had ever before known in her life. She suffered from postnatal depression and her eating habits deteriorated so much she found she didn't want to eat at all. Her moods swung erratically and her relationship with Charles plummeted from a wonderful, all-embracing love to despising the man who was ill-equipped to cope with such behavior.

Diana lost twenty-eight pounds after the birth of Harry. The bones of her shoulders stuck out, her neck looked thin and scraggy, and her body and legs lost shape. She still remembers the Herculean task of rebuilding what she described as "my shapeless lump of a beanpole" after the years of battling alone with her eating disorders, suffering alternately from anorexia nervosa and bulimia.

Today Diana recalls, "I cannot think how awful I looked. I was ashamed of the way I looked, so thin, flat-chested, with no shape to my legs, and looking as miserable as sin. I couldn't even look at myself in the mirror without feeling dreadfully depressed."

Now, at the age of thirty-four and with no special man in her life, Diana finds that she needs to turn heads to lift her spirits and give herself the confidence to continue her lonely life. She will stand happily in front of her bathroom mirror totally naked to check how she is shaping up and whether she approves of what she sees. Two or three times a week she will make a detailed inspection of her body, but she also has the confidence to give herself a quick up-and-down check whenever she finishes drying after taking a shower. If she believes some muscle needs more tone or views the faintest hint of cellulite, she will discuss it the following day with her gymnastics teacher.

She told one girlfriend, "Sometimes I occasionally like what I see in the mirror, but not very often. I have to keep up the hard work otherwise I see cellulite at the top of my legs or on my bum. And I couldn't bear to see any flab at the top of my arms. That's really yuk. Lately, I have been finding the wrinkles mounting up around my eyes no matter what I put on to counteract them. To hide the wrinkles I just make sure I smile a lot or wear dark glasses, then no one's the wiser."

Laughing, she went on, "I wouldn't dare to let my hair return to its natural color because I'm sure it would be full of gray hairs after all I've been through."

Diana was determined to keep herself superbly fit during her break from royal duties and charity work that she announced to the world in December 1993. And yet the break would bring her a never-ending saga of dramas and public humiliations over her relationships with various men. During the first nine months of 1994, Diana relaxed, tried to enjoy herself, get fit, make more friends, and more importantly, sort herself out and decide her future. Her good intentions, however, would end in yet more tears.

She would train more often at the Chelsea Harbour Club, mostly playing tennis and swimming and doing minor workouts in the gymnasium. Afterward she would relax over a cup of coffee, usually a cappuccino, while she sat at the back of the cafe area at table number 8, which she all but commandeered as her own. From that vantage point she could see the arrivals and departures while remaining discreetly in the background.

Of course, Diana was being more than a little naive if she believed that she could ever again remain unnoticed in a cafe or a shop or anyplace else. At the Harbour Club every member present and the entire staff would always be aware that the most loved, talked about, notorious, and tantalizingly beautiful woman in Britain was in their midst. They all enjoyed basking in the reflected glory, for Diana's presence would cause a buzz of excitement, an undercurrent of tension that helped give the club a spark, as well as served as a never-ending subject of gossip.

She would have a coffee or a juice with her sports advisers and coaches and on occasion with other women who frequented the club that she had come to know well. She really enjoyed her time there. Occasionally she would have a chat with one or two of the young men who attended, but not too often. Most weeks she would visit the club three times, and on occasion more often.

In the early spring of 1994, Diana noticed a ruggedly built young man of about thirty. His face seemed familiar. She noted his broad back, his rippling muscles, and his stout legs and wondered where she had seen him before. He had a confident air, and she watched him, somewhat taken by him.

Some weeks later her elder son, William, wanted to watch the England Rugby Union International, televised live that Saturday afternoon. He persuaded his mother to sit with him. There on the screen, his face in full view, was the same man she had seen at the club. He was Will Carling, the celebrated captain of the England rugby team, probably the most famous rugby player in Britain.

She had met him before. On two occasions she had been the guest of honor at rugby internationals in which Carling had been the captain of the England team when she had been officially introduced to the teams as they lined up to be presented before the match.

The next time she saw Carling at the gym she said hello as she passed by, and Carling was rather taken aback at being spoken to by the Princess of Wales. A few days later she again approached his table and they began to chat. Later, on another visit Diana invited him to her table for an orange juice. They chatted about rugby, about the Harbour Club, and Diana told him that her sons hero-worshiped him. Carling liked that, smiled and blushed, appearing somewhat embarrassed as he sat eating his toast and talking to the Princess of Wales.

During the following few weeks the two would meet every so often, but Carling would wait for Diana to approach him, not wanting to impose himself on her. One day Diana simply walked up to Carling's table and asked, "Can I join you? I feel so conspicuous sitting on my own."

Carling was flattered and delighted. They would talk mostly about the club, keeping fit, working out, and their respective programs. No mention was made of their private lives. Carling, a former Army captain, did not tell Diana he was living with a beautiful, slim, blond girl, named Julia Smith, who had her own thriving public relations firm, Hands On PR, in London.

Will Carling had first met Julia at a dinner party in 1989 shortly after being appointed captain of the England rugby XV. Julia's love life had been high profile, for she had moved into guitarist Jeff Beck's home just after she left school. Following six years of enjoying "married" life in the quiet of the country, Julia then conducted a much-publicized affair with the guitarist Eric Clapton. From the first, Julia's effervescent personality and flirtatious nature, coupled with her serious side, appealed greatly to Carling. He would not forget her. Three years later they met again at a dinner party. At the time Carling had been dating a tall, beautiful, blonde, Victoria Taylor-Jackson, a real estate agent, and they were living together in Carling's basement apartment in London.

Victoria talked of their sensational two-year-long relationship, of Carling's likes and dislikes and his insatiable appetite for sex and women with firm bodies. "Will has always been a ladies' man who can't resist powerful women. He's mad about sex and has an obsession for blondes. He can't resist them. His previous girlfriend before me, a girl called Nicky, was a blonde. I'm a blonde, Julia's a blonde, and we all know the color of Diana's hair."

She went on, "What Will really liked about women was if they were into fitness and had strong personalities, like Diana. He would always tell me he loved women with good firm bodies. He would fantasize about having kinky and open-air sex with me, and he would sign his love letters to me with the words 'Big Willy.' He seemed to love writing me very sexy notes, detailing the sex we would have together when he returned from an overseas trip with the England rugby team."

Victoria and Carling were living together when Julia appeared on the scene. "During a party we threw in January 1993, I walked into our kitchen and found Carling whispering in Julia's ear. I thought nothing of it. Then I discovered that Julia, a close friend of mine, was sending him faxes every other day, calling him by the pet name she gave him, Bum Chin. "We were getting on brilliantly when the breakup happened. We were having fantastic sex and thoroughly enjoying life together. One Sunday he simply went cold on me, like an iceberg. It was as though he had flicked a switch and turned off the machine. His love had gone and he told me our affair was over, finished."

Victoria confessed to being upset and in a state of shock for several weeks while she sorted out her life without Carling. She recalled, "A few days later I picked up a newspaper to find Will pictured with Julia telling the world, 'This is my new girl friend.'"

She went on, "I was absolutely livid. I phoned him in a rage and told him he had behaved like a complete shit. He didn't have an answer and behaved very sheepishly. So that was it. In four weeks he had gone from telling me I was the only girl in the world for him to going out with somebody else."

Carling would be so captivated by the willowy, bubbly Julia that one month later he asked her to marry him. In June 1994, Carling and Julia were wed, three months after Diana and Carling had begun their regular, informal meetings at the Harbour Club.

When Carling met Diana a few weeks after returning from his honeymoon, Diana said, "I understand congratulations are in order."

"Yes, that's true," Carling replied. "Thank you very much."

"And who's the lucky girl? Have I met her?"

"No," replied Carling, adding with a smile, "she has to

work in the office while I'm working out at the gym. Someone has to bring home the bacon."

At that time, Carling was fast becoming one of Britain's top sports earners, driving a $150,000 Aston Martin while garnering endorsement deals that brought him more than $350,000 a year. He had also launched his own management consultancy company, Insight.

For several months the princess and the rugby captain continued to meet at the club. Slowly, Carling learned to relax in Diana's presence, and she would go out of her way to make him feel at ease. Their meetings began to take a more serious turn. They would arrange when they would meet, at what time and on what days. Always, the couple would laugh and joke together. The get-togethers seemed totally innocent. Carling began to tease Diana, telling her that she should become really fit rather than just playing at being fit. She rather liked that.

Principally, Carling would tease Diana about the shape of her body, telling her that her biceps were like sparrow's legs, thin with no muscle. He even began to call her "my little sparrow." She loved the nickname. On a more serious note Diana also asked him what she should do to give herself some real muscle, adding with a laugh, "But I have no wish to look like Arnie Schwarzenegger."

"I'll take you to my special gym," Carling told her. "They'll sort you out."

Carling took Diana to the BiMAL, a medical and sports rehabilitation clinic, a center Britain's top sportsmen attend for physical problems they have been unable to overcome with the help of their own physiotherapists. There, Diana was provided a training program designed to give her more upper-arm muscle, but no visible biceps. Diana would become a regular visitor, arriving at 8 A.M. most Fridays for a thirty-minute session.

Carling would also tease Diana about her wardrobe. Like everyone else in Britain who followed the fortunes of the Princess of Wales, Carling knew that Diana had the most amazing wardrobe, with literally hundreds of expensive, fashionable items costing thousands of dollars. However, on many occasions when going to the gym, Diana would arrive in a pink Martha's Vineyard sweatshirt, black cycle shorts, and white trainers. Carling would smile at her and crack a joke, suggesting that the poor princess was really a Cinderella with no other clothes to her name. Diana would blush and look shy, but loved being teased. It made her feel wanted.

As a joke, Will had a little two-inch china pig made with black shorts painted on it and a pink sweatshirt emblazoned with the words "Martha's Vineyard." The pig was lifting weights. Carling gave it to Diana's chauffeur, Steve Davis, to hand to the princess anonymously. Diana opened the present and roared with laughter. She knew precisely who had sent it.

Diana invited Carling to Kensington Palace during the summer of 1994, telling him that Prince William and Prince Harry were eager to meet their rugby hero. Carling went along. It would be the first of many visits to Diana's private apartments at the palace. She began inviting Carling for a drink and the occasional meal at the palace. The registration number of his car was logged into the police computer at the palace gates and Diana gave him her private direct phone numbers so his calls could bypass the switchboard.

During their meetings at the palace Carling would be introduced to several of Diana's assistants, including her butler, Harold Brown, her secretary, Patrick Jephson, as well as a number of others who kept her diary, helped with her clothes, and cared for the two princes. Caroline Wicker, an attractive, intelligent young woman, had joined Diana's staff in 1990, employed solely to open, sift, and catalog Diana's mail, which would arrive by the sackful most weeks. One day in September 1994, she told Carling, during idle chatter, that she needed another, more fulfilling job, and Carling offered her a position. But he had neglected to seek Diana's permission to approach her.

Diana was furious. Royal protocol dictates that Royals can fire staff whenever they wish, but no one, not even other Royals, are permitted to poach staff or ask whether they would be interested in another job before asking their royal employer for permission to do so. Carling, unaware of such royal protocol, had committed a cardinal error.

But there would be more. Caroline Wicker, in her twenties, is a bright, lovely-looking girl, and Carling had offered her a job in his own office working close to him. Carling would tell one of his pals later, "God, you would have thought I had nicked the crown jewels or something. She was furious with me. It became clear later that it was jealousy more than the breaking of protocol that annoyed Diana. I apologized and told her that I had no idea of the correct protocol, but it took some weeks before she totally forgave me for the gaffe."

Diana, however, would not forget. She would not present Caroline Wicker with the customary departing gift, a signed photograph of the royal household. And Diana ordered she be instantly struck off the Christmas card list.

One person who followed the escalating relationship between Carling and Diana was his former personal assistant, Hilary Ryan. She says, "For a while Diana and Will didn't even speak when they met at the Harbour Club, but Will would go at the same time as before just to see her. During those weeks he seemed awfully downcast." "But by February 1995 everything seemed to be back on track, and Will and Diana would meet three times a week for coffee and a light breakfast after working out. He would tell me that he would be out for several hours, and I understood that together they would be at Kensington Palace.

"Carling ordered a special 'hot' line telephone to be installed, which I was instructed must not be used or answered by anyone in the office, not even me, his PA [Personal Assistant]. I knew the phone had been installed for Diana so she never had to go through the switchboard. On occasions they would chat on the phone for an hour or more, laughing, giggling, cracking jokes, and, on occasions, deep in quiet, intimate conversation."

Carling had been captivated by the alluring, flirty Diana. Her attention flattered him; the very fact that they were having a relationship filled him with pride and self-importance. Already, as captain of the England rugby XV, Carling had considerable self-assurance. Now, less than a year after marrying Julia, Carling knew that the relationship with Diana had taken on an importance that never, for one minute, had he dreamed would be possible.

Diana began giving Carling pecks on the cheek when they met and a kiss on each cheek when they said goodbye. She would put a hand on his shoulder and offer her face to be kissed, gently, courteously, as one would kiss a close friend, but not a lover. In public when saying farewell, they would shake hands, but Diana's hand began to linger and she would give Carling a penetrating look that said more than any kiss.

Carling realized what was happening and loved it. He was becoming involved. Whenever he was with the Princess, Carling felt special, enjoying their time together whether they were snatched moments or hours of chat, tittle-tattle, having a drink, or discussing workouts. They gave each other pet names: Carling called Diana "The Boss" while she called him "Captain."

Carling decided to return to the mystic guru he had first consulted some years before when he was dating Julia and before he had even met Diana. By trade, Charlie Chan, thirty-seven, is an avant-garde society hairdresser with a salon in London's Piccadilly. But he also has a first-class reputation for reading astrological charts as a hobby, advising the rich and famous.

Chan said, "I told Will that he should never have married Julia. I still don't think the marriage will work. With their combined charts I don't think their marriage will ever work. They're just not matched."

During the early part of 1995, Carling returned to his guru friend to ask him what the stars were saying about his future and the future of a Cancerian friend of his with the birth date of July 1, 1961.

"I knew he was referring to the Princess of Wales. I just knew it," said Chan. "I told him that Diana was having a good year and he seemed happy with that. I also told him that he was having an extremely happy year but was ready to move on. Will is Sagittarian with Scorpio rising, so he's in a good position. I have told Will that there is no point in looking back. He has to go forward and I think he will."

Chan was adamant that he had never advised Carling to leave his wife. He said, "Julia is Pisces with Virgo rising and in a poor astrological position. She is fortunately very strong. The whole situation is very simple. If you love something, then you hold on tight and fight for it. If you don't love it, then push it away and move on. It's the only way."

In March 1995, two months before the Rugby Union World Cup finals were to be played in South Africa, Carling arranged for William and Harry to attend a get-together of the England rugby squad where they kicked a ball around and played with the squad members. The boys were in seventh heaven.

Diana began telling Will, as she would often phone him, of the problems that beset her. He would encourage her to get everything off her chest and was only too happy to be the man she wanted to help overcome the pressures and torments of her life. He would listen and advise and sympathize until Carling found himself wanting to throw his arms around her protectively, providing a shoulder to lean on, a collar to cry on.

On occasion the tears would erupt and Carling would feel sad and an affinity to someone who desperately seemed in need of friendship, support, and more importantly, warmth. Carling would happily provide tender, loving care for the lonely Diana. She warmed to that side of the man, though to many Carling had more often seemed a cold fish. Diana also appreciated his confidence and self-assurance, which seemed to give her strength.

And yet Diana would, on occasion, look at Carling and wonder why she had become so attracted to him. He was too stocky for her liking, too short, too muscular, and too young, being four years her junior. Sometimes he would also appear too arrogant. And yet she found him appealing, exciting, and she realized she found Will Carling sexually attractive. On occasion Diana and Carling would attend cocktail parties together, and people noted that Diana found it impossible to keep her hands off her hunky man, touching his arm, flicking a hair from his jacket, and just standing close to him, watching his every movement and listening intently to his conversation. She seemed smitten.

Sometimes when alone together at Kensington Palace, Diana would be so overcome with emotion that she wouldn't want Carling to leave her, lest she dissolve into floods of tears. She would beg him to stay, to hold her, comfort her, sometimes to cuddle her as one would a child. On those occasions Carling felt like her big brother. That made him feel good and he was happy, indeed felt privileged, to play such a role to the Princess of Wales.

Carling found himself becoming more involved, spending more time with her, more time on the phone, and less and less time with his wife. In the meantime Julia had become extraordinarily busy, running her PR consultancy and taking on more work, modeling clothes and discussing with producers the possibility of hosting radio and television shows. She had become a woman in demand and she luxuriated in the attention.

Before flying to South Africa to take part in the Rugby Union World Cup, Carling spent three hours alone with Diana at the palace saying farewell. During the tournament, Diana and Will Carling talked frequently on the telephone, sometimes three or four times a day. And, of course, he also called Julia. His wife, however, had no idea that Carling was calling the Princess of Wales.

Diana watched every game that England played during that series of matches, cheering whenever England scored and yelping with enthusiasm whenever Will Carling played particularly brilliantly. Staff would know what was happening during the games just by listening to the shrieks from the Princess of Wales. When things went badly for England, they would hear loud wails of "Oh, no, oh, no." That usually meant the opposition had scored, or Carling had been injured.

On his return from his six-week tour of South Africa, Carling and Diana spent more time together. The rugby season was over, and though Carling still kept in trim, he had more time to devote to his business, to the machinations of the rapidly changing rugby world, and to Diana. Everything was going well, particularly between Diana and Carling. The world at large had no idea the two had become lovers, but their secret affair, and their good fortune, would not last.

Hilary Ryan, who had been hired by Carling in 1994 at $35,000 a year as his personal assistant, was fired, allegedly for being too confrontational in the office, making waves where Carling wanted a quiet, smooth-running operation. Yet, on the day she was dismissed, Carling gave her a magnificent reference describing her as "highly efficient, very reliable and totally dedicated to the company."

A month after Will Carling's return from South Africa, Rupert Murdoch's sensational Sunday tabloid the *News of the World* splashed across its front page in big, bold letters, "Di's Secret Trysts With Carling." The accompanying story detailed in brief the couple's secret meetings and the relationship that had built up over an eighteenth-month period. The story created a furor and provided Britain's tabloid readers with weeks of speculation and prurient gossip. It would cause Carling's twelve-month-long marriage to break up and make Diana look more like a femme fatale than an innocent princess who was above suspicion.

A week later the strong-willed Julia Carling, thirty, pulled no punches in a vicious attack on Diana. She seethed, "This has happened to her before and you hope she won't do those things again, but she obviously does."

She added, "She picked the wrong couple to do it with this time because we can only get stronger from it. It's a horrible thing to go through. But it does make you stronger no matter how much someone is trying to destroy what you have. Our relationship is very strong anyway—and thank God for that."

Carling, too, seemed to want to end his relationship with Diana, stating publicly, "I have been incredibly naive, absolutely stupid. Diana is sad about it and says it's happened to her time and time again. But it hasn't happened to Julia and myself before, and I never want it to happen again."

He appeared to want to end the rift with his wife and do all in his power to continue his marriage. "My main feelings are about what it has done to people around me, the people I really care about and love," he said. "My wife, Julia, for example, look what's it done to her. That is unforgivable. I love my wife more than anything."

He insisted, however, that the relationship with Diana had been wholly innocent. "It was a perfectly harmless friendship with the Princess of Wales. Maybe I was just stupid."

Diana went to seek advice from her old friend and sister-in-law, Sarah Ferguson, the daughter of Charles's former polo manager Maj. Ronald Ferguson, the young woman with a past who married Prince Andrew in 1986 and separated from him five years later.

But Andrew and Fergie remained close and would spend time together with their daughters, Beatrice and Eugenie. The more Fergie saw of Andrew, the more Diana and Fergie discovered they had much in common. Once again they would come to rely on each other for friendship and shared interests, phoning each other for advice and long heart-to-hearts over their topsy-turvy lives. Much of the time discussions would revolve around their relationships with their husbands, other members of the Royal Family, lovers, and prospective lovers. It wouldn't always be deadly serious for sometimes they would be convulsed in laughter at one of their misdemeanors.

The relationship between Diana and Fergie has been far from steady. When Sarah Ferguson began dating Prince Andrew in the early 1980s, Diana and Fergie became a close couple, swapping stories, having fun together, teaming up to challenge the fuddy-duddy image of the Royal Family. They wanted to put some fizz into the House of Windsor and to show that life could be enjoyable even if one had become a part of the Royal Family. Fergie would help Diana overcome her bulimia, and they shared details of each other's escalating marital problems.

Diana, however, would be advised by Sir Robert Fellowes, her brother-in-law, to keep clear of Fergie. He explained that she seemed hell-bent on bringing the Royal Family into disrepute, determined to enjoy her life as she saw fit and not as a member of the Royal Family was expected to do, judiciously, correctly, her private life above reproach. Diana also frowned on Fergie's sexual encounters, first with the American Steve Wyatt, with whom she fell in love when pregnant with Eugenie, and secondly, and more importantly, when Fergie fell under the spell of Johnny Bryant—an American businessman she met through Wyatt—who boasted to the world of his sexual encounters with Sarah Ferguson.

Diana never liked Bryant, believing him to be an uncouth loudmouth. Fergie, however, was swept off her feet in an extraordinary four-year-long sexual affair with Bryant, unable to say no to his demands, which she found passionately exciting and wild. But Bryant would let her down, boasting in the most intimate detail to friends and strangers alike of their lovemaking, detailing Fergie's sexual proclivities. He would also speak of his lust for Princess Diana, saying, "I love Diana. I see her quite often and she's a wonderful girl. She's so sexy and attractive. I'm thinking bad thoughts whenever I see her!"

During 1995, Sarah would come to realize that her affair with Bryant had harmed her relationship with Andrew and, more particularly, with her daughters, Bea, seven, and Eugenie, five, who were fast growing up. She began to distance herself from her former lover, and Andrew and Fergie would spend more time together. Constantly, Andrew, Fergie, and their daughters would be seen together on some outing or attending school together as a family, and people noted how happy Fergie and Andrew appeared to be when together. There seemed nothing strained or awkward about their relationship, and the nation wondered whether a reconciliation would be possible.

Some cynics asked whether Fergie had finally realized that she would be much better off married to Andrew than living the life of an estranged, single mother with two daughters. Fergie herself commented to friends in the summer of 1995, "Andrew wants me back. I love him and we both love the girls. I don't know what's stopping us."

Encouraged by Diana, a new Fergie would take shape during 1995. In October 1994 at age thirty-four Fergie weighed nearly 170 pounds and would be seen wearing loose-fitting, shapeless dresses. By October 1995, after a year's programmed exercise and dieting, Fergie looked like a different woman, her weight down to 135 pounds and wearing size 10 (British size 10) dresses. "I've given up dairy products," she boasted, "even ice cream!"

Diana told Fergie about her relationship with Carling. And she insisted that despite all the hullabaloo, the innuendos, and the incessant gossip, the basis of their relationship had been fun and friendship. Diana would not tell Fergie whether they were lovers, but telltale comments made Fergie believe the relationship had become far more serious than straightforward fun. Diana also confided that Julia Carling's unprovoked attack on her had made her see red. Diana was furious that the "jumped-up little worm"—as she described Julia—could have the temerity to make such slanderous attacks when she knew nothing of Diana's relationship with Will Carling.

In the view of the general public and most of the newspaper columnists, Julia had won the first round in what was seen as the battle between two powerful women for the right to Will Carling's undivided attention. Never before had any wife whose husband had been attracted to the Princess of Wales openly attacked Diana or publicly accused her of trying to destroy their marriage.

The British public was agog at the comings and goings of the three participants in the extraordinary saga, fueled daily by fresh revelations pouring from the tabloid press. In no previous instance had Diana been involved in such a tug-of-love drama over a man. That Carling was one of the nation's best-known and most-respected sports idols only added to the interest. But few knew what was going on behind the scenes in Kensington Palace.

In fact, Carling had informed Diana that, like her, his marriage, too, had been going through a bad spell, even though he and Julia had been married for little more than a year. He told

Diana that he understood how ghastly her breakup with Charles must have been and commiserated with her.

Diana replied, "If I can be of any help, you must let me know. It's at times like that you find you desperately need friends, and somehow there are none around. I'm here whenever you need me."

Carling told Diana that he hoped that would never be the case, but he thanked her for her concern, adding, "If ever I need a comforting shoulder, I'll come running. I promise."

Julia continued her media blitz, telling newspapers that husband Will had decided to end his friendship with Princess Diana. "I didn't give him an ultimatum," she said, smiling broadly and looking remarkably confident. "The decision to end the friendship was Will's alone."

She added, "As far as we are concerned, it's over. It's a completely closed shop. That was an episode in our lives and you have to get on with things. Diana's business is her business. What is important is Will and myself."

Julia Carling seemed to enjoy her fifteen minutes of fame, her picture splashed over the newspapers, her name hogging the headlines day after day, rivaling Diana for the media's attention. Despite the fact her marriage was going through a crisis, Julia glowed in the spotlight of publicity.

For the talented, ambitious Julia Carling the timing could not have been better. London's Carlton Television announced that Julia would be taking over as host of their highly rated weekly daytime magazine show, *Capital Woman*. And her PR company launched a new beauty product for eye wrinkles, selling at a premium price, $300 a tube. Since she became Mrs. Carling, Julia's career had taken off, landing her lucrative modeling jobs, numerous TV and radio appearances, as well as bringing in business for her PR firm, including some topflight clients such as Mick Jagger, Paul McCartney, and Tina Turner.

She herself admitted with commendable honesty, "The fame thing has happened for me because I'm Will Carling's wife."

Throughout the drama, Julia would happily pose for photographs, and comments slipped daily from her lips. "If Diana tried to renew the relationship with Will, she would have a tough time," she boasted, adding, "Will would think it was a really stupid thing to do renewing the friendship with Diana. He's regretted it enough as it is."

In answer to journalists' questions the following day Julia Carling commented, "I have no sympathy for Diana. I don't know whether she has put this episode behind her. I don't really feel anything for her, that's her business. I wouldn't choose to have her as a friend, probably because of who she is. She seems to pick her friends badly, but that's not for me to dwell on—it's for her to sort out. You've got to learn to deal with your problems, and unfortunately she probably can't."

Diana had other ideas. She had decided that she wanted Will Carling for herself; that they had discovered they found each other exciting and both wanted the relationship to continue. At first, Diana refused to accept a cloak-and-dagger affair and would continue to meet her lover at the BiMAL Clinic and the posh Harbour Club. Within forty-eight hours of Carling's declaration that his relationship with the Princess of Wales was at an end, the two of them had breakfast together at the Harbour Club, giggling and laughing in full view of the other members, as if nothing whatsoever had been said.

The meeting was no accident. Diana arrived looking stunning in a tight-fitting white body T-shirt with jeans and went immediately to the cafe. Ten minutes later Carling walked in and went straight to the Princess, sat down, and ordered orange juice and toast. Neither had been working out or using any of the club's amenities; they just met for a late breakfast.

For the first few minutes Carling seemed tense, looking around the near-empty cafe, but Diana appeared in sparkling form, leaning her elbows on the table and looking directly into Carling's eyes as they chatted and laughed. They talked for about forty-five minutes, while other members did a double take when they saw the two of them sitting together. Somehow, this meeting would remain secret, Julia unaware the two were spending so much time together.

A couple of weeks later the wretched Julia Carling would be lost for words. Will Carling had phoned Diana to tell her that some presents he had promised her sons had arrived and asked whether he should deliver them to Kensington Palace.

"Of course you must come," she said. "It would be lovely to see you again and the boys so adore you."

Carling wondered whether he should bring the presents personally or have them sent round in case photographers were lying in wait. Diana pleaded with Carling to bring the presents—England rugby shirts—himself, and finally he agreed. He told her the time and the day he would arrive.

On Monday, September 4, 1995, Carling drove up to Kensington Palace, this time at the wheel of his wife's blue Range Rover, hoping the vehicle might fool any photographer, who would expect Carling to arrive in his Aston Martin. However, two newspapers had been telephoned by an anonymous caller telling them when Carling would be visiting Kensington Palace later that day. Carling was stunned when he drove up to the policemen on duty only to discover two photographers outside. Carling stayed only twenty minutes and Diana was not even there. Yet the visit would cause more trouble.

Later, Carling told reporters, "Julia knew I was popping round, although she didn't think it a very good idea. She knew I had a long-standing commitment to leave presents for the young Princes, and while in retrospect it was not such a good idea, she knew I was going. There was no question that this was something underhand or done without her knowledge. After all it was quite innocuous. I had made a promise and I didn't want to let people down."

Julia's only comment would be, "I am getting a little tired of all this."

Diana read the following day's papers with a smile on her face. "Will's at It Again," screamed the headlines. Diana grinned broadly when she noted Julia Carling's dusty comment. Diana had not forgiven "the worm" for trying to smear her name, making her appear as some femme fatale. Nor would she forgive her. Diana believed the upstart Julia Carling should be taught a lesson.

That day, her eyes blazing with anticipation and determination, Diana closed one of the tabloids, looked again at the front page, and commented, "The little worm hasn't seen anything yet. I haven't even started."

# 14

## *"Home Wrecker"*

———— ❧ ————

AT EIGHT O'CLOCK ONE MORNING toward the end of September 1995, three weeks after Carling's visit to Kensington Palace, Diana arrived at the BiMAL Clinic for her weekly Friday workout, continuing her never-ending, self-imposed ritual of strengthening and toning her muscles. Diana worked out so ceaselessly and enthusiastically primarily because she feared that she would once again turn into the "lumpy beanpole" she felt she had become during the years following Harry's birth in 1984 when eating disorders dominated her life.

During the past twelve months a secondary reason had emerged that made the drudgery of workouts far more interesting and sometimes positively rewarding. By attending both the Harbour Club and the BiMAL center she could continue her relationship with Will Carling, the man who had become more important to her than she had ever envisaged during their early encounters. Now, the hunky Carling had become even more of a challenge. For much of the time, Diana rather enjoyed the headiness of the exciting, tantalizing duel.

She parked her Audi sports coupe, threw a towel over her shoulder, grabbed a small bottle of mineral water from the front seat, and almost bounded into the clinic, a spring in her step and a big smile on her face. As usual for such sessions Diana was casually dressed in a loose-fitting V-necked sweater, black cycle shorts, and trainers. Photographers were there to snap the Princess as she arrived and went inside. Fifty minutes later Will

Carling arrived at the wheel of a borrowed BMW and casually walked inside for a physiotherapy session to treat a trapped nerve in his hip.

Twenty-six minutes later Diana emerged alone looking angry, depressed, and red-eyed, so very different from the happy young woman who had walked into the clinic with a skip and a step. She climbed into her car, slammed the door, and drove off, accelerating hard as if wanting to escape from the scene as quickly as possible. Carling emerged a minute later, checked twice to see if any photographers were about, then walked to his car, his hands deep in his trouser pockets, his face like thunder.

During their brief encounter Carling told Diana that Julia wanted to make a fresh start, and he suggested that he and Diana spend some time apart, "to see what happened."

Forty-eight hours later Carling's wife would hear of the secret meeting, for the *News of the World* splashed the story on page one under the headline "Will and Di at It Again," giving minute-by-minute details of what the newspaper claimed had been another of their secret trysts. But they had no idea what had been discussed.

Carling protested, "I did not know the Princess was there. I did not see her. I was upstairs having treatment and someone told me that she was there working out in the gym below."

He went on, "I have discussed all this with Julia this morning. Any suggestion that the Princess and myself set up a meeting is crazy."

Later that day Carling would be seen to have spoken too hastily. He knew of Diana's schedule. It had been Carling who introduced Diana to the clinic, a no-nonsense sports organization run by highly qualified physiotherapists for sorting out the problems of Britain's high-profile sportsmen, athletes, and footballers. The gym has no swimming pool, no smart cafe area, no bar, and its reputation is based on high-tech equipment and the skill and advice of qualified physiotherapists experienced in rectifying stresses and strains of injured muscles.

Carling knew that Diana visited the clinic virtually every

Friday morning at 8 A.M., staying for more than an hour, before driving herself back to Kensington Palace. They had met there on a number of occasions during the previous six months. From time to time, they had left to breakfast together somewhere else.

When Julia arrived home later that Sunday she immediately contradicted her husband, insisting that her husband had not talked to her about the alleged meeting. "I've got a hangover," she told reporters, "and I've nothing to say."

Within hours of Carling's forthright denial, Princess Diana also contradicted his statement, confirming that she did have a meeting with Carling at the clinic. A senior palace spokesman said, "The Princess of Wales and Mr. Will Carling met at the fitness center on Friday, but it was by accident."

Diana spent most of that weekend with her younger son, Harry. On Friday afternoon she drove alone the forty miles to his boarding school in Wokingham, Berkshire, then brought him back to London, and they spent the remainder of the day together at the palace. On Saturday Diana took Harry go-carting in Chelsea, and later they drove to Windsor to see Harry's elder brother, William, play rugby at his new school, Eton College, England's premier private school. On Sunday, Diana and Harry, having spent the night at Kensington Palace, drove over to the home of the Duchess of York. Later, Diana took Harry back to school before returning to spend the evening alone at the palace.

Throughout the weekend Diana made sure she read all the newspapers, which were full of her secret trysts and the problems facing Julia and Will Carling. She would also spend hours on the phone, particularly when driving to and from Harry's school. Despite the problems she had experienced using mobile phones in the past, Diana would still drive along happily chatting.

Julia would comment the following day, "I am standing by my husband, despite everything. He's my husband and I am behind him all the way. I believe everything he has said. I don't believe there is anything going on at all."

Diana consulted friends of mine suggesting she should contact Julia Carling through an intermediary and that the two should meet to discuss the whole matter. On one occasion Diana said, "If I met Julia, I'm sure we would be able to thrash things out and then we could forget the whole affair."

She immediately giggled. "Oh! I shouldn't use that word *affair* should I? I meant *relationship*."

Friends made discreet inquiries and advised Diana that she should not even suggest a meeting for they believed Julia would refuse. They hinted that Julia could go further, telling the world that she had turned down a peace pact put forward by the Princess of Wales.

Diana was determined that everyone would see the Princess of Wales enjoying life, no matter the hulabaloo surrounding her private life. She would show that the fuss surrounding Will Carling and his wife were no concern of hers.

Diana telephoned a close friend, one of her special advisers, two days later. "I'm going to be a little naughty today," she said, giggling coquettishly. "I have written a poem about all the rubbish going on and I'm going to read it out today at the *Literary Review* lunch of the year."

The adviser asked if the poem was risqué or imprudent. "Oh, no," Diana replied, laughing, "nothing like that. It's about me and Will Carling and secret trysts, that's all."

At the annual lunch of the *Literary Review,* a magazine devoted to poetry and other literature, Diana, the guest of honor, looked stunning in a smart bright red suit. She smiled and waved to the cheering crowds who greeted her at London's Cafe Royal where she would make her speech.

She did not appear in the least apprehensive or nervous as she addressed the gathering of notable men of letters. "I feel privileged to be allowed to join a highly exclusive gathering of intellectuals," she said. "Apparently, some people are wondering what Diana, that notorious illiterate, is doing at a distinguished scholarly occasion such as this. So I've made time between therapy sessions and secret trysts to attempt a reply."

She cleared her throat and delivered her limerick:

*The Princess was heard to declare,*
*Let gossips poke fun if they dare,*
*My real inspiration,*
*Is Bron's invitation,*
*Stick that in your tabloids,*
*So there.*

The poem, read with gusto, was greeted with laughter and great applause, especially by Auberon "Bron" Waugh, the noted columnist and son of the late, celebrated author Evelyn Waugh. It was Bron who founded the *Literary Review,* which he now edits. Bron commented, "Today's prize is for poetry that rhymes and scans and makes sense, and so Diana's fitted in well. It was a limerick in the ancient tradition."

Diana was thrilled with the reception given to her poem. University professors, asked by the media to comment, praised her little limerick. But there was another reason for the smile on Diana's face when she read the tributes the following day.

During the previous few weeks much had been written about the brilliant Julia Carling, the girl who had the courage to tackle the "marriage wrecker" Diana head-on and show the world that she was the woman Will Carling loved and wanted, above anyone else, including the Princess. Julia Carling had been happy to tell the media that she, like Diana, was from a wealthy background; was brought up in the country, like Diana; had never taken drugs, like Diana; had lost her virginity at the mature age of eighteen, only a year earlier than Diana; and remarkably, had chosen to live with a much older man when she was still a teenager, just as Diana had decided to do with Prince Charles. There were other similarities Julia happily stressed. She, too, is an extraordinary mix of the naive and the knowing; she, too, can portray the shy little girl with the soft voice and engaging innocence.

Other people noticed more similarities. Both Diana and Julia are slim, attractive blondes who have the capacity to make themselves look like a million dollars. They both dress well and attractively and have a certain presence about them. They both love wearing expensive clothes and enjoy the power to turn heads. Julia, however, is smaller boned than Diana, just 5 feet 5 inches tall and weighing under 120 pounds, while Diana is 5 feet 7 inches tall and weighs around 130 pounds.

Their personal lives had also taken remarkably similar paths. Julia spent six years with the guitarist Jeff Beck, a star of the 1960s, who was thirty-nine when they began to live together. Julia had just turned eighteen. Jeff Beck had taken Julia to live in a lovely, big country house, but she, like Diana, had found herself growing more unhappy with her relationship, cut off from young people, from friends and from the hurly-burly of everyday life that both Diana and Julia had missed. It seemed extraordinary that Julia's relationship with Beck had lasted six years, about the same amount of time that Diana had managed to maintain her relationship with Charles.

There the similarities ended. For Julia had only to walk out of her relationship with Beck while Diana had become a lonely prisoner, more depressed with every passing year. Able to escape her relationship, Julia had never suffered from anorexia or bulimia as had Diana. Somewhat apologetically Julia would tell interviewers that she never goes to the gym to get fit or tone her muscles. "I hate the gym and I don't need it," she would say, leaving the interviewer to decide whether her remark included a deliberate gibe at the Princess of Wales. She would add, however, "But I do enjoy full body massages. They make me feel a new woman."

Julia would also proudly tell of her educational accomplishments, having passed eight O (ordinary) level examinations at school and three A (advanced) level exams, though she would drop out of university without taking her degree. She knew that Diana had an abysmally poor educational record, passing no exams, even failing those she sat again. It is a failure that has always embarrassed Diana.

Diana phoned friends the following day, eager to know what they thought of her poem, and received warm praise, even from those who normally doubted her mental ability. Teasingly, she asked one girlfriend, "Do you think Julia Carling would have enjoyed my poem? I hope so because she doesn't think I have any brains."

Diana had hoped that by poking fun at her secret trysts with Carling she would help to defuse the situation, which she believed was out of hand. Some columnists had cast Diana as a "home wrecker," accusing her of deliberately targeting married men with no thought for their wives. That tag hurt Diana. She maintained it was most unfair, as well as being untrue.

During the furor over the Carling affair, Diana had returned to her old habit of reading every newspaper and magazine piece written about herself, Julia, and Carling. Every mention of Diana as a "home breaker" or a "home wrecker" made her furious. She would storm around her apartment screaming obscenities and yelling, then erupt in tears of anger and frustration.

"How can they?" she would plead to Sarah Ferguson and other close girlfriends. "How can they say such things about me? It is so unfair and so untrue. Why do they pick on me? Why do the papers say on one day what a wonderful person I am and then the following day accuse me of being a home wrecker? Why are they being so beastly, so unfair?"

During the following few days, staff would know that Diana had become an unhappy woman. One minute she would be sweet and kind, the next angry and vitriolic about anyone and everyone who crossed her path. Her staff were well aware of Diana's violent swings of mood and would understand that during these phases it was advisable to keep their heads down and say nothing. Once again Diana was showing serious signs of paranoia, but none of her friends would tell her that.

Diana also let people know that she believed Julia Carling to be a "bitch on the make" who was trying to "use" Diana and the alleged affair with her husband to benefit her career. Privately Diana would say, "I've watched that woman on TV, and she's so wooden. She needs all the publicity she can get, and she is deliberately making the most of this rumpus to feather her own nest." To others Diana would be more outspoken: "Just because her marriage wasn't working, the little cow is trying to put all the blame on me. She's got a bloody cheek. She is some trumped-up PR woman who thinks that by using me she is going to become a celebrity."

Newspapers and magazines were thoroughly enjoying what they saw as a battle between two beautiful modern women, one the Princess of Wales, the other a bright, highly successful career woman with a bright future. The prize, the love of the England rugby hero. Others believed the three members of the triangle had their separate and different reasons. Diana wanted to demonstrate that she had the power and the sexual attraction to combat any rival, particularly Julia; many believed Carling thought he and Diana would become an item and that he would walk off into the sunset with a rugby ball under one arm and the Princess of Wales on the other; some thought Julia Carling was desperate to make the most of a marriage that had gone wrong and was happily milking the Diana link for all she was worth. They believed Diana had become caught up in the bad marriage and had enjoyed an affair with a man she found attractive and fun.

Diana's jokey limerick at the literary lunch, however, had singularly failed to ease the situation, for Julia Carling's bitterness would not be so simply assuaged. Six days after the controversial meeting-that-never-was at the fitness center Will and Julia Carling issued a joint statement that shocked their close friends and would begin TV news programs:

"Will Carling announced with regret tonight that he and his wife, Julia, have agreed to spend some time apart. They both believe that they need space and some peace for the time being. "They want to emphasize that nobody else is involved, and they hope that by allowing themselves time apart to reflect, they will be able to get back together as soon as possible."

Diana watched the TV news that night and confessed later that the news made her smile, giving her a feeling of triumph and satisfaction over the young woman who had dared to challenge her. Diana knew from Will Carling that Julia had been determined to show the Princess of Wales, and the British public, that she could not only compete with Diana but would prove more than capable of keeping her handsome hunk of a rugby hero as her husband despite any attempt by Diana to steal him away.

The love triangle had become a most public affair, and the world had witnessed Julia's contempt and bitterness toward her rival. Diana smiled because she believed Julia Carling had grossly exaggerated the relationship between Will and herself, and had made herself look foolish.

The statement, which made front-page news, appeared beside a photograph of Julia taken the previous day at the launch of an electronic beauty product her PR firm handled. She looked stunning, smiling, laughing, engaging in animated conversation, showing no sign of the turmoil in her private life. Later that evening, as the statement was making headline news on Britain's TV stations, Julia turned up unexpectedly at a party to celebrate the first anniversary of the cable-TV pop-music station VH-1 where she hosted a weekly show. She appeared in great form, chatting and drinking for two hours with everyone.

Julia was showing Will, Diana, and the media that she was a true professional PR consultant down to her well-manicured fingernails. "In the instant-broadcast age," she commented while the furor raged around her marriage, "it's not what's really going on that matters but how you make it look publicly."

Some thought that statement the height of cynicism, revealing that Julia equated her job on the same plane as her marriage. It made others wonder how serious Julia Carling's commitment could be to her marriage. Some suggested that the decision to separate, for however long, seemed remarkably hasty when only days before Julia had said, "We have even considered counseling, but there's not enough of a problem to sort out." She had paused and then added, "Look, if it ever came to that— well, it would have to be really severe. We wouldn't need someone to sort out any problem because Will and I are straight enough with each other."

Some of the in-depth interviews that Julia gave to the media would be avidly read by Diana. She would sometimes laugh out loud at Julia's remarks, for Will would have told her a different story to the one Julia was telling the media. Diana also loved reading what Julia had to say about Will.

On one occasion Julia commented, "I think it's a real advantage that Will and I are so different. We hardly share any of the same interests. I hardly ever go and watch him play rugby. I prefer to go home at night and listen to music, while Will prefers to go out with the lads. I like really up-to-date music, while I grimace at Will's taste, which is more the sort Princess Diana likes—Phil Collins and the like. "Will and I have always been straight with each other. We know what's going on in each other's lives. We may not live in each other's pockets, but we talk on the phone five or six times a day."

Julia admitted that Will had changed her. "Will has made me a better person. We were both pretty selfish people—I was spoiled by my father—and we have made each other less selfish. Well, you have to, when you have a relationship with someone else. Will's a calming person—he doesn't get neurotic about things, which has been very good for me."

Diana read that last sentence and wondered whether Carling's calm approach to matters was one of the reasons she had fallen in love with him. She respected him for never losing his temper, always staying cool and in command, the opposite to Diana's temperament, one moment in the blackest despair, the next happy and smiling.

The Carlings' decision to separate, however, cast a totally different light on the entire matter and worried Diana. From everything Will Carling had told her throughout their relationship, it seemed extraordinary that Julia would demand a separation to sort things out. Carling told Diana that he had been "flabbergasted" by his wife's demand to spend some time apart, suggesting to the world that his relationship with the Princess had been far more intimate and serious than had been the case.

Within twenty-four hours Julia would go out of her way to squarely blame Diana for the marriage breakup. She issued a statement saying, "I confirm that my husband and I have separated. It saddens me deeply that this has happened, but the recent pressures and tensions have produced this situation. I had always valued my marriage as the most important and sacred part of my life, and it hurts me very much to face losing my husband in a manner that has become outside my control. I have given total support to Will and this has unfortunately proved to no avail."

Understandably, most newspapers viewed her statement as a direct and open attack on the Princess of Wales. "I Blame Di" was the headline in some of the tabloids. Others went further, interpreting Julia's words to mean that she was branding Diana a "marriage wrecker."

"The little bitch" were Diana's words when she read the statement the following morning. "How dare she blame me for what's happened in her marriage? My God, what nerve. Who exactly does Julia Carling think she is?"

Carling warned Diana that they should not meet anymore for fear of the newspapers discovering their "secret trysts" and making their relationship front-page news again. He also told her that he didn't think it fair to Julia for the two of them to continue to meet, not at their sports clubs, not even for coffee or a snack, which might be interpreted wrongly by the public and certainly would be by the media. Diana disagreed, arguing that they should act as if nothing had happened, to show the world they enjoyed a friendship, and nothing more. Carling, however, would remain adamant.

Diana pressed Carling, telling him that if he had been kicked out of his house by Julia, then there could be nothing wrong with his occasionally seeing her, either publicly or in private. Quietly Carling told her it would be more diplomatic if they didn't see each other until the storm had settled and they could all resume their normal lives.

Julia would go home to her parents' house in an idyllic Northamptonshire village eighty miles from London. And yet the next day she would be snapped by a paparazzi taking her young niece for a walk in the country. The photographer had been tipped off when Julia would be there. Carling, mean-

while, stayed at the home of Colin Herridge, the media liaison
for the Rugby Football Union, a close friend of Carling's for
many years, who issued statements on his behalf.

After the separation statement, Herridge added, "Carling
has promised that he will definitely not be seeing the Princess
again. I don't think the relationship was an affair; it was a
friendship. Will is determined to sort out his domestic affairs
and is hoping for a speedy reconciliation. He is also determined
to play his rugby."

Diana would be tempted to forget about Carling, to turn
her back on him and let him sort out his life, with or without
Julia. Despite all the thousands of words written about Diana
and her relationship with Carling, only she knew the whole
truth. She would tell it to only a tiny handful of people.

In essence, Diana told them that the relationship with
Carling began in all innocence for she knew that her sons would
love to meet Will Carling, their hero. She and Carling had met
at the Harbour Club and he had agreed to visit Kensington
Palace and meet the boys. He had also arranged for them to
meet the England team prior to the World Cup. Her sons had
idolized the England rugby captain, finding him wonderful.

But the relationship developed. She and Carling would
meet three times a week at the club, and she found herself
becoming attracted to the man she had not originally found
sexy.

Friends of mine who saw Diana and Carling together at the
club suggest that Diana is not being totally honest about the
relationship. Diana would walk up to Will's table with a big
smile on her face, openly flirting with him. She would invite
herself to sit down, and at first, Carling would look rather
sheepish. The more he gained in confidence, the more he
enjoyed her approaches. Before long, club members noted a
definite sexual attraction between the two—the way they
chatted, looked at each other, and gave each other attention.
Their body language screamed they wanted each other.

Carling would wait to see her at the club, wanting to join
her for coffee and a snack, helping her with workouts and

programs to develop her body. Diana loved the attention of the man she was becoming strongly attracted to. For Diana this affair would be far deeper and more meaningful than any she had enjoyed since James Hewitt. Diana had known that her relationship with Hewitt had blossomed, then gone out of control, because she had then desperately needed love, attention, some warmth, and emotional involvement, and Hewitt had been on hand, eager to oblige.

Diana admitted that on most days she and Carling would talk frequently on the phone, sometimes four times a day. At first their calls would be jovial and fun, but over time, their attitudes to each other changed. They gave each other pet names, joked and teased, but underneath the high spirits, a more serious relationship was developing.

They both realized they could not go on in that way. Without saying a word they both knew that, if they continued being so close and so intense, they would soon become lovers. Diana noted that throughout their relationship, even at the beginning, Carling had hardly ever mentioned Julia. And she had wondered why.

Diana told how she invited Carling to Kensington Palace. And the invitation both worried and flattered him. During most of his daytime visits Diana's staff would be working as they chatted over coffee or tea. Then Diana phoned inviting him to drinks one evening. Carling was flattered and was even more surprised when he discovered he was the only guest. Carling thoroughly enjoyed that first evening alone with the Princess of Wales, who flattered him and flirted and insisted on pouring the drinks. Diana, too, enjoyed that evening and realized she rather liked having Will Carling as a companion, with his sense of fun and humor.

More invitations followed. Sometimes they dined alone, and on occasion Carling would stay late into the night. They would drink a bottle of wine or champagne, listen to music they both enjoyed, and suddenly, naturally, find themselves in each other's arms. One thing would lead to another.

She believed Carling had fallen in love, and they agreed

spending more time together would be enjoyable. The more involved Carling became with Diana the less he appeared to pay attention to Julia and seemed to be living a more independent life. The ambitious Julia would spend more time concentrating on her career while Carling found life with Diana more frivolous, more relaxing. Carling would tell Diana all this saying that he did not know what to do about Julia. Diana told Carling that she didn't want to know about Carling's marital problems. She would tell him that he had to sort them out himself.

When their close relationship became known, Diana told Carling that he would have to make difficult decisions. She promised him nothing save the relationship they had, a friendship based on lots of fun, shared interests, enjoying time together whether in the gym or back at the palace. She also knew that Wills and Harry would not be too pleased if their hero no longer called round to the palace. The boys had no idea of the amount of time Carling was spending with their mother.

Later, Diana would explain that Carling could not decide what to do. He felt like a cork bobbing about on the ocean, thrown hither and yon by events and the two women in his life. He knew that both women were much stronger than he could ever be, but he couldn't make up his mind. He told of furious rows between himself and Julia over his association with the Princess, arguments that left him exhausted and unsure what to do. Julia, however, made up his mind for him by demanding a separation.

Diana felt that Carling had shown such weakness in the face of the trauma that it would probably be far better if they forgot everything and he returned to his true loves, playing rugby and spending evenings with his rugby mates. By the time of the Carlings' very public separation Diana had become less enamored of Carling, for he had proven not to be the man she had hoped for, lacking strength and determination, his gifts physical, never mental.

And yet Diana knew that she and Carling were ideally

suited, for they laughed and joked at the same things, liked the same music, and were undeniably sexually attracted to one another. Diana also realized that he provided something she desperately needed and had never found with Charles or James Hewitt, a strong shoulder on which to rest her head and a man on whom she could rely.

But the Carling affair would bring unwelcome repercussions for Diana.

One day in the summer of 1995 she walked into the ladies' locker room at the Chelsea Harbour Club and heard two women talking. Though not visible to them, Diana could hear everything they said.

The first asked her friend what she thought of the Julia Carling affair.

The second replied, "I think she is behaving like a perfect bitch."

"Why do you say that?"

"Will Carling and Julia had been married for less than a year and along comes Diana, who thinks she can have any man she wants. In my opinion Diana has behaved like a bitch."

"And Carling?"

"He didn't stand a chance. Diana took a fancy to him and that was it. Diana knew what she was doing."

The women's reaction to her affair with Carling made Diana angry and confused; angry that they should call her a "bitch" and confused because she believed she had done nothing wrong.

Meanwhile, Julia Carling seemed determined to milk every ounce of publicity she could from the love triangle. From the moment of the separation, on which she had insisted, Julia was seen in public, relentlessly photographed. She seemed to thrive on the media's intrusion into her marriage and its problems.

Despite the fact she had no professional singing career, Julia recorded her own version of "Stand by Your Man," which the record company hoped to produce for the Christmas market. She then posed for some quite extraordinary pictures of her with a DJ, Richard Allinson, her cohost on VH-1, showing Allinson with his head in Julia's lap, gazing up into her eyes as she strokes his hair.

Ten days after the separation, a paparazzi caught Julia taking a Sunday walk with her parents and her brother Adrian on Barnes Common, on the outskirts of London. The photographer was there purportedly by chance. The same would happen again a week or so later when Julia and a hunky friend, hairdresser Daniel Galvin, emerged from a late-night dinner at the trendy Julie's Restaurant in Holland Park. This time two photographers were on hand to snap Julia as she leaned forward, facing the cameras, to kiss her friend good night. *The Sun* tabloid had been phoned anonymously that morning tipping them off about Julia's secret date.

Julia Carling, however, didn't have only the publicity she wanted. Carl Pickford, the former assistant manager to one of Diana's old favorite pop groups, Duran Duran, had enjoyed a passionate ten-month relationship with Julia after meeting her at a party in 1990. He would kiss and tell in *The Sun,* a Murdoch tabloid, detailing their affair and advising Carling that he would be mad to let Julia go because she was so fantastic in bed. "Julia is as positive about what she wants in her love life as in her career. We would make love all night. It was great. The best sex I've ever had. During a two-week holiday at her parents' Spanish apartment Julia was insatiable. I couldn't believe her appetite. Sometimes she wanted sex twelve times a day."

He told the newspaper that Julia enjoyed making love in public places, especially on airplanes. "On almost all the flights we ended up making love in one of the tiny washrooms. She wanted it throughout the flight. We hardly even had time for the complimentary drink."

Diana would read the intimate details revealed by Julia's former lover, wondering whether her rival would be embarrassed by the accounts of her wild and "insatiable" sexual appetite. Diana believed that perhaps Julia welcomed such publicity, believing the old adage that any publicity is good publicity.

"I'm sure she hopes I read the article," Diana commented, adding, "the little tart."

Carling's fling with Diana appeared to have put an end to his marriage to Julia. The blond PR consultant would later comment that she felt "betrayed" and "hurt" by both her husband and Princess Diana. Some weeks later she confessed, "I can't compete with a princess. I feel so let down. Will is a changed person since he met Princess Diana, and I wonder if he'll ever be the same again. You can't change a person back, can you?"

For Diana, however, the time had come for decisive action. She did not want to be seen as a marriage wrecker but as the loving, caring princess the public still adored. She decided to continue her affair with Carling in the strictest secrecy until the storm had blown over.

She stopped frequenting the BiMAL Clinic, and Carling would not appear at the Harbour Club. They would not be seen together for several months, though Carling would continue to visit Diana at Kensington Palace, usually arriving and leaving under cover of darkness. To the public at large, and even the prying eyes of the paparazzi, Diana's affair with the rugged England rugby captain had apparently ended.

Many doubted that Carling and Diana had been lovers. But Sarah Ferguson and two or three of Diana's closest confidants knew the truth and realized that Diana had triumphed in her battle for Carling's affections, even though it had been necessary to face the anger and vitriol of a woman her own age, risking condemnation from the public, whom Diana was desperate to keep on her side. For Diana realized that she needed to retain the love and respect of the nation if her secret plans for her future were to succeed. And she was determined to push ahead with those plans to forge a new, independent career outside the jurisdiction of the Royal Family.

# 15

## *Angel of Hope*

———— ❦ ————

Despite the criticism and the scandals that have swirled around Diana in the past few years, no one can deny that she has touched millions with her compassion for the sick and disadvantaged. And since the collapse of her marriage she has devoted herself tirelessly to helping and caring for others, bringing happiness and joy to thousands she has met.

Many who have judged Diana before ever meeting her testify that after spending some time talking to her they have been won over by her personality and warmth. One of Diana's earliest and scathing critics was the right-wing writer Auberon Waugh, the son of the novelist Evelyn Waugh, who would write caustic remarks about her in *Spectator* magazine. Since meeting her, Waugh admits to being stymied by her beautiful manners and sweetness, happy to retract his unkind and uncalled-for words.

Perhaps hitting the right note, he commented, "She has this genuine warmth, humor, and recklessness. That's what slays people. Men aren't complete fools, you know."

That is the essence of Diana's remarkable personality. For she does possess this extraordinary ability to win over people, for once having met her, many find their earlier criticism unjust. Most acknowledge that they have misread the strength of her character and her disarming charm and come away knowing that Diana is the epitome of womanhood.

Without doubt, many people grossly underestimate the Princess of Wales, including not only Prince Charles, the

Queen, and Prince Philip, but most of the senior courtiers, who believed Diana to be mentally unstable. But the time was fast approaching when the new, more confident Diana would make them all sit up and take note. A caring, loving person who looks down on meaningless royal duties and wants to help others, Diana brings hope and light to many sick people.

This author has attended lunches, dinners, cocktail parties, and informal get-togethers at polo clubs where Diana has been a guest. And I have also watched her closely during official royal visits to hospitals, children's homes, factories, armed services headquarters, as well as grimy towns and innocuous villages. On all these occasions she has exuded the most remarkable talent for attracting people and making them feel special in a single moment of attention. People smile when Diana smiles. They laugh when she does, and patients in hospitals and homes who speak to her say openly and honestly that Diana seems to care for them as no one has before.

Frequently, I have chatted with people who, a few minutes after speaking to Diana, would say, "She's special, she's some-thing else." They would often add, "I don't know what it is; she said nothing different to me, nothing remarkable, yet she made me feel special."

With all the criticism, implicit and explicit, that has been made of Diana during the past few years, it is remarkable that she has retained the knack of making people, even those to whom she is not speaking directly, feel that she has an interest in them. During lunch and dinner gatherings Diana will sit at the top table, seemingly only interested in the few people seated around her to whom she can talk. At the same time, without its being apparent, she will scan the room, catching someone's eye and holding the look for little more than an instant, as if registering that person is someone special to her.

Friends of mine who have never met Diana face-to-face will say, "I saw the Princess across the room and, for little more than a couple of seconds, our eyes met. I have thought about her since and don't know whether she was flirting or simply registering me in her mind, yet knowing I would go away wondering if she did want to engage me in more than a fleeting look. It's uncanny, yet at the time, very real. If that same look had been given to me by another young woman, I would have considered the glance to be flirtatious, inviting me to approach her and perhaps start a conversation. Diana's look is that ambiguous, both disarming and devastating."

And it is not only in the United Kingdom that Diana wields her charms so successfully and so seductively. I was a guest at a dinner in Paris in 1989 celebrating the French bicentenary at which more than four hundred people were present. I watched Diana closely that night. She did in fact appear more nervous and shy than usual, but as the evening progressed, she became increasingly confident and began to use her eyes in her inimitable way, looking at people sitting at other tables, sometimes nodding gently to someone, throwing a quick smile at someone else, and giving that searching look, suggesting mild flirtation, to yet another person.

That particular night Diana appeared to be going out of her way to prove to the glamorous, sophisticated Parisians that she, too, could flirt as well as any of the beautiful young Frenchwomen. The following day the French newspapers were full of pictures of Diana, and the commentaries were all flattering. She had won her spurs in the most critical capital in the Western world.

On most occasions Diana is careful to show that her interest in someone, be it a hospital patient, a soldier, factory worker, or dinner host, is personal, not something that the two of them want the world to know about. That is of course part of Diana's attraction. On other occasions Diana loves to throw herself headlong into a relationship, in which she takes pleasure in the fact that the person who adores her is someone in whom she believes, as well as a person whom she knows others admire and respect.

Some of those people she admires include the brilliant dancer Wayne Sleep, with whom she loved to dance at every opportunity, or world-famous stars such as Luciano Pavarotti. In September 1995, Diana was invited by the world-renowned tenor to his hometown of Mòdena in northern Italy to make a guest appearance at a concert raising money for his personal charity, musical therapy for the children of Bosnia. Diana was only too happy to help Pavarotti, whom she adores, repaying him for flying to London on two previous occasions to raise funds for her charities.

Fifty thousand Italians watched on giant TV screens and millions watched on nationwide television as Diana arrived, looking more like a blond Italian vamp than a princess of royal blood. She was dressed in a $4,000 white Gianni Versace dress, the hem well above the knee. The wolf whistles echoed around the stadium as the glamorous Diana, with a deep-cut bodice and thin shoulder straps, kissed Pavarotti on both cheeks and hugged him closely.

Never before had one of Diana's dresses revealed so much cleavage, and the Fleet Street fashion writers were determined to discover for their readers the secrets of Diana's uplift. They revealed that Diana hadn't been wearing a Wonderbra but an old-fashioned, built-in corset! The fashion experts showed how the white silk crepe dress was cut to cling to all her curves and focus on the low neckline, which had been trimmed with diamanté buckles. The bodice had concealed boning in the lining and the shoulder straps acted as a lifting lever, creating, as they put it, a "cleavage to kill for."

And yet Diana has the ability to create that frisson of understated sexuality before a crowd of fifty thousand excited, ardent young Italians and, on other occasions, win over highly intelligent and high-brow diplomats and politicians. Britain's former foreign secretary Douglas Hurd is a most serious, well-respected, and mature politician who has been charmed by Diana's personality and presence. Hurd and Diana met on a number of occasions at the Foreign Office when he was the secretary of state and she was seeking his support to become a roving royal ambassador, traveling abroad to pursue her ambition of becoming more involved in international charities. She hoped that Douglas Hurd would become her wise counselor, and he in turn believed that Diana's magnetic personality and allure could be of great service for overseas charitable causes.

Hurd strongly supported Diana's plan against the advice of
senior aides in Buckingham Palace, who felt her idea might
detract from the role of both the Queen and Prince Charles and
might even cheapen the monarchy in people's eyes. It was
strongly suggested in palace circles that Douglas Hurd had
become "besotted" with the young Diana. Not surprisingly,
with such opposition the plan would be dropped.

Members of the House of Lords, clergymen, scholars,
industrialists and business leaders, men of letters, and serving
British officers have all in their turn found themselves captivated by Diana, who has held their attention and won their
admiration. She appears to have a similar effect on people
whom she meets around the world. Former U.S. presidents
Ronald Reagan and George Bush found pleasure chatting with
Diana during visits to Britain; President Jacques Chirac of
France, Henry Kissinger, Gen. Colin Powell, have all come
under her shy influence, which seemed magnetic and certainly
enchanting and elusive. They all discovered they wanted to
continue to converse with her, slightly taken aback by her
disarming quality.

Diana wins so many hearts not only among the recipients of
her charitable works but also among the administrators and
managers of charity organizations, as well as the men and
women who work within those organizations at every level.
She will walk into a room of perhaps forty or more people, of
whom only two or three will have disabilities of one type or
another. Within minutes of meeting the officials and as though
by instinct, she will have discovered the sufferers, who may be
at the back of the room, and will spend some of the time talking
to them. She will go out of her way to make them feel wanted
and important, that they have as much to offer as anyone else in
that room.

Every year Diana holds a reception at Kensington Palace for
the charities of which she is either the president or royal patron.
Perhaps the chief executive and senior manager of each charity
attends with one or two of their disadvantaged people in

attendance. Usually, more than two hundred people attend, and Diana makes sure, each year, that she spends more time talking with the disadvantaged than with the executives. She will tell them, "We talk at meetings, but this day is for them, so you will excuse me, won't you?"

Afterward, the patients will talk for days, weeks, and months about their few minutes' chat with the Princess. That meeting becomes one of the highlights of their lives. More importantly they will say that they found the Princess "warm and caring."

Mr. Barry Brooking became chief executive of the Parkinson's Disease Society in 1995 and has seen Diana at work during visits to patients of the charity, where she has been the patron for the past six years. He said, "When I took this job, I had no preconceived idea of how the Princess would be to deal with on a personal basis and how she would interact with patients. But within months I was totally won over by her knowledge, her expertise, her professionalism, and the warmth she exudes whenever she is talking to patients. And the effect she has on patients must be seen to be believed. And although cynics sometimes suggest the Princess is not being sincere when dealing with disadvantaged people, I can only say that I believe she is absolutely sincere. And I have witnessed her talking with them time and again. She is quite remarkable."

On a number of occasions Barry Brooking has held discussions with Diana both at Kensington Palace and at the society's London headquarters concerning problems as well as future projects of the charity. "She is tremendously keen to help in any way she can," Brooking said. "And she tells us openly that if there is anything that she can do, any way that she can help, then all we have to do is to ask her and she will do whatever is possible to help. One cannot ask more of a patron. And when one considers Diana is patron to more than one hundred and twenty separate charities, her offers are remarkably generous given the limited amount of time she can give to every charity."

Brooking has also been surprised at Diana's knowledge of Parkinson's. Wanting to learn more about the problems and the progress in research toward possible cures, Diana asked to meet Prof. Peter Jenner. Jenner is the head of pharmacology research at King's College, London, director of the Parkinson's Disease Society's research laboratories, and codirector of the Neurodegenerative Diseases research center. In 1995, Professor Jenner was awarded $500,000 by the National Parkinson Foundation of Miami for future research into the disease. Together, Diana and Brooking visited Peter Jenner at his research headquarters to see firsthand the progress being made. For more than an hour she talked to Professor Jenner and other research staff as well as a number of trustees and sufferers of Parkinson's disease.

Brooking said, "If people who doubt the Princess of Wales's intelligence had been present, they would have been forced to rapidly change their opinion. She showed not only great interest in the research going on but also a remarkable and genuine knowledge of the subject. The research team were surprised at the extent of her understanding of the disease and the research, showing that she must have studied Parkinson's quite thoroughly."

While at the laboratories Diana spent some time talking to Mrs. Janet McNelly, a trustee of the society and one of the youngest sufferers of the disease. Mrs. McNelly said, "I was only forty-three when I contracted the disease and that was five years ago. Diana wanted to know how I managed being a housewife, cooking meals, cleaning my house. She wanted to know how I coped with the drugs, and the drugs' side effects. She encouraged me to keep chatting to her and explaining everything, telling me to take my time and not to feel under any pressure. I found her surprisingly easy to talk to; so natural and relaxed, and she made me feel as though we had known each other for years. She was so understanding and warm, and I felt she really cared. I had never met anyone who seemed so genuine and kind since I contracted the disease. She is a remarkable young woman and people should understand that."

Diana will do whatever she can to assist one of her charities. The Parkinson's Disease Society plans to hold a charity lunch in

Wales this year, 1996, to raise $50,000 toward the cost of funding two specialist nurses to care for Parkinson's disease patients. Before Brooking had completed the sentence outlining the scheme, Diana said, "I know what you are about to say. If you want me to host the lunch, I will do so with the greatest of pleasure. I now understand that it is hugely beneficial for specialist nurses to be involved in the treatment of patients and is something which must be encouraged."

Ms. Ali Knowles is appeals manager of seeABILITY, a charity that helps those between nineteen and one hundred years of age with multiple disabilities, such as multiple sclerosis, ME (myalgic encephalomyelitis), cerebral palsy, and other diseases as well as blindness or visual impairment. Diana has always had a soft spot for seeABILITY. In 1983, when she decided to become a royal patron, she selected this particular charity to be her very first.

"The Princess of Wales comes to our residential-care home once or twice a year to see and talk to the residents," Ms. Knowles said, "and she is so warm and natural with them all. She makes their day, their week, almost their year, whenever she makes an appearance. Her warmth is so genuine and sincere. And the staff all love her for the manner in which she cares for people and always concentrates on the very ill patients, the ones who need support and encouragement."

Bethany, twenty-three, suffers from spina bifida, is blind and confined to a wheelchair. Bethany said, "She is wonderful. She touched me and held me and treated me as an equal. She made me feel so relaxed and confident."

Another resident, Ann, fifty-three, who also met Diana during one of her visits, said, "She seems so down-to-earth, so natural, and she seems to understand all our needs."

The comments are typical of sufferers, victims, and patients, as well as the staff who work for charities, in their praise of Diana, not simply for being a royal patron and giving of her time, but for the quality of her approach, her attitude, and the empathy she exudes when dealing with all of them.

Ms. Knowles added, "The younger residents appreciate

what Diana does and admire her for it, but the older residents really love her for the warmth, the care, and the individual attention she gives them. No other stranger ever gives them such a high. It's wonderful to see."

In the fall of 1986, some months after Diana had agreed to become the patron of Help the Aged, she went on her first visit to a small residential home, Moorhouse near Staines, Middlesex, about thirty miles west of London. The twenty elderly residents had been told that Diana was coming to visit, and they were all seated in one room when she arrived. Diana walked into the room with officials from the charity and went to a group of residents. She sat down on the floor, held the hands of two of the elderly people, and said, "Hello, I'm Diana. What are your names?"

John Mayo, director general of the charity, who was present, said later, "In an instant she had won their hearts and their admiration and put them all at ease. Most of the residents had been somewhat of a fluster waiting to see her, wondering what this young person, then not thirty, would be like meeting them. Diana was nothing short of brilliant. She met every one of them, shook them by the hands, and chatted to them individually. She smiled, made little jokes, held their hands, and comforted some of the very old. She was magic."

Mayo has also toured India and Africa with Diana in her capacity as a patron of Help the Aged. He recalled, "In 1992 she visited one of Help the Aged's residential homes in Hyderabad where about fifty very elderly and most infirm people lived. They knew who she was and she brought smiles to all of them. She went round the entire home shaking hands with every single person, comforting some, smiling with others, and encouraging others. She stayed for one and a half hours chatting to them all, asking about their families and their lives in the home. All I can say is that they loved her. She put them at their ease and they responded to her understanding and warmth."

John Mayo continued, "In Africa, in July 1993 we visited a Mozambican refugee camp in Zimbabwe where about fifty thousand refugees were living. We went to the area run by Help the Aged for the very elderly and infirm. Once again she was brilliant. She watched them making sandals out of old tires, tending their vegetable patches, weaving clothes, and cooking their food. She went into some of their tiny, darkened huts and chatted to those too ill or infirm to come out into the sun. She brought great smiles to their faces, she encouraged them in their work, asked questions, and became involved with them. They responded wonderfully to her. It was a joy to watch her with them."

Diana has become a world figure, not only through her overseas tours with or without Prince Charles but because of the magic of the fairy-tale wedding and the extraordinary numbers of magazines and newspapers that splash her photograph on their covers. John Mayo remembers being astonished to discover color photographs of the Prince and Princess of Wales stuck on the walls of straw and wooden huts in a tiny village at the upper reaches of the Amazon in Beni, Bolivia, in 1984. He said, "It simply emphasizes the extent of Diana's appeal throughout the entire world. It is truly remarkable."

John Mayo is also aware of the remarkable effect Diana's patronage has on the finances of Help the Aged: "I will give you one example. Each year we hold a Golden Awards lunch, usually at a large London hotel, and people pay to attend, swelling our coffers. Sometimes Diana will attend, but of course she cannot be there every year. In November 1995 she was able to attend the annual dinner held at the London Hilton. When it was learned Diana would be present, the six hundred and forty seats available were sold within hours."

Diana's name seems inexorably linked with one particular British hospital that tugs at the heart strings of the nation whenever its name is mentioned. The Great Ormond Street Hospital for Children cares for sick children under eleven years of age and is world renowned, not only for its quality of care, but also for its research unit and capacity for dealing with the most difficult cases. Diana is not only happy but proud and privileged to be the hospital's royal patron.

Robert Creighton, chief executive of the hospital, is full of praise for the work Diana does on behalf of the hospital and also for her encouragement and efforts to raise funds. He said, "Having the Princess of Wales as patron is hugely beneficial to the hospital, not only in public relations terms but also in helping us raise money for our many projects."

Once a year Diana will make a public visit to the hospital, trailing in her wake TV crews, newspaper photographers, and journalists, who are permitted to follow her for a short while as she tours one or two wards talking to staff and some of the sick children. The TV stations and the newspapers love the photo opportunity, and the nation sees her chatting and playing with one or two youngsters.

But the media and the nation do not realize that during the year Diana also visits the hospital on two or three other occasions in an entirely private capacity. She arrives alone, without even her secretary or a lady-in-waiting and with no camera in sight. On those visits she wants to spend time with the children, their parents, and the staff without the media circus.

Robert Creighton commented, "For eighteen months we cared for a poor little Bosnian girl, Irma, who was aged eight, who had been seriously wounded when a bomb exploded near her during the fighting in 1993. Irma was paralyzed from the head down and we tried to make her life easier. Diana came to visit her once or twice during the time she was alive. And then, sadly, on March thirty-first, 1995, Irma died. The following day Diana phoned asking whether she could come and meet the staff, all the staff, who had spent the previous eighteen months caring for Irma. There were probably a core of about a dozen doctors and nurses who had been closely involved with Irma, and she came and met each and every one of them. It was a sad, moving experience for everyone, including Diana. But the staff really appreciated that she wanted to come and say thank you to them for all their care and nursing of the poor little girl.

"That is typical of the Princess of Wales. She feels for people and understands them. She adores coming here in private without cameras and the press when she can sit and talk and encourage some of the sick children, most of whom know who she is because they have seen her on television. She also likes to visit when parents are with their children so that she can talk to them also."

Creighton continued, "I have witnessed Diana on a number of occasions now, meeting parents and sick children, and I must tell you that it is a remarkably moving experience. They seem to instinctively gravitate towards her and warm to her as though they have known her for ages. Usually, children take time to adapt to a stranger, but not Diana. She has a certain rapport with them that is warm and natural, and children respond to her. It's wonderful to see."

Diana also takes a close interest in the research carried out at Great Ormond Street into eating disorders among young children. In 1995 she made a private visit to the hospital's research unit to talk to the doctors and staff and also some of the young children who were suffering, encouraging them to eat, and telling them that she understood, more than anyone, the trauma and pain they were going through because she had experienced it herself.

In talking to sick children and other people who suffer, as well as the disadvantaged, Diana finds some of the happiest hours of her life. She hopes that her presence helps them and gives them encouragement to fight their battles and endure their pain and suffering. When pressed, all she will say on the matter is, "I understand them, I know how they feel, what they're going through. And they all need help."

Centrepoint, the London charity for young people at risk— the homeless and unemployed and those in danger of becoming drug addicts and prostitutes—appeals especially to Diana. It helps 2,500 young people under twenty-five every year. They are found places to live, whether they are seeking shelter for the night or more permanent accommodations. Many are also found places in educational and training centers; some are found jobs.

Ms. Mo Houlden, head of Centrepoint's fund-raising, has been with Diana on a number of her visits to see the charity at work. Some of the visits have been with media crews, but others have been private where Diana meets as many of the young people as possible.

Ms. Houlden says, "She gives them encouragement and hope for the future. Most of our youngsters have no homes, no jobs, and nowhere to live. Their futures appear to them to be very bleak, but they will open their hearts to Diana in a quite remarkable way.

"Usually we do not inform them that the Princess of Wales is visiting, just that a visitor is touring their accommodation or place of training. They are rather taken aback when Diana walks in, and at first most are shy. Within minutes, however, Diana has won their confidence and they open up to her, chatting happily and naturally. They confide in her, telling her things they would never tell the staff. Indeed, we nearly always tell Diana at the end of her visit that whenever she wants a full-time job with youngsters, she should come and work as a volunteer because she manages to persuade the young people to open up. She is very, very good."

Mo Houlden has seen Diana ring promises from teenage heroin addicts that they will try to give up their addiction. "And afterwards those kids have told us that they will try to do so because they made her a promise," she said. "We are not saying they succeed, but they try, and that is a start. "Most of them tell us the same story of how natural, how easy, how genuine Diana is, so very different from the person they imagined her to be. In every way she is a marvelous boost to the charity and the kids. They love her."

In October 1995, Diana visited King's Cross, London's most notorious red-light district, frequented by hookers and the homeless of all ages as well as vagrants, drunks, and junkies. She decided to see for herself the atrocious conditions in which they lived after a briefing from Centrepoint staff relating the problems facing many young people in London. This would be her first official visit into such down-and-out territory. The press were not informed and no media were present, but photographs were organized by the charity and later offered to newspapers.

Dressed in a warm red sweater and tight black jeans, Diana appeared in good spirits for her midnight tour, chatting to a number of people as she walked around King's Cross. To one, she quipped, "It's a good thing the press aren't here... they would think I had a new job walking the streets."

The young and the old were equally impressed. Diana happily shook hands with the homeless, the drunks, and the junkies. One junkie told her, "You've got some guts shaking hands with everyone around here. Half of these kids have got needles and lots have HIV."

Diana happily chatted with anyone she met and continued to shake their hands. She concentrated particularly on the young teenage girls, some of whom were pregnant, many being hookers, and told them that Centrepoint was trying to establish a new night shelter for the homeless in the area. A group of young teenage hookers asked Diana if she could do something to stop the pimps from taking most of their money, complaining that the pimps would give them a beating just for kicks. Diana looked pained and visibly winced, but she could hold out no such hope for them.

One drunk managed to spoil the occasion, shouting at Diana, "What do you know about the homeless, you live in a fucking palace. Why don't you give us some of your money?" Diana smiled and walked on. To a charity worker she commented quietly, "He does have a point."

The feedback Diana receives from talking to disadvantaged people, especially the young and those suffering acutely, gives her an inner strength to face the media onslaught that never ceases to bewilder her. Few people realize the time and effort she devotes to her 120-odd charities. She believes that she can do so much more for people by committing her life to charity work than she could every have done undertaking a never-ending round of royal duties that often bored her to death.

Diana would say, "I cannot understand why we have to visit the same places, the same institutions, meeting the same people year in, year out, when there is so much more vital and necessary work to be done caring for people who are the unfortunates of society. Nearly all the people I have to meet on royal duties are the privileged, the wealthy, and the successful ones, never the poor, the homeless, the sick, and those suffering from incurable diseases who cry out for help and support."

Perhaps her greatest talent is found in the remarkable relationship she establishes with children of all ages. Watching Diana with young children, whether she is talking, playing, hugging, or simply having eye contact with them, is to witness an immediate understanding between Diana and the child. She seems to bring a sense of joy and spontaneous happiness into their lives. Most of the children she meets have problems, caused by illness, accidents, of birth, or background.

Anne Houston, director of ChildLine Scotland, says, "We were all struck by her understanding of children's problems when she visited us in Glasgow. She has an amazing empathy with children and showed great interest in the training our volunteer counselors receive."

Stories of Diana's personal relationships with children are legion. Blond-haired Emma May, ten, suffers from a rare chromosome disorder called Turner's syndrome, which will necessitate difficult and painful stretching surgery. Already she has spent many months in hospital, but she now has a princess as a special friend. Emma met Diana in 1994 and they now write to each other. "She is wonderful," comments Emma. "She's my very own special friend. I don't call her princess. I just call her Diana now because we're friends. She calls me Emma."

Six-year-old Sian Marks has spent the last four years in hospital suffering from a virus that caused kidney failure. She has nearly died on a number of occasions. She asked to give Diana some flowers when she visited Great Ormond Street Hospital but became too nervous on that day. Diana bent down, talked to her, held her until Sian found the confidence. Then held her hand. Sian warmed to her almost instantly.

Her father, Peter Marks, commented, "Now she talks about Diana all the time. She seems to gain strength from that brief relationship. Diana just showed warmth and kindness that day and Sian understood. She is truly remarkable."

Shortly before twelve-year-old AIDS victim Bonnie Hendel died in hospital, she told her mother, "I don't need medication anymore, just lunch with Princess Diana every day." And Bonnie had never met Diana but had simply written to her, telling her she was in hospital and dying of AIDS. Diana sent her a short letter and a signed photograph of herself, which Bonnie kept by her bedside and would kiss good night.

Doctors at St. Mary's Hospital, Paddington, phoned Kensington Palace asking that Diana be informed that Bonnie was only hours away from death. Diana was out, but as soon as she returned she went immediately to the hospital, arriving two hours after Bonnie had died. Diana apologized to her parents, but they told her, "You were a heroine to Bonnie. She loved you."

Minutes later Diana was seen leaving the hopsital, unable to control the tears that ran down her cheeks.

During her self-imposed retirement from the limelight Diana decided to dedicate her life to charity work in all its forms. She knows she can help raise funds for any number of charities, and she hopes that her presence and personal approach to sufferers and the disadvantaged makes them feel better and brings a little cheer and encouragement to their wretched lives. She also wanted to do something worthwhile with her life rather than be categorized as nothing more than a fashion icon, married to the heir to the throne, whose life revolved around meeting important people, undertaking royal duties, and being seen for what she was rather than what she could do for others.

# 16

## "They Made Me Feel Like a Leper"

———— ❧ ————

To MANY, PRINCESS DIANA lives a hectic life. It appears that her photograph is always in the daily newspapers, whether she's at some charity event, tending the sick and dying in hospital, or her name is in screaming headlines suggesting her involvement in yet another scandal. In reality nothing could be further from the truth.

Before she cut back on her charity work in 1994, Diana's life had become one mad whirl of activity in which she would be working perhaps four days of the week. But her life was no nine-to-five job. She would need to plan her expeditions in great detail with her team—with the police, local dignitaries, the charity involved. She had to make exact traveling arrangements so as to always arrive on time, no matter where she had to travel in the United Kingdom.

Diana might have to carry out three or four separate royal duties in one day, perhaps flying four hundred miles north to Glasgow for two events, the next in York, one hundred and fifty miles nearer home, and perhaps the final one of the day in Birmingham, another hundred miles nearer Kensington Palace. After that she would then travel another hundred and fifty miles by rail or car to London. Often, Diana would not arrive back at the palace before 9 P.M. That day had probably started at six in the morning, meaning fifteen hours when she had to appear immaculately dressed and alluring virtually every minute of every hour.

Diana also has to appear happy, relaxed, and smiling on all

her public occasions no matter what her mood. She finds dealing with people on a one-to-one basis invigorating and interesting and loves to feel she is helping ordinary people come to terms with an illness, a handicap, or a problem. But whenever she becomes the center of attention with great groups of people surging around her, trying to greet her, wanting to meet her, and to touch her, she becomes embarrassed and awkward. And though she tries to look as relaxed and comfortable as possible, she in fact hates being gawked at, on display for everyone to look and point at and to criticize.

And the cameras would never leave her alone from the moment she put her head outside Kensington Palace. They would follow her every waking hour wherever she went, sometimes thirty or more photographers, as well as a number of TV crews, catching her every move, her every glance, her every word.

In December 1993 she decided to withdraw from public life for several reasons. Diana felt exhausted and drained, physically and emotionally. She found it more difficult to maintain the pace and the pressure with the number of duties she was expected to carry out mushrooming almost monthly. Since her separation from Charles a year before in December 1992, her royal duties had contracted substantially yet her public life had become considerably more demanding. Now she had to make all the decisions, the arrangements, the speeches; she had to lead discussions, hold interesting and intelligent conversations with people she had just met, on subjects about which she seemed to know very little. People had come to expect so much of her that she found the work tougher and more exhausting than she had ever imagined. She needed to give herself a break, to retreat from the limelight, which, during the years leading to the separation, had become unbearably bright.

Overnight, or so it seemed, Diana disappeared from the front pages of the newspapers and the nation's television screens, and her name and her picture cropped up far less often in the glossy magazines.

Diana told one of her colleagues, "I can remember waking

the morning after announcing my decision and realizing that I
didn't have to rush off somewhere or other to some charitable
function or royal duty. I lay there feeling wonderful. I can
remember soaking in a long, hot bath and realizing that I had
simply stopped my madcap life, the life that used to give me
nightmares. I could see myself on this treadmill, which was
going faster and faster and which it was impossible for me to
stop or get off. I would find myself exhausted but unable to
stop. Then I would wake and find myself in a dreadful sweat as
though I had been running flat out."

Diana had been nervous the day she made her historic
announcement primarily because she was suffering from ex-
haustion. For months she had been on a knife edge, fearful that
something awful would befall her now that Charles had demanded an official separation, casting her adrift from the
family and leaving her to fight her own battles and lead her
own life.

She didn't want Charles to see that she couldn't cope for he
had always teased her, almost from the first months of their
marriage, that she couldn't boil an egg or organize a tea party.
And she could remember how the teasing became more vicious
as their marriage disintegrated. A look of disdain would cross
his face as he would interrupt another of her tearful sessions to
tell her to "pull your socks up" and "sort yourself out."

And then there was the Queen, who Diana felt had always
treated her as an interloper, someone to be tolerated because she
had married the Queen's son and had done "jolly well" to
produce two boys—an heir and a spare—as Diana was informed. She was determined to prove to her mother-in-law that
she could manage perfectly well on her own without Charles.

More importantly, Diana didn't want Wills and Harry to see
their mother unhappy and miserable, for they had observed the
tears in her eyes on far too many occasions during their young
lives. She was determined to show her happy, smiling, loving
side, not the anguished mother who always seemed on the verge
of tears. She wanted to show them that their mother was made
of sterner stuff.

By retiring from the limelight and royal duties, Diana, at a stroke, cut herself off from the Royal Family and the palace courtiers, who seemed to take such a delight in running her life. At first she felt lonely, somehow missing the hectic life.

During those first few months of 1994, Diana became a new woman. But it had taken her longer and the task had been harder than she had envisaged. Despite the newspaper stories saying how stunning she looked, she could see in the mirror the wrinkles coming, the bags under her eyes, the acne on her chin, all brought about by her jangled nerves, lack of sleep, and constant, nagging worry about her life, her future, and more especially, what would become of her and the boys.

Yet she couldn't shake her fear of a life of permanent loneliness. She would lie awake at night and think of her sons in their beds at their respective boarding schools, cut off from their mother for most of the year. She was jealous of the life they shared with their father. Now it seemed, besides Charles, the rest of the family would turn their backs on her because she had dared to argue and not play the role of the little princess. In the end, she thought she would pack her bags, leave Kensington Palace, and live a quiet life in some mansion deep in the countryside, far away from the bright lights, the cameras, and her adoring fans and supporters.

And the Royal Family had cut her off completely. The phone never rang from any member of the family; no invitations came from the Queen for tea or dinner, none from Philip, Princess Anne or Andrew or Edward, and of course, none from Charles. She never heard from the Queen Mother or any of the other Royals. Diana began to feel that the Royal Family were treating her in the same way as the House of Windsor had dealt with an epileptic child, Prince John, born to King George V and Queen Mary in 1905. On orders of the German-born Queen Mary of Teck, young John was removed from the family and incarcerated in a small house on the royal estate at Sandringham, never to be seen in public, never to be accepted as part of the family, never included in any family gatherings, and never visited by his parents, brothers, or sisters. He died in

1919, aged fourteen, virtually unmourned except by a nurse who had devoted her life to him.

Diana would say, "Ever since the separation the Royal Family have made me feel like a leper."

She would tell the few friends she could trust, "I know they can't forgive me for what I've done. In their eyes I've committed the greatest sin imaginable, daring to challenge the Royal House of Windsor. They want to rub my face in the dirt, make me realize how stupid and wrong I have been demanding to lead my own life, organize my own charity events, rather than wanting to carry out their royal orders, attending the same boring events year in, year out. I know how the family works. Once someone has crossed them, they will never forgive and never forget. They want to see me suffer."

Later Diana became more courageous and she happily told people her thoughts of the treatment being handed out to her by the Royal Family. And she would say, "I can take everything they throw at me. They want me to crawl away from their lives and disappear somewhere, preferably thousands of miles away so I will be no further trouble. The Queen, Philip, and Anne, as well as some of the others, believe I have been stupid to behave as I have done. They believe I should have put up with whatever happened, kept my mouth shut, and carried out my royal duties. For the Queen and Philip believe it to be the highest privilege imaginable to be a member of the House of Windsor."

Wickedly, Diana would add, "But I can tell the world it isn't the greatest privilege. I've tried it."

At first the fact that no member of the Royal Family ever contacted her hurt. However, as the months rolled by, the isolation gave her an inner strength since they were all acting in concert to break her, and she was absolutely determined that they would not do so.

# 17

## The Lonely Princess

———— ❧ ————

DIANA AWOKE ON JANUARY 1, 1994, determined to fulfill a host of New Year's resolutions. For years she had read the magazines suggesting how to become a "new woman" by exercise, sensible dieting, various therapies, and leading a sensible, stable life. Now she would put into practice all she had read. Diana had told one of her men friends, "This year I am determined to sort myself out and get really fit. Do you realize that I'm going to be thirty-three this year, which means that in 1996, I'm going to be nearer forty than thirty?"

Mockingly, Diana exclaimed, "Oh my God! What will I do?"

First priority would be to get her body into shape once more. She knew that swimming, which she loved, helped her tone her muscles and keep fit. She would swim up and down the pool until exhausted, which gave her a feeling of satisfaction. She increased her regular exercise schedules in the gym, getting an adviser to program her workouts, concentrating on the muscles Diana wanted to tone. In particular she wanted to make sure no cellulite appeared on her thighs or buttocks or upper arms. "I can't bear that," she would tell her adviser. "One thing we must stop is that cellulite."

She continued to play tennis with her trainer and enjoyed matches with other friends. She enjoyed her coaching lessons enormously for it had always been one of her ambitions to be good at tennis. She loved to play singles against world-class players like Steffi Graf, not because she considered herself anywhere near their level but because she wanted the thrill of playing someone really good, a professional from whom she hoped she might be able to pick up some tips.

After her matches with topflight players Diana would seem embarrassed and become shy, saying, "Thank you very much. I hope it wasn't too awful for you. You've been very kind."

Afterward they would always chat and have a fruit juice together, and Diana would ask them to pinpoint the poor areas of her play that they believed she should work on. If any of the players didn't think it correct to criticize her play, Diana would insist, telling them, "I need the help, so please, pull no punches."

Most of the class players Diana encountered on court were in fact surprised by the quality of her play, particularly her service, which she had practiced and honed so that even her coach, Rex Seymour-Lyn, told her she was in danger of "becoming seriously competent." And he meant it.

More than anything, Diana reveled in her newfound freedom, knowing she could do whatever she wanted, day in, day out, spoiling herself in shopping sprees, talking clothes, discussing styles, hair, and makeup without having to rush. In a matter of a few weeks she began to feel better, more in control of her life than she could remember. She began to spend more time indulging herself. She had the money to do so, and now she had the time and the inclination. She would read of the latest fad, an interesting therapy, a new remedy, the attributes of an avant-garde treatment she had not known about, and more importantly, she found herself increasingly interested in feminist books.

Some newspapers and magazines suggested that Diana had become a "therapy freak," constantly indulging herself in a great variety of different therapies, repeating all of them once or more a week. She would alternate or drop some treatments for a while.

Aromatherapy is certainly one way Diana loves to indulge herself, and she receives regular treatments at the expert hands of Sue Beechey of Aromatherapy Associates in Fulham,

London. Diana always feels relaxed and happy with the world after a session and encourages Sue to vary her treatments with different oils.

On occasion Diana has experimented with acupuncture. An Irish specialist, Oonagh Toffolo, will visit Kensington Palace when Diana is feeling particularly nervous and stressed. In the 1980s, Oonagh helped Diana overcome her anorexia nervosa and bulimia. Diana once said, "I think Oonagh saved my life. She certainly saved my sanity."

One of Diana's favorite treatment and therapy centers is in Beauchamp Place, near Harrods, where Chrissie Fitzgerald carries out more exotic treatments for Diana. Under Chrissie's expert hands Diana undergoes the occasional colonic irrigation, the water treatment some people find difficult to understand and appreciate. The treatment is frowned upon by doctors, who say that people should not undergo it unless they have a specific bowel problem. Diana has no such health problem and yet she will, from time to time, indulge in the practice. She believes it clears out the "angst" and the "aggro" that builds up inside her, making her feel more relaxed and more at peace with the world.

Another of Diana's luxuries is reflexology, the treatment that involves massaging specific points of the feet to stimulate blood supply and nerves and, hopefully, relieve tension. This treatment is much favored by Japanese men and women, principally for relieving tension. Once again Diana relies on the expert hands of Chrissie Fitzgerald. Sometimes the treatment can be mildly painful, but those who enjoy reflexology say the relaxation and the draining of tension from the body make ample amends for the pain.

Diana occasionally enjoys osteopathy, which aims to correct supposed deformations of the skeleton that cause disease. This therapy is also gauged to help aches and pains caused by stress, including tension headaches. Her osteopath is Michael Skipworth, whom she will sometimes phone in near panic, asking for an immediate appointment, so severe are some of her headaches. Diana once believed she suffered from migraines, but she has been told her headaches are not migraines. As a result, she now has the confidence that her headaches will respond to treatment within thirty minutes in Michael Skipworth's soothing hands. She has known Skipworth for nearly ten years. She first began visiting his clinic for her recurrent backache, which has affected her, on and off, since her teens.

Two other treatments Diana will turn to occasionally, but certainly not weekly, are psychotherapy and hypnotherapy. During psychotherapy the patient transfers emotions connected with people from their lives onto the analyst in a bid to deal with the past, and eventually to forget those emotions that have caused the patient so much stress. Hypnotherapy can be used for many different aspects of someone's health. Diana undergoes sessions to treat her stress, and sometimes finds sessions useful to control her eating. Understandably, Diana is determined not to allow her eating to ever get out of control again. She wants no repeat of the pain, anguish, and feeling of desperation she had when suffering from anorexia and bulimia.

Anger therapy is another treatment Diana has tried, but she is not convinced that it works too well. She knows she loses her temper far too easily, shouts and swears when things go wrong for her. But she also believes those bouts of anger and rage are part of her personality. And although she hates to lose her temper, she does believe it sometimes gives her a feeling of wonderful release. In earlier efforts to contain her swings of temper Diana tried anger-release therapy and kick boxing. During anger-release therapy clients are encouraged to shout, scream, and punch inanimate objects, like beanbags. Kick boxing is a similar treatment, but here the client uses her feet to kick a punching bag.

When totally frustrated, Diana will usually go to her bed and thump the pillows, on occasion burying her head in the pillows and screaming at the top of her voice, the goose down drowning the noise so that no one can hear her rages.

During the past couple of years Diana has consulted one or more astrologers, rather than always relying on the same person for predictions. Nowadays, she puts less faith in their readings than she did in the 1980s. She fears that some astrologers, knowing her identity, treat her more gently, even putting a gloss on predictions they would not have for a stranger.

During many of her therapies Diana will peruse the latest magazines that are provided for clients. She will always read the articles concerning the latest health fad or therapy, which, she realizes, has become the religion of the nineties. Many people in Britain believe Diana to be the patron saint of therapy for as a result of all the publicity surrounding her various treatments, therapy has gripped the wealthy British, who have the money to indulge themselves.

In the past five years membership in the British Association of Counselling has risen by a remarkable 300 percent to ten thousand. In Britain in 1996, it is estimated that fifty thousand people work as therapists with a further half million people serving as volunteers, providing the backup for a new, thriving industry. Many therapists acknowledge that it is the publicity surrounding the Princess of Wales and her interest in so many varied therapies that has created the astonishing increase in business.

Diana will also try many beauty treatments that she has read about and thinks might help her. She is adventurous, believing these "new" therapies should be tried. She is determined to use whatever treatments she believes will help her stay and look young. "I am determined to fight age all the way," she has said with a smile, "and anything that I can do to help put off the aging process I will certainly try."

As a result of that determination Diana has undergone computer-aided cosmetology, otherwise known as the face-lift without surgery, at regular intervals at the hands of Chrissie Fitzgerald. Minute electrical impulses are sent through the skin to the roots of the muscles, recharging the tissue and purportedly easing fine lines. Diana knows that the lines of the middle thirties are starting to show around her eyes and hopes this treatment will help keep them at bay.

So successful were her workouts, swimming and tennis, her therapies and treatments, that Diana began to feel like a new woman. Only she couldn't conquer the feeling of loneliness.

Without making any announcement or even informing the senior courtiers at Buckingham Palace, Diana decided in the early summer of 1994 to end her self-imposed semiretirement and throw herself back into the limelight, but concentrating solely on her charitable responsibilities.

She would say with a certain glee in her voice, "The family will hate seeing me on the front pages again, particularly Charles. They will realize their campaign to silence and flatten me has failed and I'm alive and kicking. And they will note that I'm fit and healthy, ready to undertake many, many years of public duties for every charity that wants me."

There were, however, other reasons. Diana had become bored and frustrated. And rather annoyingly for Diana, her love life had not been going at all well. She had become involved with a couple of men, enjoyed one or two flings since splitting from James Hewitt, but only Will Carling had provided Diana with a serious relationship. She hoped that in Carling she had found the right man to stimulate her, to make her feel loved and wanted, and to provide the anchor to her life that, in her heart, she desperately pines for.

To only a few people Diana has confessed her feeling of loneliness and isolation. During the summer of 1995, Diana told one of her great close friends whom she has known for fifteen years how miserable she found living alone. "I try to pretend that I enjoy life on my own, but I don't. I hate being at home at night on my own when everyone has gone. And it seems I can't be seen out with anyone I fancy, so my relationships have to remain secret, which is very trying and not conducive to a lasting, fulfilling affair."

In the same tone, as tears welled in her eyes, she continued, "I drive through the streets and see couples everywhere and wonder what is wrong with me that I have no one. I see couples going shopping together to the supermarket and envy them; I see couples in their cars with the children in the back and wish it were me. I just want to enjoy those ordinary, everyday events, which I never enjoyed with Charles because we never lived like any ordinary couple. We never did anything together. Never went shopping. Never took out the children on our own. None of the things every other couple in the world does naturally, together, as a family. And now I wonder if I ever shall and it hurts. Life is flying by and I have no one to share it with."

She adds, "I wish I could just meet some man who would love me for what I am. Every time I look at a man nowadays I find they're married and their wives go berserk if I even talk to them. The women can be so hurtful towards me. I sometimes wonder if I'm destined to be an old maid, living my life alone."

After talking in such a vein Diana will usually snap out of her doleful demeanor, apologize, and say, "I'm sorry I'm being pathetic. I must stop feeling sorry for myself and get out there and find someone before it's too late." And a half smile will cross her lips as she fights back the tears.

It seemed to Diana that every new close relationship with any man was doomed to end in failure, unhappiness, bad publicity, and recriminations. She had begun to believe that she would be unable to form a stable relationship with a man for fear of the paparazzi, and the disastrous effect exposure would have on any meaningful affair.

A number of distinguished psychiatrists would question Diana's need for such a variety of therapies. Some considered that Diana's desire for constant grooming reflected an unease that bordered on self-indulgence, neuroticism, and narcissism, rather than a cry for a sound, loving relationship.

Dr. Raj Persaud is a lecturer in psychiatry at the prestigious Maudsley Hospital in London. Dr. Persaud worried that people with a narcissistic personality disorder, which some had suggested could be part of Diana's problem, mistake the attainment of perfect appearance with that of forging happy relationships. "It is really the extension of adolescent fantasy: 'If I can be perfect, I will marry the person of my dreams.' Often they cannot understand that, even though they are magnificently turned out, relationships founder. But the person they are trying to attract senses their self-absorption and fears there will be no time left over for them."

When Diana worried about her disastrous and near-empty

love life, she would become morose and would think back to the days when she could always pick up a phone and speak to the one man she had been able to trust, her beloved father. Even today, more than three years after her father's death, Diana still wishes he were there for her. She could always talk to him during those horrific years when she could see her marriage had failed and had no where to turn.

Sometimes, when in a reflective mood, Diana will say to a close friend, "I still miss him. When he was alive, I always knew he was there in the background, always supportive. I knew I could phone him at any time and we could chat about whatever was troubling me. He would always give sound advice and make me feel wanted and special. No one has been able to take his place since, and his death has made me feel more lonely than I ever did when he was alive."

When in one of her somber moods, Diana will still shed tears for her father, wishing she could bring him back, so that she could talk to him. And she has admitted that since his death she will, on occasion, particularly when feeling depressed, talk to her father as though he were still there. She knows he isn't and doesn't for one minute believe it is possible to speak to the dead, yet she finds comfort in the hope that he could be there. Diana knows that if her father were still alive, she would have greater confidence in her future.

# 18

## *Her Private World*

━━━━❧❧❧━━━━

BUT OTHERS NEEDED DIANA. Senior executives of many of the 120 charities that boasted Diana as their patron were disappointed when she announced in the fall of 1993 her need to escape from public life to seek some privacy. They knew that Diana's presence, even if only once or twice a year, had become the major event in their charity's life, eagerly anticipated and always well attended. And most charities also recognized that Diana's patronage meant healthier bank balances to help fund their work.

Diana held a council of war at Kensington Palace, calling in her private secretary, Patrick Jephson, the former Royal Navy lieutenant commander; Anne Beckwith-Smith, her trusted friend and chief lady-in-waiting; her "unofficial" press officer, the Australian Geoff Crawford, who was based at Buckingham Palace; and her equerry, Royal Marine captain Edward Musto.

Her right-hand man, Patrick Jephson, now thirty-nine, had been Diana's equerry for some years before being promoted to private secretary in 1990, succeeding Diana's great friend and confidant Anne Beckwith-Smith. It is difficult to overemphasize the importance of Anne Beckwith-Smith's role. She had met Diana before her engagement to Prince Charles, and the two had formed an understanding. Ten years older than Diana, the mature, sensible Anne showed by her diplomacy and sound advice that she would make the perfect lady-in-waiting for the Princess of Wales.

Anne would be one of only three members of the staff of

forty-one employed by Charles and Diana at the time of their
wedding in 1981 who would survive the dramas and traumas of
those first seven years of the royal marriage. Indeed, the more
Diana and Anne worked together, the closer they would
become. At the end of Diana's first royal tour in 1983, Diana
spontaneously threw her arms around Anne's shoulders and
gave her a great hug before presenting her with a lovely brooch.
"I couldn't have done it without you," Diana whispered to her.
They were no empty words.

When Diana finally succeeded in getting rid of Oliver
Everett, her first private secretary, she asked Anne to take the
job. Anne accepted, and the two women forged a close bond
that would last for more than ten years. During the dark days of
the marriage Diana would frequently flee to Anne's
Knightsbridge apartment and talk to her for hours, pouring out
her heart. On occasion, Diana would even stay overnight rather
than return to Charles at the palace. She would come to have
absolute trust in Anne's friendship, loyalty, and sound common
sense.

Anne is no yes-woman. She is known to have had a major
influence on Diana and is happy to act on her behalf whenever
necessary. She is also quite capable of making strong and honest
arguments when she disagrees with the Princess and is not
frightened to tell Diana when she believes Diana is going about
things in the wrong way. On occasion they will argue, but if
Diana cannot be persuaded that she should change her mind,
then Anne will say, "Well, if you are determined, then that is
your choice. But it is my job to warn you."

Those words would usually make Diana stop and think if
the course of action she has decided on is the one she should
carry out. Often Diana will reply, "I know, I know. But on this
occasion I think I know what is best."

Diana values Anne's views, her advice, her integrity, and
her diplomacy. In those first nervous days after the marriage
Anne, too, found she was on a learning curve. She had to find
out how to play the courtiers at Buckingham Palace, who
tended to treat the young Diana and her ladies-in-waiting as

immature, inexperienced young women who had to be taught the ways of the royal world. At first Anne and Diana's other friends whom she had appointed ladies-in-waiting did take advice from those who had been in senior positions with Charles.

Later, however, Anne became proficient at holding her own in arguments with senior Buckingham Palace aides, some of whom continue to look upon Diana's small team of friends and staff as amateurs playing on a sophisticated stage where only professionals should be tolerated. Since the separation, some senior courtiers patronize the Kensington Palace staff, but Anne has won a sound reputation as capable of putting in their place those she calls "the snobs at the palace," valiantly defending Diana.

During those first few years of the marriage Diana had been cared for by some of the most experienced palace staff. It is untrue, as Diana has repeatedly alleged, that she was given no training, no advice, no help, to settle down in her new role as the Princess of Wales. Prince Charles had asked Michael Colborne, one of his secretaries, a man with whom he had become close during his years with the Royal Navy, to teach her the ropes during those first few years. Colborne, then in his forties, agreed to help, and Diana looked to him during the first three years for advice on a wide range of matters. Colborne, who had been in Charles's private office since 1975, knew how the system worked, and he imparted as much advice as possible to the young Diana.

Prince Charles had also drafted another experienced royal hand to help the untutored Diana. Oliver Everett, a former polo-playing friend of Charles's and another of his secretaries, had quit royal service to resume his diplomatic career in the Foreign Office. He was working in Madrid, with the prospect of a great future in the service, when Charles urged him to return and become private secretary to the young Diana. He agreed, but his relationship with Diana would soon founder.

The Queen's principal lady-in-waiting is the vastly experienced and kindly Lady Susan Hussey, an intelligent woman who has been in royal service close to the Queen for twenty years. Almost daily during those first years Susan Hussey would telephone to ask Diana or Anne whether she could be of help in sorting out any problems. She bent over backward to aid and advise the young Diana. And yet Diana would later deny that all this help and advice had been offered.

Both Everett and Colborne also helped Anne Beckwith-Smith, who would become the most loyal and long-standing adviser to Diana. Some wondered whether Anne had deliberately sacrificed her chances of marriage and motherhood to remain by Diana's side. Ironically, Anne and Diana nearly fell out when Diana sacked Oliver Everett after eighteen months in the job. At first, Diana believed Everett to be her best friend and great at his job. But she would become suspicious of him, believing he was too close to Prince Charles. Diana also felt he patronized her. Anne argued forcefully for Diana to keep Everett, but Diana was adamant. Two days before Christmas 1983, Everett was forced to resign and Anne was rewarded with his job.

For ten years Anne worked tirelessly as Diana's personal and private secretary, her confidant and her friend, the one person, perhaps more than any other, who helped Diana combat her anorexia and bulimia and who tried to calm the Princess of Wales when she became overwrought and anxious. But Diana had come to rely more on her own judgment, and Anne felt her advice no longer carried the weight it had during their earlier years together. She would remain Diana's principal lady-in-waiting, though there was no special title and she would find employment in the celebrated Victoria and Albert Museum, half a mile from Kensington Palace.

Diana asked her war council if there was any reason why she should not quietly and without fuss resume her full load of charity work. She had never in fact ended all charity work, but to all intents and purposes the general public felt she had retreated behind the walls of Kensington Palace. They had most certainly noted her absence. Jephson thought it would be better if Diana asked Buckingham Palace to issue a statement, but

Diana had no intention of allowing such a move. She believed the senior palace staff would not want her to reenter the public domain.

She would say nothing of her inner thoughts to her team. She knew Charles would be annoyed, Philip angry, and the Queen quietly incensed at Diana's return, for they had encouraged her to center her life on her two sons. Indirectly it had been suggested to Diana that she take a lovely house near Windsor, in striking distance of Eton, where her sons would be educated during the next seven years. Diana had declined the invitation for she had no wish to be sidelined. She knew when her decision had been passed up to the senior aides and the Royal Family, they would be disappointed that another ruse to remove her from the spotlight had failed. The thought brought a wicked smile to her lips.

Patrick Jephson greeted Diana's decision to step up her charity work with some relief for he had seen the Princess becoming more frustrated and less focused, wallowing in self-indulgence. But he realized full well the consternation Diana's decision would cause at the palace, and he discussed the diplomacy of such a move with Diana.

"It's my life," Diana told Jephson. "And you know the charities want me back on the scene. The phone never stops."

Diana also had a secret yearning to throw herself back into the fray. Meeting people, seeing their faces light up, gave her a feeling of being wanted, and loved, which had sustained her during the dark years of the marriage. She now needed that comfort above all else.

There was, however, another personal reason for Diana's wish to return to work. In May 1994, Prince Charles had information leaked to the press detailing his wife's annual bill for her "grooming." In the year following their separation Diana had spent $5,000 a week, a total of $250,000 that year!

Apparently these accounts covered all her clothes, casual wear for the boys, her increasing interest in alternative therapies, makeup, hairdressing, and a few gifts. Charles drew Diana's attention to the high expenses, and Diana, too, had been shocked at the amount, believing she had cut down since ending her royal duties at the end of 1993. The press of course expressed surprise, with pictures of Diana in a range of her latest, expensive haute couture outfits, which the tabloids described as her "spend, spend lifestyle." They detailed her new therapies, her clothes, her clubs and restaurants, and her way of life, which some described as "outrageous." It was pointed out that the $250,000 did not cover any day-to-day living expenses, staff, cars, travel, or holidays. They were all extra.

Charles leaked the information because he was "absolutely furious" that Diana should spend so much money on herself for, what he perceived, was no good reason. When informed of the annual bill, Charles had flown into one of his infamous rages, shouting and swearing, kicking the furniture in his fury. Diana, too, would explode when she saw the details of her lifestyle splattered all over the newspapers, courtesy of her own husband.

"The spiteful little shit," she exclaimed. "How could he wash all my dirty linen in public?"

Diana of course knew that part of the huge expenditure had nothing to do with wanting to spend money, but was a natural reaction to the loneliness and the frustrations of her life, all of which had come about because of the disgraceful behavior of Charles himself and his demand that they separate. She always knew that Charles had little idea of how a woman's mind worked.

Shaking her head in disbelief, Diana said to Sarah Ferguson, "Doesn't he realize that any woman without a man in her life, with a failed marriage and no one to love her, would behave in the same way, trying to find some happiness in spoiling herself?"

Diana did, however, have her supporters. The "ladies who lunch," the euphemism for the wives of Britain's rich and famous, believed Diana's $250,000 annual bill was somewhat above average but certainly not in the superleague of spenders. None thought the amount outrageous because Diana had a certain standard to maintain as the Princess of Wales.

Diana recognized that the publicity would, more than likely, harm her image with her adoring public, who would not want to see her taking advantage of her situation, spending so much money on herself. She knew that most ordinary British house-wives, checkout girls, factory workers, and office drudges, who are her most adoring fans, wouldn't spend $2,500 a year on their clothes, let alone $250,000. They would also recognize that Diana had decided to take early retirement, living in a palace full of servants while still a young woman in her thirties. There she would indulge herself in some therapy while her sons were away at boarding school. The last thing Diana wanted was publicity that saw her as taking as much money as she could from Prince Charles but not doing anything, not even charity work, in return.

Even the straitlaced *Financial Times* found it necessary to comment, "The princess was reported to be embarrassed and contrite and to have set in train cost-cutting measures. Perhaps, given the political and economic climate, she was wise, even valorous, to opt for discretion. But if ever a woman was encouraged to become a spendthrift, it was Diana. She married into a family which elevated dowdiness to an art form."

Three days after the story of Diana's spending spree reached the media, as though to order a remarkable story appeared on the front page of the *Daily Mail*, by Richard Kay, a reporter who had become Diana's most trusted tabloid confidant. "Diana Rescues Drowning Man," ran the headline, and the story outlined how Princess Diana helped save the life of a drowning man in a dramatic rescue operation in London's Regent's Park. Allegedly, Diana rushed to the water's edge and helped pull out an unconscious tramp, hauling him onto the bank, where he was given mouth-to-mouth resuscitation.

Kay reported that Diana was "praying for the recovery of the man," Martin O'Donaghue, forty-two. She had since visited him twice in hospital where he was "fighting for his life." The experience of saving the man's life had "affected her deeply," and the man's welfare was "uppermost in Diana's mind."

The heroic story gripped the nation. As dusk was falling, the Princess was being driven through the park after having gone jogging. Her car was flagged by a group of tourists, who reported seeing a man fall into the lake. Having told her driver to make a 999 call on her mobile phone, Diana, still in shorts and trainers, ran back to the lake. She was standing by the parapet looking into the water when a Finnish student ran to the scene, climbed over the parapet, plunged into the water and dragged the man to safety. Having pulled the man from the water, the music student, Kari Kotila, twenty-nine, checked the man's mouth for blockages and gave him the kiss of life, pounding the man's heart between breaths. Later, police confirmed that Mr. Kotila had brought the man back from the dead.

Diana had not been the heroine of the moment but rather had simply joined a group of people looking over the parapet as the man struggled for his life in the icy waters of the lake. Mr. Kotila said later, "I was surprised that no one was trying to rescue the man. People were standing around looking, but doing nothing. I gave my backpack and wallet to this woman who was standing there because she looked honest. It was only later that I realized it was Princess Diana."

As the conservative *Daily Telegraph* pointed out in an editorial, "The first impression of the heroine plunging from her car into the icy deep had to be modified following further inquiries. The Princess's chief role, it emerged, was to hold the wallet of a Finnish student while he trawled for the waterlogged tramp. But the story may be added to a growing list of the Princess's neighbourly acts, many of which involve stopping her car to comfort victims of breakdowns, smashes and other mobile misfortunes.... The good deeds may enhance the Princess's reputation.... But the most impressive acts of charity are those undertaken without everyone knowing about them."

No newspaper mentioned that this revelation emerged within days after Diana's public image took quite a battering as she was exposed as the spendthrift princess. Nor did they know that during her second visit to the hospital to see the vagrant

Martin O'Donaghue, Diana left him a paltry £5 note ($7.50) as a present.

Diana enjoyed being back at work. She felt a new zest for life and determined to spend more of her time with the charities that particularly appealed to her. She had already decided to carry out fewer media-grabbing functions, such as appearing at glamorous film premieres or being pictured chatting to the disadvantaged. She had, it seemed, taken to heart the remarks of the *Daily Telegraph* editorial writer. She had always enjoyed the quiet, private visits she had made to many of her charities, for she felt it brought her closer to those she was seeking to encourage, to help, and to cherish. Now she would indulge in still more private charity work. It would become a vital part of her new life, giving her a feeling that she was undertaking worthwhile work, while hopefully bringing a little cheer to those who suffered.

In her new, more hectic existence, the Princess of Wales is usually out of bed and into her shower by seven o'clock each morning, listening to pop music on the radio. When swimming or going to the gym, she will leave the palace by eight o'clock, driving herself to her rendezvous. She may work-out or swim, or both, for an hour or ninety minutes, before taking another quick shower and having an orange juice and croissant before heading home to start work.

At ten o'clock she usually holds her first meeting of the day with Patrick Jephson, when together they go through all her correspondence as well as her diary for the next seven days, checking details, confirming dates, times, appointments, and discussing what she should wear. Diana has become a stickler for attending to her correspondence, making sure that people who write letters to her will, without fail, always receive a reply. And she hates formal letters being sent to anyone who has bothered to write to her. She always tries to make her replies personal, informal, and friendly. She understands letter writing is a wonderful contact with the public, those people who admire and support her. A small staff of three women attend to her correspondence, logging the letters and typing the replies on a computer.

In yet another break with royal tradition in June 1994 Diana dispensed with her equerry, wanting to become even more independent than all other senior Royals, who are always attended at official functions by an equerry. Diana decided she no longer needed someone to hold her umbrella, park her car, or wait in attendance, believing equerries to be outmoded.

On occasion one or other of her ladies-in-waiting will sit in on her early-morning meetings, as well as her dresser, who needs to know every minute of Diana's day so that her clothes can be pressed, prepared, and laid out in good time. After her meetings Diana will then have long discussions with her dresser, debating what she should wear for every outing.

Although she loves spending much of her spare time in casual wear, Diana still admits to the thrill of putting together an ensemble in which she feels confident. She knows that people want her to look special, even stunning, and she tries to oblige whatever the occasion. She plans each outfit with meticulous attention to detail and real deliberation, sometimes discussing possible variations and accessories with her team for ten or twenty minutes, wanting to make sure what she wears is absolutely appropriate. Some days Diana may change her clothes half a dozen times.

When asked about her clothes, Diana will nearly always say, "I love wearing casual clothes. For me it is a real pleasure because of the times I have to dress correctly to suit the occasion, the place, and the people I will be meeting."

After her working schedule has been decided, Diana usually conducts meetings arranged in Kensington Palace where she will sit with charity organizers to discuss plans. These meetings may last for two hours or more for she has become far more involved in the activities she supports. In those meetings Diana will stress two important points. First, she asks organizers to think of specific ways that she, personally, can help their charity, which, she realizes, is her primary task. She hates being just a figurehead and tells them so. She also urges the organizers to make sure that when she visits their headquarters, she meets the people for whom the charity is devised, not simply the charity workers. Diana wants to be sure she never loses touch with the people the charity is designed to help.

During the school holidays, when the boys are staying with her at Kensington Palace, Diana cuts down on her meetings, her charity work, and her workouts and concentrates on finding various things for the boys to do while making sure they ask friends to come round to the palace to play or for meals. Sometimes Diana will organize outings for Wills, Harry, and two or three of their friends.

Diana will usually invite the boys' friends' mother or father, or both, to the palace for a chat and a coffee or perhaps a snack lunch or evening drink so that she can keep in contact with her sons' school friends and their families. Diana tells the parents of her concern for Wills and Harry. "This is their home," she says, "and I want them to realize that they can invite whomever they want to share it with them. The last thing I want the boys to think is that they live in some palace, devoid of the realities of life and divorced from the real world. It's their home first and foremost."

When the boys are not at boarding school, Diana will try to arrange a lunch date with one or more of her friends, sometimes a man but more often a woman. Lunch is usually taken with a friend. She will usually select one of her favorite restaurants, Launceston Place, an intimate, quiet restaurant behind Kensington High Street, and Bibendum in Fulham, a slightly more trendy establishment, or perhaps an old haunt like San Lorenzo's in Beauchamp Place.

Since the separation Diana has tried to entertain at Kensington Palace, throwing an informal dinner party on alternate Saturday nights. Invitations asking her to house parties in the country or to lavish dinners or dances in London are now far fewer. The number of hostesses who want Diana at their gatherings has dropped remarkably from the days when Charles and Diana were invited to any number of events, the hosts falling over themselves to try to persuade the Prince and Princess of Wales to be their guests.

The Prince of Wales, and of course his wife, are by far the star attractions in British society. Hosts also realize the Queen and Philip much prefer to eat quietly at home on their own or with just one or two old friends.

Diana understands the new order. She knows that Charles and Camilla, accepted as an item by the Wiltshire set and others, have attended weekend house parties together ever since the late 1980s. The last person hosts could invite would be Diana. And understandably, Camilla's pals are only too eager to help encourage the relationship of their friend with the Prince of Wales, the heir to the throne.

Diana did not establish her own social circle. She had been too young before she met and married Charles, and understandably, his friends became her friends as well. She did not seek her own circle of friends, save for some younger wives, but they have mostly moved to the country. And since Charles left Diana to reside at Highgrove, nearly all his friends have remained close to him. Diana feels that loneliness and believes some of her erstwhile companions deserted her because she and Charles separated. To them it didn't matter that he had cheated on Diana and returned to his former mistress, for they all believed that Charles would one day be king and, more likely than not, Diana would not be queen. They preferred to stay where they predicted power would ultimately lie.

Those desertions hurt Diana. She would come to despise those women who had sought to be her friend but had discreetly moved away when they realized the marriage was over. Sometimes she would weep at their two-faced attitude, but on other occasions the thought of their treachery gave her added strength, so determined had she become to wage war on her husband and the rest of the Royals who wanted to disown her.

Faced with the necessity of building a new set of friends, Diana began her own Saturday soirees, when she would invite a number of people to Kensington Palace for a relatively informal dinner, music, drinks, and a chat. She will usually play the hostess on her own with no man as a support. She will invite those old friends who haven't gone to the country for the weekend, some enjoying a "girls' evening" without their husbands or men friends. Sometimes they are all-female parties, which Diana's contemporaries say they thoroughly enjoy away from their menfolk where they can dictate the topics of conversation.

One thirty-six-year-old married society lady commented, "I have been to four of Diana's Saturday-night dinners in the past six months. They are wonderful and relaxing. There were just eight women present, and because there were no men in attendance, we could all enjoy a wonderful bitch. I think the girls love those evenings, especially in such beautiful surroundings. And Diana is a wonderful, friendly hostess."

Most evenings of the week, however, are rather sad affairs for the Princess of Wales. When the boys are at boarding school, which is thirty-five weeks a year, Diana usually stays at home on her own for the entire evening. Sometimes she entertains the occasional visitor, and on occasion, one of the lovers with whom she has become involved since her break with James Hewitt in 1991. She also invites a girlfriend round for a snack and a chat. In these instances she will have her butler and a maid on hand for most of the evening. If she is alone, Diana usually sends them home around 7:30 P.M. and then has the vast Kensington Palace apartment entirely to herself. Diana finds it increasingly difficult to cope with this lonely existence.

When really bored at night, Diana will spend some time on the phone, but she soon discovered that most women do not have the time or the inclination to talk during the evenings for they were busy relaxing with their menfolk, entertaining, or simply having a quiet dinner at home. So, unable to find friends to talk to, Diana will be reduced to turning on the television, perhaps a television soap or a film. She will often watch the latest video release for she has become quite a film buff since living alone. Fed up with the "box," she will read

magazines and listen to her type of music, the seventies hits,
which she first enjoyed as a teenager.

Even today Diana is no great bookworm, preferring the
instant, short editorial pieces found in magazines. During the
past two years, however, under the guidance of her psychotherapist and friend Susie Orbach, Diana is reading more
serious literature, much of it concerning women's interests and,
in particular, feminism. She also enjoys the occasional special-
interest book such as homeopathy, health food, or other such
therapeutic interests. The novels she used to enjoy no longer
hold the same interest.

Often, Diana will take a hot, scented bath as early as 9 P.M.
and then spend an hour or more reading magazines in bed or
propped up by pillows watching TV until she falls asleep. More
often than not Diana wakes at around midnight or 1 A.M., turns
off the TV, and puts down her magazine before falling asleep
once again.

Quite frequently Diana resorts to sleeping pills because she
finds sleep so elusive, but they make her feel drowsy the
following morning, and she dislikes that feeling. She much
prefers to be wide-awake and raring to go at first light rather
than having to struggle awake, forcing herself to dress before
driving half-dazed to the gym.

The one activity that Diana still adores is shopping.
Throughout most of the year she will always find time to shop
at least twice a week, perhaps a couple of hours one day and two
or three hours later in the week. Much of her shopping entails
chatting with representatives of the haute couture brand names,
learning about their new designs for the following season and
wondering if they will suit her. She still loves to browse,
wandering through shops unrecognized, if possible, finding the
odd knickknack or accessory that she feels may provide a
highlight that, combined with one of her outfits, will attract
the attention of the media, the public, and the fashion buyers.

She now enjoys buying casual gear for her sons when they
are back home from boarding school. Ever since they have been
toddlers, Diana has refused to go along with the royal tradition

of putting secondhand clothes on the boys, hand-me-downs from older royal children. Charles, Andrew, and Edward were all dressed in clothes worn by other members of the family.

The thrifty Queen Mary and the Scottish Queen Mother, still going strong at age ninety-five, believed in the principle. Not Diana. She has ensured that both boys are always treated equally, and young Harry, two years younger than William, is never given his older brother's castoffs.

Even in small, insignificant ways Diana wants to distance herself from the Royal Family. She knows she must remain on terms with Charles for the sake of the children, though she still finds it extraordinarily difficult, for she openly despises him. But Diana has plans for the future, not just for her own life, not just for the boys, but for Prince Charles.

# 19

## Diana's Perilous Gamble

———❧———

Around nine o'clock on the morning of Tuesday, November 14, 1995, Prince Charles's forty-seventh birthday, Diana lifted the telephone in her palace apartment and asked to be put through to Sir Robert Fellowes, the Queen's personal and private secretary, the most senior aide in the Royal Household.

"Hello, Robert, it's Diana here. I have something to tell you."

"Yes, what's that?" Sir Robert asked politely.

After a second's hesitation Diana took a deep breath and said, "I've done an interview for *Panorama* [a serious, high-profile BBC current-affairs program]. I'm phoning you to let you know that it's going out next Monday, November the twentieth."

For a moment there was silence. "You've what?" asked Sir Robert, his voice incredulous and questioning. "You've given an interview to *Panorama*? What about?"

"Me. It's an hour-long interview about me and my marriage. Just me, talking about everything."

"Does HM [the Queen] know of this?"

"No, she knows nothing. Nor does Charles."

"Do any of your staff know, Jephson [Diana's private secretary], Crawford [her press adviser]?"

"No. They know nothing. I have told no one. You are the first to know."

"Will you be around later? Because I will have to inform HM immediately. I might need to get back to you."

"Not till much later because I am going to Broadmoor [a top-security jail for the criminally insane] on an official visit."

The contents of the conversation between Elizabeth and Sir Robert Fellowes is not known. Later, palace sources confirmed that Elizabeth had been shocked by the news. After questioning Sir Robert and other senior aides she would become absolutely furious that Diana had had the temerity and the impertinence to give such an interview without her express permission. Nothing like this had occurred before in Elizabeth's lifetime, for no other Royal would ever have had the audacity to undertake such a venture without the Queen's express permission. Without exception, all members of the Royal Family, through their private secretaries, would always clear any TV, radio, or press interview with senior aides at Buckingham Palace. They would only give permission after consulting the Queen.

Elizabeth immediately called Charles, who was on a five-day official royal visit to Germany, and asked him if he knew anything about the interview. He knew nothing.

What had enraged Elizabeth was not only that, in secret, Diana had given an interview without telling anyone, but that the BBC had agreed to Diana's express demand to keep the matter secret until she had informed the Queen. For the chairman of the BBC was Sir Marmaduke Hussey, whose wife, Susan, has been the Queen's chief lady-in-waiting and constant friend and adviser for more than twenty years.

The fact that Diana had chosen Charles's birthday to inform the Queen, and for the BBC to make a formal announcement later the same day, was not lost on anyone. Charles's staff with him on his royal tour, as well as those back home at St. James's Palace, were devastated. "The little bitch" and "the little vixen" were two of the polite comments made about Diana's remarkable coup.

Charles and his team, however, were in no position to complain for Charles had given his own two-hour television interview in June 1994 when he confessed to committing adultery with his longtime mistress, Camilla Parker Bowles.

Charles had been roundly condemned by the Queen, Prince
Philip, and his sister, Princess Anne, for agreeing to the TV
appearance, but he had first discussed the matter with his
mother before agreeing to the television spectacular. They
thought it was wrong, in principle, to permit the TV cameras
into his life. And they told him so before the interview took
place. It had been Charles's decision to go ahead. Afterward,
they all chided him on how stupid he had been to confess to
adultery.

Diana had taken the only course open to her. She had to
adopt secret tactics to ensure the interview ever took place. She
knew that the Royal Household, including the Queen herself, as
well as Charles's office, would have moved heaven and earth to
prevent such an interview from occurring if they had known
about it in advance.

"I had to carry out this operation in secret," Diana confessed. "Otherwise they would have put a stop on it."

In such situations Sir Robert Fellowes would have had a
private word with the BBC's director general, Sir John Birt,
asking to be informed if the Princess of Wales had suggested an
interview. The director general would then have been obliged to
inform the palace of the deal brokered between Diana and the
editors of *Panorama*. The palace would then have said they did
not think such an interview would be appropriate "at this
time," and the BBC, which operates under royal charter, would
have felt obliged to drop the proposed program.

In her heart Diana believed that the palace had done all in its
power since the official separation to keep her in the background, so that attention would focus on the dutiful, responsible, hardworking Prince Charles. Palace mandarins had
rejoiced when Diana chose to retire from public life. Her
reemergence into public life had been seen as a catastrophe, for
the media's attention had once again focused almost exclusively
on Diana. Her picture was back on the front pages; TV
programs screened every photo opportunity. Once again,
Charles would be relegated to virtual obscurity.

During those three years, Diana had come to believe that a

number of senior courtiers were actually plotting against her, trying to smear her image with the public and make her appear irrational. She talked openly to all her friends, as well as her staff, telling them how advisers to Charles and to the Queen were conducting a war against her to drive her out of the Royal Family. During many conversations, Diana would refer to them openly as "the enemy," and she would pull no punches describing their actions as deliberate machinations to destabilize her situation and make her feel alone and unwanted.

Diana knew one of those she described as "the enemy" very well indeed. Royal Navy commander Richard Aylard, forty-three, had been Diana's equerry between 1985 and 1988. He had been by her side throughout those three years whenever she ventured forth from Kensington Palace on both royal and charity occasions. And there had been hundreds of such functions to attend. And yet when an opportunity arose to become Charles's asistant private secretary, he leapt at the prospect. He proved himself so attentive and eager that when the top job—Charles's private secretary—fell vacant in 1991, he was promoted. He proved a worthy royal servant and struck up a good relationship with Charles, who came to rely more and more on his advice. He organized the Prince's life and was a prime mover in the Dimbleby TV documentary of June 1994 in which Charles admitted to adultery. Diana believes Commander Aylard to be primarily responsible for what she views as a concerted campaign to undermine and discredit her.

He has also changed the Prince of Wales's and the Royal Family's tradition of "never complain, never explain" into participation in the minefield of public relations with its sound bites, photo opportunities, and off-the-record briefings. He is viewed by the Queen and Prince Philip, and many of their senior courtiers, as a man who has tried to propel the Royal Family into the twenty-first century at too fast a pace and, as a consequence, brought discredit to the House of Windsor.

Diana heard that the fiercely ambitious, twice-married Aylard had apparently developed a nervous twitch and was in the habit of shutting himself away in his office, hardly speaking

to his staff, who felt cut off. Aylard was also concerned about
Charles's personal valet, Michael Fawcett, thirty-three, who
Aylard believed wielded an ever-increasing influence on Prince
Charles. Fawcett had become a junior valet to Charles in 1985
and won a reputation among staff for giving remarkably good
impressions of Prince Charles. But since those days he has
emerged as a considerable power, influencing Charles to a
degree that worried not only Aylard but a number of other
senior royal servants who have been with Charles for many
years. Charles listens most attentively to Fawcett, a married
man with two children.

From the moment Diana decided to retire from public life,
she had been cut out of all royal programs. No longer would she
be called upon to represent the Queen, as she had in the past.
She was, of course, still the Princess of Wales, but now her
work was restricted to her own interests, the 120-odd charities
of which she had become a patron.

During 1994 the only royal event in which Diana was
invited to take part, along with every other member of the
Royal Family, was the fiftieth-anniversary celebrations of the
D-day landing. And in 1995 she was asked to attend celebrations marking the fiftieth anniversaries of VE Day (Victory in
Europe) and VJ Day (Victory in Japan). Diana was happy to
have no further royal duties for it meant she had the time to
concentrate on her many charitable engagements. She had so
much more freedom now that she was no longer at the beck and
call of the senior aides at Buckingham Palace.

The more Diana realized that Buckingham Palace and St.
James's Palace were determined to keep her out of the newspapers and off the nation's TV screens, the more concerned she
became about her future. Time and again Diana had received
invitations from charities to visit their overseas projects. On
numerous occasions she had asked permission to travel abroad
to visit charities, but usually some excuse had been forthcoming from Buckingham Palace refusing the request.

The Red Cross had wanted Diana to take a high-profile
position throughout their yearlong 125th-anniversary celebra-

tions, participating in a number of Red Cross events around the world throughout 1995. Within days of the news being published, discreet intervention by Buckingham Palace put an end to the plan. Diana was upset and angry. Later, Diana would be asked to undertake work as an ambassador on behalf of the British Red Cross. That, too, was diplomatically turned down after the request had been passed to Buckingham Palace. Diana of course knew the reason. But she would still become furious at the thought that the Queen and Philip, along with their senior advisers, were doing their damnedest to bury the Princess of Wales.

Throughout 1995, Diana considered how best to counter such a deliberate policy, which she was convinced had the approval of both Charles and Elizabeth. It was enough that Diana was the darling of the British people, eclipsing every other member of the Royal Family. The last thing the Royals wanted would be for Diana to steal the royal limelight overseas as well.

Diana invited PR chiefs, former cabinet ministers and members of Parliament, newspaper and TV executives, captains of industry, and marketing experts to a series of power lunches. She would seek their advice, asking in what direction they felt her career should go. She would inform them of the problems she faced with senior aides blocking her ambitions.

The power brokers and influence makers would offer advice and come up with ideas for a new direction for Diana's talents. This author was invited, with two others, to put together a possible scenario for the Princess for launching a new career. We decided that a charity—perhaps to be named The Princess of Wales Foundation—could be one solution.

The foundation would have Diana as president with a director general, offices, and a small, full-time staff. The charity would be involved in whatever area Diana preferred— caring for the homeless, the disadvantaged, the unemployed, the deaf, blind, or mentally ill. The main point would be that Diana herself would become actively involved, perhaps spending two days a week at the foundation's headquarters, spearheading the charity, hosting lunches, and chairing meetings where she would persuade the leaders in all strata of British society to support her foundation. More importantly, we felt it would provide Diana with a real job on which to focus her life, direct her energies, and utilize her remarkable qualities. After the plan was put to her, Diana said she would study the project, which she found "most interesting."

At the following meeting Diana revealed that she had decided her future lay in working overseas and said that she had set her sights on becoming a royal ambassador, communicating directly with victims and the disadvantaged. She revealed that becoming a worldwide royal ambassador—jetting around the world visting charitable organizations, raising money for good causes, and helping the victims of society—had been her secret ambition for years. She had now decided to bring her dream to fruition as soon as possible.

As her plan developed in her mind, Diana began a new series of lunches and meetings, inviting a number of key people whose combined influence in the realms of psychotherapy, image grooming, self-esteem, and media know-how would provide the necessary expertise if she did decide to make her bid for her new career.

Close friends that she took into her confidence included Annabel Goldsmith, wife of the multimillionaire Sir James Goldsmith. Annabel, a mature woman, seems to have taken over as Diana's mother figure in place of Diana's close friend of many years, Lucia Flecha de Lima, the wife of the Brazilian ambassador who had moved from London to Washington with her husband. Angela Serota, the estranged wife of Tate Gallery director Nicholas Serota, has been an intimate friend of Diana's for five years, and they lunch together frequently. Diana would also discuss every detail of her plan with the woman who had become her closest confidante, her psychotherapist, Susie Orbach.

The wealthy, warmhearted, tousle-haired Susie Orbach, forty-nine, is the one person in the world who knows all Diana's secrets. Ever since a strong relationship developed between the two women in 1994, Susie Orbach has become the most dominant person in the life of the Princess of Wales, advising, guiding, and comforting her as no other therapist has before. The key to their closeness lies in Orbach's feminist stand, which she has advocated since writing her bestselling book *Fat Is a Feminist Issue*, which was published in 1978. In the book Orbach identifies the obsession with weight, shape, and food that haunts so many Western women and lays the blame squarely on men for controlling women within unequal partnerships.

She wrote, "Fat is not about lack of self-control or lack of willpower. Fat *is* about protection, sex, nurturance, strength. . . . it is a response to the inequality of the sexes."

Diana read and reread the book, which is punctuated with case histories of women suffering at the hands of men. For Diana, brought up in the patriarchal aristocracy to marry by arrangement, produce a couple of heirs, and withdraw quietly, relating to Orbach's writing came easily.

Much of Susie Orbach's evangelism stemmed from her experience of a course on compulsive eating. Having learned that women's needs are not contemptible, Susie was able to reject the rules society was hurling at her—and her body dutifully shrank. Her pattern of dieting and binge eating was broken.

Diana felt a sense of awakening after she met Susie and listened to her theory. To educated women Orbach's theory may now be commonplace, but to the innocent, uneducated Diana here was someone who understood her urge to control her body and who knew what it was like to gorge on chocolate and dry cereal.

Orbach suggests she had an uneasy relationship with her parents, who had an unhappy relationship. The daughter of a Labour member of Parliament and a mother who taught English as a foreign language, Orbach felt isolated as she was growing up, in the same way that Diana did. At fifteen, Susie had an abortion and was expelled from school. After failing to complete her degree at London University's School of Slavonic and East European Studies, at the age of twenty-one she escaped to America, "found herself," qualified as a therapist, and returned to London where she cofounded the Women's Therapy Center, renowned for teaching women to support each other. Having now written six books, Orbach is recognized as a highly reputable therapist who speaks with integrity. Diana became her willing pupil.

Orbach, too, had an unhappy marriage at a young age. In 1970, Susie married Manhattan architect Alan Feigenberg, but divorced him within eleven months following bouts of compulsive overeating. But she had always remained silent about that marriage. She has, however, enjoyed a twenty-three-year-long relationship with Joseph Schwartz, a physics and psychology professor turned psychoanalyst. They have never married. He is the father of her two children.

But Susie Orbach has her critics, who wonder if she is the best person to advise the Princess of Wales, responsible to a great degree for guiding Prince William, the heir to the throne. Orbach is a known left-winger who disdains the traditional family. In one of her books Orbach looks forward to an increasing narrowing of the gap between the sexes, a world where the conventional nuclear family may well disappear to be replaced by "an alternative way of living." She asserts that future generations will be the products of a completely different structure of parenting, that communal living will be accepted as conventional along with single parents and homosexual couples.

To these select few friends, Diana confided that if the Royal Family and the Establishment put a stop to her plan of becoming a royal ambassador, then she would seriously consider moving to the United States and setting up a permanent home there. She told of conversations she had held with prominent Americans in various walks of life who told her that she would be most welcome to live in the United States, suggesting she take an apartment in New York and a house in the country.

From New York she could then proceed with her plan of

becoming a royal ambassador, touring the world, working for any number of charities who would welcome her with open arms.

Diana told her friends, "I am deadly serious. This is no idle threat for I am determined to do the job for which I believe I am uniquely equipped. And if the Royals won't let me carry out that work, then I will go and live where I will be able to."

She told how she would plan her life if she did move to New York. She would spend school terms in the United States or working for charities in foreign countries, and holidays at home in England with her sons. She explained that both boys, at boarding school, often preferred to play games on Saturdays rather than be at home. As a consequence they were already seeing less of their parents. Diana would comment, "And if they need me, London is only a Concorde flight away. I could even buy a season ticket."

One of her principal advisers, a man on whom Diana has come to depend to a remarkable degree, is a highly intelligent, witty, irreverent, bald and overweight Australian TV chat show host by the name of Clive Vivian Leopold James, known universally as Clive James, the king of the put-down.

Clive James came to public attention as a spectacularly rude television reviewer for the *Observer* newspaper after studying at Cambridge University. But he desperately wanted to appear on the box himself. Eventually he became a highly successful host mainly by witty flourishes, clever put-downs, cynicism, and savaging those who appeared on television. Ironically, at the time of Diana's wedding he wrote a satire about it that did not receive rave reviews. Friends believe he would have "died" for an invitation to the wedding, but one would not be forthcoming. Clive James persevered, and finally, in the early 1990s, he met Diana, the woman he had admired from afar for more than a decade. His time had come.

When Charles and Diana separated, Clive James wrote a serious article in the *Spectator* urging the Prince and Princess of Wales to stay together—just like the Spitfires and Hurricanes of the war—to save British private life from the Nazis of the popular press. But he went further, many judging his wit had become obscene, for he compared the estrangement of Charles and Diana to the Holocaust, though he agreed the estrangement was "inherently more trivial."

He would assist in schooling Diana for her TV epic; he wrote some of the lines; he went over her replies to probable questions; and he advised her how to behave on camera, looking straight at the interviewer, speaking in short sentences. He advised on what she should wear and her general demeanor. He suggested she smile and laugh and crack the occasional joke to lighten the proceedings.

Since becoming a confidant, Clive James has also become fiercely loyal: "I would almost rather climb a ladder of swords than tell you about any little tête-à-têtes I have with Diana. . . . I would rather swim naked through a lake full of crocodiles than tell you about those."

At lunches with Diana and others he will be full of bonhomie and jokes, using his famous style of put-downs and mock savagery. Clive James is bright, some suggesting that he may be too bright for his own good. But he helps his lunch companions by laughing at his own jokes at the right spots, just to make sure the other guests haven't missed one of his witticisms. And he would give Diana great support.

Sometime during the summer of 1995, Diana decided the only way to achieve her ambition would be to make a direct appeal to the British people. She realized that such a cri de coeur would have to be made over the heads of the Queen and Charles and all their royal henchmen, otherwise she was convinced they would use their extraordinary, though subtle, powers of persuasion to squash her plan. Diana believed that the only way of achieving her objective would be via television, where she could gain so much popular support for her ambition that the Establishment would be unable to put a stop to it.

Unlike Charles, Diana could not just ask the BBC or any other TV channel to organize an interview, for that would be politely stopped by Buckingham Palace. Keeping the project secret would be vital, though difficult. She had never done anything like this before in her life and she had no idea whether it would be a success or a failure. But those attending her lunches agreed to do everything to help her, including writing most of the answers to questions that would be agreed to by the interviewer beforehand.

She never told those she invited to her innumerable lunches the real purpose for their visits, and they would leave Kensington Palace convinced that the Princess of Wales was being victimized by the Royal Family—her efforts to carve out a new career for herself blocked at every turn—with Diana trying to combat a totally unfair and unfounded smear campaign suggesting she was "unstable, mentally unbalanced, and suffering from paranoia."

The intimate lunches, usually one or two a week, took place throughout the summer and fall of 1995, usually held around a small circular table. Diana, relaxed, charming, and attentive, would entertain perhaps only two or four people on each occasion. She felt that small lunch parties would ensure that her message got through loud and clear, that she would be able to ensnare, seduce, charm, and persuade her guests to understand her terrible predicament, and, if possible, to advise her how best she could break out of such encirclement and lead a worthwhile life.

At the end of each lunch, Diana would seek advice, inviting her guests to phone or pop back for another chat if they felt they needed further information to reach a conclusion. She would impress on her visitors, "All I want to do is help people. I feel I have a role to play helping people, the disadvantaged, the homeless, the poor, the disabled. I would really appreciate it if you have any ideas how I could achieve this."

And she would refer quite openly to the senior courtiers and aides at Buckingham Palace and St. James's, where Charles had his official London headquarters, as "the enemy" who, she claimed, were determined to stop her from fulfilling her true potential as the Princess of Wales.

Nearly all would leave her presence believing that they had been given a mission to help the beleaguered Princess. Most would come under her spell, which they found remarkably arresting. Many thought they had been selected by her, privileged beyond reason to help this beautiful, misunderstood, lonely, aggrieved woman to find a role for herself. In the fullness of time, however, most would be disappointed; some would even feel cheated.

In the fall of 1995, Diana would invite others to Kensington Palace: her therapists, who had advised and helped her during the past twelve months to revitalize herself. They realized that Diana's problem was unique, for as a member of the Royal House of Windsor, she was enmeshed in what they all recognized to be one of the principal dysfunctional families in the land. And the most important of all her therapists was Susie Orbach. Another adviser who helped shape her thoughts was the American motivation guru Anthony Robbins.

Others invited to lunch, taken into Diana's confidence, and sworn to secrecy included Lord Attenborough, the director of *Gandhi* and *Chaplin*, who gave Diana extensive advice before her TV interview. Film producer Sir David Puttman would be another, along with Sir Gordon Reece, who helped to change and mold Prime Minister Margaret Thatcher's television technique.

But throughout those months her most important adviser would be Susie Orbach. Diana would drive to Ms. Orbach's $750,000 home in Swiss Cottage, North London, and Diana would be tutored in her approach to Prince Charles, the Queen, and the courtiers who run Buckingham Palace and advise the monarchy. More than anyone else, Orbach was responsible for preparing Diana for her forthcoming ordeal.

"Without Susie Orbach I would never have even considered doing a television interview. She gave me the strength I needed," Diana has said to many people since the remarkable TV epic.

By September 1995, Diana felt sufficiently prepared to face an interviewer. She had learned her lines well, rehearsed answers to possible questions with her therapists and advisers, and felt confident that she would give a good account of herself.

Diana had received a number of requests for an in-depth profile from TV interviewers, including Barbara Walters, Sir David Frost, and Oprah Winfrey. She felt they were all too high-powered and preferred someone less well-known. She had met Martin Bashir, a quiet, rather introspective, yet charming thirty-two-year-old *Panorama* reporter, a former sportswriter, and believed he would keep silent about the interview until the big day.

Bashir would spend three days with Diana going through the questions, one by one, line by line, taking one part of her life at a time until she was happy with the questions and she could concentrate on her answers. Her only demand was that no questions be asked about her relationship with Will Carling. She sought advice and stuck to it like glue. Her answers were always brief and to the point, exact and never rambling or hesitant. The interview was shot over five hours with many breaks so that Diana could check the next question and prepare her answer. She would leave nothing to chance.

News of the interview caused dismay, not only in Buckingham Palace, St. James's Palace, and Downing Street, but in every newspaper and TV office in Britain. It had come as a shock to everyone because no one thought Diana would have the courage, the intelligence, or the strength of character to carry through such a plan. Some newspapers described the secret filming as "deceitful and underhand." Others went further, the tabloid *Daily Mirror* asking on its front page, "Has She Gone Mad?" suggesting the Princess of Wales had committed an act of treason by undertaking the interview without seeking permission from the Queen.

The BBC played down the contents of the interview, but when it was shown during the evening of Monday, November 20, 1995, most people were taken aback by the content, Diana's remarkable performance, and the honesty of her replies. More than 23 million people in Britain watched the show, which many believed to be the most extraordinary and damaging royal statement since the abdication of King Edward VIII in 1937.

Diana's appearance in a dark suit with a simple white top was low-key and serious, so unlike the clothes in which most people see Diana. She wore dark makeup around the eyes, emphasizing the seriousness of the occasion. Within minutes in the hour-long interview Diana showed how much she had changed and matured. Her composure and fluency were remarkable. Pat, polished, and articulate, Diana showed no sign of her old self. Gone was the interviewer's flushed and flustered nightmare, with her flat voice, fiddly hands, and hesitant sentences.

No question took her by surprise and no answers were fluffed. Her honesty was compelling when she spoke of her eating disorders. She said, "It is true that I suffered from bulimia, bingeing and vomiting, for a number of years. It's like a secret disease. I was crying out for help. You inflict bulimia on yourself because your self-esteem is at a low ebb, and you don't think you're worthy or valuable. You fill your stomach up four or five times a day—some do it more—and it gives you a feeling of comfort. It's like having a pair of arms around you, but it's temporary. Then you're disgusted at the bloatedness of your stomach and then you bring it all up again."

She spoke of the postnatal depression after giving birth to William in 1982 and the effect it had on her marriage. "Well, it gave everybody a wonderful new label—Diana's unstable and Diana's mentally unbalanced. And unfortunately that seems to have stuck on and off over the years."

Bashir asked about her self-mutilation. Diana replied, "When no one listens to you, or you feel no one's listening to you, all sorts of things start to happen. For instance, you have so much pain inside yourself that you try and hurt yourself on the outside because you want help, but it's the wrong help you're asking for. People see it as crying wolf or attention seeking, and they think because you're in the media all the time, you've got enough attention. But I was actually crying out because I wanted to get better in order to go forward and continue my duty and my role as wife, mother, Princess of

The man with whom Diana enjoyed a
passionate three-year affair, Maj. James Hewitt
(Express Newspapers)

A paparazzo caught Diana and
Major Hewitt kissing in 1990
(London News Service)

Will Carling with his wife, Julia, outside their London home in May 1995, just twelve months after their marriage (London News Service)

The lovely Julia Carling, who fought a bitter tug-of-love battle with Diana over hunky Will Carling (Express Newspapers)

Arriving at a gala night at the
London Coliseum, June 1993...
(London News Service)

...and at a cancer charity
event in London, December
1995 (London News Service)

Prince Charles with sons, William and Harry, in Klosters, Switzerland, 1994 (Express Newspapers)

Diana enjoying a skiing holiday with Wills and Harry in Lech, Austria, in 1995 (Express Newspapers)

On an early morning visit to
the Chelsea Harbour Club,
1994 (Express Newspapers)

Princess Diana in her bikini
enjoying the Caribbean surf
and sun, January 1993
(London News Service)

Learning to in-line skate in Kensington Gardens in November 1995. She would be castigated for not wearing a helmet or protective gear for knees and elbows. (London News Service)

Psychotherapist and feminist Susie Orbach, the woman who keeps all of Diana's secrets. (Express Newspapers)

Princess Diana with Prince Charles, Prince William, and Prince Harry at the official VE day celebrations in London, May 1995 (London News Service)

Princess Diana with Prince Harry during the official VJ day celebrations in London, August 1995 (London News Service)

Wales. So, yes, I did inflict upon myself. I didn't like myself, I was ashamed because I couldn't cope with the pressures."

Bashir: "What did you actually do?"

Diana: "Well, I just hurt my arms and my legs. And I work in environments now where I see women doing similar things and I'm able to understand completely where they're coming from."

She spoke of the devastating effect she felt after learning that Charles had renewed his relationship with Camilla Parker Bowles, in 1986. "I took refuge in rampant bulimia, if you can have rampant bulimia, and just a feeling of being no good at anything and being useless and hopeless and failed in every direction. For I knew that my husband loved someone else."

Diana explained that she knew of Charles's adultery and love for Camilla, not only through her own intuition but also through friends who cared about the marriage. And that made the marriage increasingly difficult.

She said, "Friends on my husband's side were indicating that I was again unstable, sick, and should be put in a home of some sort in order to get better. I was almost an embarrassment."

Bashir: "So you were isolated?"

Diana: "Very much so."

Bashir: "Do you think Mrs. Parker Bowles was a factor in the breakdown of your marriage?"

Diana: "Well, there were three of us in this marriage, so it was a bit crowded."

For most of the interview Diana appeared serious and concerned, though willing to answer all the questions openly and honestly, obviously wanting to clear the air. Sometimes she smiled, occasionally she laughed. She would keep eye contact with Bashir throughout, as if TV interviews were for her an everyday occurrence. She had been well schooled, and it showed.

Many people were shocked that Diana confessed to her three-year-long adulterous affair with Capt. James Hewitt.

Asked about the relationship, Diana said, "He was a great friend and he was always there to support me, and I was absolutely devastated when a book appeared, because I trusted him. . . . "

Bashir: "Were you unfaithful?"

Diana: "Yes, I adored him. Yes, I was in love with him."

Diana also praised Charles for admitting his own adultery during his TV interview in June 1994, saying, "I admired the honesty because it takes a lot to do that."

It was, however, Diana's remarks on the monarchy, on Prince Charles and "the enemy" ranged against her, that caused the most consternation in Buckingham Palace. In a bellicose reference to what she sees as the Establishment, Diana said that she was now motivated by the old adage, "'Always confuse the enemy'; the 'enemy' being Prince Charles's staff."

But Diana aimed her most deadly remarks so as to injure Charles, the husband she has come to detest and whom she is determined to ruin if at all possible. Her replies to questions about him revealed the bitterness within her, a malice bordering on hatred. With great subtlety Diana managed to impress on the viewers that her husband was not really fit to be king. And she achieved that ambition without saying one nasty word about him. Diana knew full well that to criticize another's ability to do his job, particularly one that has taken a lifetime of training, can be devastating. And she knew the savagery of that attack can be even more destructive if delivered in a small, quiet voice.

Bashir: "Do you think the Prince of Wales will ever be king?"

Diana: "I don't think any of us know the answer to that. Who knows what fate will produce, who knows what circumstances will provoke."

Bashir: "But you would know him better than most people. Do you think he would wish to be king?"

Diana: "There was always conflict on that subject with him when we discussed it, and I understood that conflict, because it's a very demanding role, being Prince of Wales, but it's an equally more demanding role being king. And being Prince of

Wales produces more freedom now, and being king would be a little bit more suffocating. And because I know the character, I would think that the top job, as I call it, would bring enormous limitations to him, and I don't know whether he could adapt to that."

Bashir asked whether it would make more sense if the position of monarch passed directly to Prince William once he becomes of age rather than Prince Charles. Diana replied, "My wish is that my husband finds peace of mind, and from that follows other things, yes."

And she hadn't finished. She would take an even greater risk during the interview, bringing herself in open conflict with her mother-in-law and her "enemies" within the palace, by daring to criticize both the Queen and the monarchy. Speaking quietly and sounding so sympathetic, Diana said, "I understand that change is frightening for people, especially if there's nothing to go to. It's best to stay where you are. I understand that. But I do think there are a few things that could change, that would alleviate this doubt, and sometimes complicated relationship between monarchy and public."

She continued, "I would like a monarchy that has more contact with its people—and I don't mean riding round on bicycles and things like that, but just having a more in-depth understanding. And I don't say that as a criticism to the present monarchy, I just say that as what I see and hear and feel on a daily basis in the role I have chosen for myself."

As they watched the program, senior aides at the palace were outraged that Diana had the audacity to feel herself sufficiently knowledgeable and competent to tell the Queen how the monarchy should operate. As one sixty-year-old palace veteran commented later, "Some were apoplectic at what they saw as an upstart's decision to go on TV and tell the Queen what to do. Others thought she must have lost her marbles. Others were resigned to the Princess of Wales's determination to destroy her husband and organize the future of the monarchy around her son William, guided, of course, by his mother, the Princess of Wales."

But cooler heads at the palace would prevail.

Yet Diana had managed to confuse some wise heads at the palace by confessing that she believed she would not become queen of England because sections of the Royal Household were determined that she should never sit on the throne beside Charles because she could not be trusted to behave with the quiet dignity expected of a king's consort. She continued, "The Establishment has decided they don't want me as queen because I do things differently, because I don't go by a rule book, because I lead from the heart, not the head."

Diana also stated, categorically, that she did not want a divorce from Charles. By stating that publicly Diana had set a trap for the monarchy and, more particularly, for Prince Charles. Most people had believed their separation in December 1992 had been instigated, even demanded, by Diana. She put that canard to rest by telling the nation that it had been her husband's decision to separate.

Diana knew that Charles would not want Wills and Harry to see their father demanding a divorce from their mother. She believed her remark would mean she could remain Princess of Wales for some years to come. But the Queen decided that Diana had been mischief making, trying to lead her own life at the same time as keeping her title and her royal privileges, but accepting no responsibilities and undertaking virtually no royal duties. So she stepped in, calling Diana's bluff, urging Charles and Diana to divorce as soon as possible.

More importantly for Diana's life, she proclaimed in quite strident language her ambition for the future, wanting to work as an ambassador for Britain, offering her unique talents to serve the victims of society across the world: "I see myself as an ambassador for this country. I would like to represent this country."

Diana explained, "I've been in a privileged position for fifteen years. I've got tremendous knowledge about people and how to communicate, and I want to use it. I think the British people need someone in public life to give affection, to make them feel important, to support them, to give them light in their dark tunnels. I see it as a possibly unique role. Let's use the knowledge I've gathered to help other people in distress."

She would go on to explain in more detail the type of ambassador she would become, saying, "I would like to be queen of people's hearts. Someone's got to go out there and love people and show it. . . . The perception that has been given of me for the last three years has been very confusing, turbulent, and in some areas, I'm sure, many, many people doubt me. I want to reassure all those people who have loved me throughout the last fifteen years that I'd never let them down. That is a priority to me. The man on the street matters more than anything else to me."

Such official overseas visits are the preserve of the Queen, Prince Philip, and Prince Charles and are always cleared by the Foreign Office, whose advice the Royal Family will always take whether to accept or refuse such invitations. Before the separation, Charles would be accompanied by Diana, thus ensuring the crowds turned out in the tens of thousands and the visits would prove public relations successes. Such overseas visits by Diana on her own would prove a considerable headache for the palace and the Foreign Office unless Diana only accepted invitations involving charities. Then the visits would be deemed personal rather than as her representing Britain. She would still need to consult the Foreign Office as well as Buckingham Palace, but at least there would be no protocol problems or official or diplomatic embarrassment.

Diana had watched her video three times before giving *Panorama* her permission to show it. She believed the interview had gone exactly as she had wished, if not better. "Brilliant," she repeated time and again. "Brilliant." She congratulated Bashir and his editor, Steve Hewlett, on "an excellent documentary."

The night the interview was screened Diana was not at home. She attended a gala dinner in London and smiled happily, some suggesting triumphantly, for the photographers who followed her every step. She looked ravishing, jubilant, dressed in a clinging, low-cut, full-length black dress with a choker of pearls. The sad, anguished woman in the interview seemed a different person than the confident woman going out to dinner that night.

Earlier that day Diana had arrived at her health club wearing clinging, sexy Lycra shorts and a sweatshirt, smiling broadly and striding toward the club confident and happy that hordes of photographers had arrived and waited in the cold November morning to get that final shot of her before the program.

Initially, the interview was hailed by the nation as a great success. Throughout, she made no vicious allegations, never overtly criticizing Charles or the Royal Family. She showed only sadness and humility despite her obvious underlying anger and bitterness. She made it clear she loves her country and her sons; the performance was compelling, undoubtedly the greatest of her life, asking the nation to judge a saintly, forgiving, understanding woman.

Within minutes of scanning the next morning's newspapers, Diana realized her life's gamble had been vindicated, indeed, accepted as a triumph. Diana read all the national newspapers, the four quality papers and the five tabloids, most of which highlighted Diana's confession of adultery with Hewitt, which she had managed to make sound both sad and pure. Most newspapers applauded "her gut-wrenching honesty," and some felt the nation had been "eavesdropping on a confessional, gate-crashing on the burial of a marriage." Others, more ominously, highlighted Diana's determination "not to go quietly."

She read the papers with growing satisfaction, bordering on jubilation. Repeatedly, she clenched her fist and punched the air in triumph as she read a piece that particularly praised her. "Done it. Done it. Done it," she said time and again.

The bouquets and the plaudits flooded into Kensington Palace during the days following the interview. "Magic," "Brilliant," "Magnificent," "Fantastic," "Congratulations to a star" were typical of the messages from friends and supporters. Her close friends were on the phone throughout the day congratulating her on a brave, fearless, and wonderful perform-ance. A Gallup poll taken the day following the program showed she had risen sharply in the public esteem. More than 46 percent thought more of Diana after the interview than they did before, and 74 percent believed she was right in giving the interview. Only 20 percent believed she should have remained silent.

Their reasons were even more interesting. Only 14 percent believed she gave the interview to exact revenge on Charles and the Royal Family; only 17 percent believed the interview was a cry for help. A remarkable 77 percent thought Diana simply set out to put her side of the story on record. Those consulted believed Diana to be strong, sincere, loving, and intelligent. They also think she is "a good mother."

Diana's performance, however, had not been entirely flawless, for 30 percent of the doubters believed Diana had revealed herself to be "self-centered, vengeful, and manipulative." Some critics immediately indicted Diana for using what they termed "psychobabble," to dismiss her performance. Certainly the influence of psychotherapy was evident throughout, from her unwavering discussion of self-mutilation and bulimia to comments on her strengths and ambitions.

Less than twenty-four hours after the interview Buckingham Palace made a peace offering, senior aides saying they wished to "see how we can help her define her future role and continue to support her as a member of the Royal Family." The offer was intended to be generous, constructive, and helpful and contained not a word of vexation. "Diana: Palace Peace Offer" was a typical headline.

With a one-hour television program Diana was convinced that she had achieved more than she had done since her fairy-tale wedding in July 1981. For the first time ever she had appealed to the British people, over the heads of her husband, the Royal Family, and the Establishment, and won their admiration and their support. She had also ruined the carefully laid plans of Buckingham Palace officials to sideline her, a policy that they had been implementing and nurturing for eighteen months. They had been confident that Diana, with her increasing number of unfortunate relationships going so wrong, would decide to avoid the limelight, concentrating solely on her charitable work, leaving the path clear for Charles to show the nation what a good king he would make.

To a few close friends Diana would talk openly, admitting that she had done much more than the man in the street realized. She had made her mother-in-law, the Queen, sit up and take note along with every senior aide who worked at the palace and in Charles's office. That realization warmed Diana's heart and made her feel more secure than she had been since her wedding day. For her message to the Establishment had been direct and to the point: "You never realised what a bright, tough woman I have become; ignore me at your peril."

Her interview caused two casualties. The first, Mr. Geoffrey Crawford, forty-four, an Australian diplomat who had joined the palace staff three years earlier as Diana's press officer, quit within twenty-four hours of her TV appearance. She had told him nothing whatsoever of the *Panorama* program. He felt humiliated at being kept completely in the dark. He had no alternative but to resign for Diana had shown she didn't trust him enough either to confide in him or to seek his advice.

Diplomatically, he commented, "I always enjoyed working with the Princess. I'll miss it. We've had some marvelous journeys together. She's brilliant at what she does. And completely natural. She's a great ambassador for Britain."

The second was Mr. Nicholas Soames, the minister of state for the armed forces and a close personal friend of Prince Charles since childhood. Within minutes of Diana's interview, the pompous Soames, a grandson of Winston Churchill, said on the following television program that the Princess "was showing the advanced stages of paranoia." He then rejected Diana's portrayal of herself as having been isolated by her husband's circle of friends and assistants and suggested that Diana's "most outrageous" contribution had been to question her husband's readiness to assume the role of king.

"I think that was the key to the whole interview," he said. "I think it has the potential to undermine very seriously the Prince of Wales's position, and I thought that it was a terrible thing to say because it is totally and utterly untrue."

The following morning Prime Minister John Major gagged his minister, telling him that he must not comment any further on the interview and suggesting his intervention had not been of help to anyone, including the Prince of Wales himself.

Diana was happy to read that her friend John Major had been so tough on the minister who had dared to criticize her. Having supported her decision to speak out on television, the prime minister would, she now hoped, support her ambition of becoming a royal ambassador. Diana knew that John Major's influence could be crucial in persuading the Queen and senior courtiers to agree to her new role.

# 20

## *A Triumphant Di*

————— ❦ —————

TWO DAYS LATER DIANA FLEW OFF in triumph to Argentina on a charity visit that had been planned months before. To Diana, the visit would be of the utmost importance. Diana had planned her interview to take place a few days prior to her Argentina trip so that her adoring public could see her in the new role she hoped to carve out for herself. By timing the broadcast before the trip, she ensured the most massive TV and media coverage imaginable.

Quietly and politely, with that wicked smile on her face, Diana commented to a friendly businessman, "I thought I would arrange things like this so the Establishment will be able to judge for themselves how successful or otherwise the trip will have been. If it's successful, then maybe they will agree to let me carry out more such visits."

The visit would be a magnificent personal success for Diana. Ninety press photographers accompanied her on her four-day visit to Argentina, whereas only the week before, Prince Charles, on an official royal visit to Germany, was accompanied by only one photographer. No other newspaper or magazine wanted to know about the Prince's trip. It was a salutary experience for Charles, a memorable victory for Diana and her ambitions for the future. And she knew it.

She flew to Argentina with a skeleton retinue of only five people: her private secretary, Patrick Jephson, her lady-in-waiting, a detective, dresser, and hairdresser. Usually, for a four-day overseas visit, including lunch with the head of state, the Queen would be accompanied by a retinue of at least twenty people. Diana had kept numbers to a minimum to demonstrate her idea of a modern monarchy that was not "so distant" from the people.

Her first stop in Buenos Aires, at a center run by the Association for the Prevention of Infant Paralysis, brought the streets around the clinic to a standstill as the crowds stopped traffic to catch a glimpse of Diana, wearing a light, cream dress. The clinic's superviser, Susana Duranona de Vila, said afterward, "The children adored her. The children were very, very emotional with her. She is so charming and understanding."

Similar scenes followed at the Garrahan pediatric hospital and a Buenos Aires rehabilitation center for the disabled. Everyone seemed to love her, though most of the children she spoke to and stroked had no idea exactly who Princess Diana was or where she came from. At the Casa Cuna hospital, Diana spent an hour talking to battered wives, child victims of domestic violence, and teenagers suffering from drug and solvent abuse. The day had seen Diana at the top of her form, enjoying the best of both worlds, giving hope and comfort to victims and enjoying the adulation of cheering crowds.

In all, Diana visited seven hospitals and clinics in three hectic days, as she was whisked at speed through the capital. The media gave blanket coverage. From this visit—her first after proclaiming her desire for a new ambassadorial role—it seems Diana will have considerable difficulty in persuading people and politicians that she can ever be taken seriously as an ambassador for Britain. All the Argentine commentators viewed the Princess as a celebrity rather than a serious representative. Save for a lunch with beleaguered President Menem, she seemed determined not to become involved in any political matters whatsoever. The question of the Falkland Islands, over which Britain and Argentina waged a short, sharp war in 1982, never arose, and Diana did not venture near the capital's central Plaza de Mayo where the mothers of those who "disappeared" during the so-called Dirty War of the military regimes of the seventies were holding a meeting. She was invited but declined to attend. Indeed, Diana behaved so discreetly and diplomatically that the leading daily newspaper *La Nación* dubbed her "the mute princess."

Argentina was Diana's third major overseas working trip of 1995. In February she had traveled, again by scheduled flight, to Tokyo as the guest of several charities. The main reason for her trip was to visit the Japanese National Children's Hospital at Setagaya-Ku, which is affiliated with London's Great Ormond Street Hospital of which she is president. She would visit other hospitals and clinics, but once again, she would not be involved in any diplomatic or political matters. That visit was hailed as a great success, winning the hearts of Japanese therapists, doctors, and administrators who met and talked to her.

In June 1995 she visited Moscow, spending several hours at the Tushinskaya Children's Hospital. That trip followed an appeal from the hospital directly to Diana asking if she would like to visit the Russian capital, hoping she would spend some hours at the children's hospital. She leapt at the invitation for Diana had realized where her future could lie—as a royal ambassador.

In September 1995, Diana flew to Paris to raise $250,000 for the Great Ormond Street children's hospital and won rave reviews for her style and elegance. On that occasion she met President Chirac, who jumped at the photo opportunity of standing side by side with the beautiful Princess of Wales on the steps of the Elysée Palace. President Chirac needed all the good press he could get as his regime had been rocked by the worldwide condemnation of France's nuclear tests in the South Pacific.

Diana's determination to build on her new role, to become a major champion of good causes around the world, knows no bounds. She is not only confident that she has the full backing of the British people in her bid to challenge the Queen, Philip, and Prince Charles and bring the British monarchy into the twenty-first century, but also feels she has the charisma to win the hearts of the disadvantaged and the victims of modern society in cities around the world.

Another reason for the timing of her *Panorama* interview was that Diana had accepted an invitation to fly to New York in December 1995 to receive the Humanitarian of the Year award at a star-studded $1,000-a-head dinner attended by nine hundred guests. The dinner, in aid of the United Cerebral Palsy of New York Foundation, was also attended by Dr. Henry Kissinger, Gen. Colin Powell, Donald and Marla Trump, Randolph Hearst, Rupert Murdoch, and America's best known and most forthright sex therapist, the diminutive Dr. Ruth Westheimer. Diana won plaudits from the New York fashion conscious for her low-cut, sleeveless, and beaded black, full-length evening gown. More importantly for Diana she would be seen mingling with the rich and the powerful to illustrate that they accepted her as a royal ambassador.

Some queried whether Diana wanted to be accepted more as an ambassador of "swank," New York's favorite fashion word for winter 1995. Diana understood that postfeminism seemed to be gaining ground fast on the East Coast, that "glam" had returned, and even fur sales had increased 20 percent, so she decided to wear more mascara, more expensive jewelry, and daringly, show much more cleavage than usual. New York's finest seemed to appreciate the Jacques Azagury couture dress in double silk georgette as well as the stately curves she revealed, the embroidered sequin lace bodice specifically made to fit Diana's 36B figure.

To achieve the eye-popping décolletage, which she hoped would be admired in New York, the bodice was stitched from separate pieces of silk, lined with layers of cotton to keep it stiff and shape her figure. The secret lay in four plastic "bones," two at the front and two at the back, stitched behind the silk crêpe de chine lining. The front bones, bent manually into the required shape, act like a brassiere, pushing the breasts forward and upward.

Dr. Kissinger, the former U.S. secretary of state, greeted

her with a bow and then two kisses, not sure where to cast his eyes. He praised her "luminous personality" and said, "She is here as a member of the Royal Family. But we are honoring the Princess in her own right, having aligned herself with the ill, the suffering, and the downtrodden."

But the enthusiasm and heady sense of achievement that Diana felt in late 1995 would be sorely tested over the following months. As the days and weeks passed, the number of critics would increase and the doubts would come not only from staunch monarchists and friends of Prince Charles, but from the general public, once they had found the time to examine, discuss, and dissect the interview.

One of the first Establishment bibles to openly attack Diana would be *Country Life*, the landed gentry's favorite magazine, which condemned her TV appearance as "a deplorable broadcast." An astonishing editorial, read mainly by the hunting, fishing, and shooting set, described her suggestion that Charles might not be king as "ludicrous" and "tragic." The editorial dismissed as "impertinence" her claim that she would like to be "the queen of people's hearts" and compared her to Helen of Troy, another "beautiful but destructive woman."

Others pointed out that Diana's *Panorama* account of her many personal problems displayed distress, unhappiness, impulsiveness, and loneliness, coupled with an enormous desire to be loved. It had also revealed a remarkable degree of self-obsession, a lack of insight and of remorse, a determination to achieve her ends without regard to the consequences for others.

In particular, she would be condemned for inflicting damage on her sons by her ruthless interview. The revelations of slashing her arms and legs, her gorging and vomiting, and having sex with Hewitt in her own bed were considered abhorrent for William, thirteen, and Harry, eleven, in their vulnerable teenage years. As one writer put it, "She has given lethal ammunition to school bullies who will surely now taunt the two boys."

And in the case of William, some commentators asked whether Diana had been wise to support her son so openly by seemingly trying to set him against his father as a future contender for the throne. They feared that Diana's deliberate act of spite against Charles could easily provide the makings of a family vendetta that could continue for twenty years or however long Queen Elizabeth reigns.

The interview raised a plethora of views and attitudes, almost dividing the nation into two diametrically opposed camps: for and against the Princess.

Those championing women's causes were adamant that the most important thing about Diana's interview was that she had given countless silent women a voice, claiming that her painful eloquence had proffered hope to thousands of victims. Diana has never seen herself as a revolutionary, but never before has a woman in her position articulated personal pain so openly. The immediate result was that she had mobilized an army of supporters. She had spoken publicly about her isolation within her marriage and within the Royal Family, explaining that her bulimia had seemed like a friend in her traumatic state, just as tens of thousands of other bulimia victims have felt in their isolation.

Above all, feminists admired her strength in challenging the Royal Family's determination to represent her mutiny as madness. Charles's friends had branded Diana "unstable" and a "loose cannon," prone to alarming episodes of depression and self-destructiveness. But in the aftermath of her interview that argument was discarded by the vast majority of ordinary women who understood her pain. They believed Diana's public protest because they knew that thousands of women have been sent to the asylum and to solitary confinement and recognized that the Establishment had been locking up women unfairly for centuries.

But Diana had decided not to go quietly. She broke the vow of silence that is the Establishment's secret weapon. On this occasion, Diana had not used her beauty to call the Establishment and more particularly the Royal Family to account, but her stamina and strength of character.

Polls and much other evidence suggested the public lined up

overwhelmingly behind Diana, but the distinctions in the kind
of support she received depended on class, income, sex, age,
and temperament. Broadly speaking, the great bulk of the
working class supported Diana. Class is still very much alive in
Britain, though many think it is no longer a significant aspect
of British society.

The officer class support Prince Charles to a man; the
noncommissioned officers and privates are behind Diana. The
middle class, now representing perhaps 65 percent of the
British people, are divided, the older citizens backing royalty
whatever happens, the younger ones understanding and supporting Diana and her demand for more space. Most in Britain
take one side or the other, and the talk in the pubs and cafes, at
dinner tables and the clubs, resounds with debate. The argument has occupied everybody's attention and seems unlikely to
be resolved for a long time.

Within weeks of her interview the Establishment were
sorrowfully shaking their heads and suggesting that any formal
ambassadorial role for the Princess of Wales would have to be
"limited" amid fears that she could find herself embroiled in
political controversy overseas. Britain's infamous lobby system—whereby the views of the prime minister and other senior
ministers are daily given on a nonattibutable basis to a coterie of
political journalists—had churned into gear.

Prime Minister John Major, who has openly supported
Diana, would discuss Diana's possible ambassadorial role with
the Queen during his regular Tuesday-evening meetings.
However, John Major would find himself agreeing with the
Queen that it would be "unfair" to place Diana in a position
where she was expected to speak for Britain on politically
sensitive issues. One unnamed minister went so far as to say,
behind the cloak of anonymity, "We could not trust her with a
political brief."

And other "facts" began to emerge, seemingly by chance, in
newspaper and magazine articles. If one simply glanced at the
British media during the last ten years, it would appear that
Princess Diana had been virtually the only Royal visiting

hospitals, opening care centers, chatting to the sick, the homeless, and the disadvantaged of society. Suddenly, establishment newspapers and magazines began to draw attention, wherever possible, to work carried out by other Royals, putting Diana's work in some perspective.

In all the deliberations over Diana's future the public's abiding impression has been of a determined, compassionate woman fighting her way through a labyrinth of protocol while battling against the Establishment to bring love to the needy, while her estranged in-laws indulge themselves in selfish isolation in Buckingham Palace.

Diana told the nation in her *Panorama* interview of the British public's need for "someone in public life to give affection, to make them feel important, to support them, to give them light in their dark tunnels." The rest of the Royal Family agrees, for that reasoning lies behind the thousands of public engagements, many of them associated directly with charities, that they carry out each year. The difference is that Diana's glamor and natural touch mean that her appearances will generate photographs and national headlines while an identical engagement by the Duchess of Kent would be lucky to make it beyond the local paper.

On the very day Diana held the world stage on *Panorama*, the Queen, Prince Philip, and Prince Charles were playing host to King Hussein and Queen Noor of Jordan; Princess Margaret was opening a Scottish lighthouse museum; the Duke and Duchess of Gloucester embarked on an official visit to Mexico; the Duke of Kent visited the Devonshire and Dorset Regiment in Germany; Princess Alexandra visited the Imperial Cancer Research Fund. Princess Anne, whose age and charitable interests come closest to those of Diana, was in Scotland as president of the Princess Royal Trust for Carers, which has projects costing $15 million throughout Britain. Not one of those events apparently merited more than a line in a national newspaper.

None of that worries Diana. She has set out her ambitions and is determined, come what may, to become a royal ambassador, visiting charities throughout the world, caring for people in her brilliant, inimitable manner. For her work she will rightly win a thousand plaudits and, more importantly, will finally have found a purpose to her life.

Within days of her TV spectacular, Diana boasted openly to a number of journalists traveling with her on the flight to Argentina, "I believe that through my TV interview I have finally won my independence."

Others would not be too sure. To achieve that the Princess of Wales may find she has to quit Britain and live elsewhere. Close friends wonder whether Diana would really want to live thousands of miles from the two most important people in her life, her sons. It would be a heartrending choice. But thirty years ago her mother faced the same dilemma—and left.

# 21

# Diana Unbowed

❦

PRINCESS DIANA IS FEARFUL of the future. And because she has
no confidence in what the future holds for her, she is confused
and uncertain of the path she should tread in her personal life.
She knows she needs a new challenge, a new job and she
believes that taking on the role of a royal ambassador would not
only give her the launching pad she needs to start a new life but
also a feeling of belonging, of being wanted. But today the grief
of her failed marriage still haunts her, and the hurt won't go
away though she has lived a separate life from Charles for nearly
ten years.

She had learned to cope with her isolation, for she still had
an identity as the Princess of Wales and the mother of the heirs
to the throne. She had successfully conquered bulimia and took
pride in becoming a really fit, healthy woman who could still
draw adoring crowds, demand the attention of most men and
the front covers of the world's glossy magazines.

The demand from Charles for a separation that she never
wanted hurt her more than she realized. But that demand could
not compare to the savage blow she felt when she opened the
letter from Elizabeth in December 1995, all but ordering her to
divorce "as soon as possible." Diana had not been prepared for
the Queen's urgent request and found life increasingly difficult
to cope with. She found herself breaking down, unable to stop
the tears that came for no apparent reason. Sometimes, to her
great embarrassment, even in public.

One night in early January 1996, Diana left the home of Susie Orbach after an hour-long therapy session and began walking toward her car. She had seen the paparazzi and wondered who had tipped them off that she was there. To the most photographed woman in the world, the sight of four photographers, their flashes lighting up the scene, usually caused her not the slightest concern. But this time she felt awkward, not wanting them to intrude on her every movement. She tried to smile but found she couldn't. All of a sudden Diana realized she was about to burst into tears and put up the book she was carrying to shield her face from the cameras.

To escape their attention, she ran toward her car, but the photographers ran after her, eager to capture the Princess of Wales crying, the tears streaming down her face. Suddenly she felt like a wild animal, trapped, with nowhere to hide, no way of escape.

As she reached her car, the tears really flowed, coursing down her cheeks. She couldn't find the strength to climb into the vehicle but stood leaning against it for a full minute, her shoulders shaking. She felt exhausted and forlorn and very, very lonely, hoping the photographers would stop their whirring cameras and leave her to cry in peace. But the torment would continue until she found the strength to open the car door, climb inside, and drive away into the night. It was one of Diana's most traumatic and public displays of emotion.

That night Diana felt betrayed by whoever had tipped off the paparazzi that she would be visiting Susie Orbach for the third time since Christmas, 1995. For some years Diana had felt that at least one or two of her staff were guilty of revealing her schedules to the media. At lunches during 1995 to which she would invite editors and senior journalists from Britain's national press and the media, Diana would ask them to tell her if they knew of the identity of the staff informants. She would say, "You have no idea how awful it is to have no private life whatsoever. And you must understand that it is terribly unfair on me and my sons. I can only appeal to you to put a stop to this sort of thing."

Most of the editors and senior journalists would nod in agreement and say they understood her predicament. But the phone calls did not cease and the paparazzi would continue to know nearly all of her movements every minute of the day. Forlornly, Diana would comment to her friend the London banker, "I hoped the editors might help but I suppose I was being naive. The trouble is that all they want to do is sell newspapers. But I do wish they would give me a break sometimes."

But in the first months of 1996, Diana had to face an even more vital problem—her divorce. At first, she decided not to take the slightest notice of the Queen's demand for an early divorce but to leave all the details to her lawyer, Anthony Julius of Mischon De Reya. She was in no hurry. She preferred to wait and see whether the Queen would grant her permission to become a royal ambassador. Diana suspected that the Queen had issued her statement so soon after Diana's public demand for the job of royal ambassador because she had seen an opportunity to force through a divorce in return for giving permission for Diana to become some sort of high-profile international charity worker.

"They might think I'm a fool," Diana would say, "but I know their game. It's as plain as a pike staff. Well, if they want me out of the way that much, they might have to pay for it."

But the going became tougher. She found herself becoming more prone to mood swings, which now seemed to affect her most days. For no apparent reason she would find herself in tears or screaming in anger at one of her staff. She also found that she was forever changing her mind. One day she would happily tell her loyal secretary, Patrick Jephson, that she intended to comply with all the demands for her divorce so the matter could be over and done with as soon as possible. The next day she would countermand her decision, telling him to have nothing whatsoever to do with the matter, even ordering him not to reply to her own solicitor's letters. And such changes of mind did not only occur with Jephson but with most of her staff, quite often over totally unimportant, irrelevant matters such as what to wear or eat for lunch.

Jephson found the situation so bizarre it was almost impossible for him to continue working at the palace. He wanted to
carry on as Diana's secretary because he realized that she would
need support and advice as details of the divorce settlement were
thrashed out. But he began to realize that his advice was not
being taken by Diana, that she seemed to be listening to other
voices, other advisers. By the end of January 1996 he could take
no more. He talked to Diana, telling her his job had become
impossible because she would not make up her mind and stick
to any decision she had previously made. Before he had
completed his argument, Diana interrupted, telling him that he
could be relieved of his duties forthwith. She simply turned and
left the room with no further remark, no pleasantries.

Always the gentleman, the former Royal Navy officer
issued a statement: "It has been a great honour to work for the
Princess of Wales, and I have very much enjoyed the challenges
of the last eight years. With a growing family [he has two
young children] however, I feel that I must now be free to
consider a new career path." He added that he had always
planned to step down sometime during 1996, but most royal
watchers noted that Jephson did not have another job.

Forty-eight hours later, Nicki Cockell, thirty-two, the most
senior of Diana's three secretaries—in palace terminology, lady
clerks—handed in her resignation. Nicki Cockell was responsible for the Princess of Wales's most important correspondence
and running the small office that is situated in the Court of St.
James's, two hundred yards from Buckingham Palace. Ironically, the office is next door to that occupied by Prince
Charles's office staff. But Charles's Duchy of Cornwall, which
makes profits from housing, real estate, land, and agriculture,
pays the wage bill for all Diana's employees. No statement was
issued, but Buckingham Palace press officers suggested that
Ms. Cockell had found her position "untenable" following the
resignation of Patrick Jephson.

Hours later, a third member of Diana's dwindling band of
employees quit. Steve Davis, thirty-two, her handsome chauf-

feur for just two years, announced that he would be leaving. Davis let it be known that he had been reviewing his position for some time and was understood to be negotiating a payoff. But Diana was not in the least unhappy that Davis had decided to quit, for the relationship between Davis and his employer had become somewhat strained during the past twelve months. Davis had found his job had become all but redundant during the past year as Diana would drive herself around London on most occasions, only requiring Davis to chauffeur her when out shopping or attending a charity function.

Before Diana announced her withdrawal from public life in December 1993, her team included a private secretary, an equerry, two detectives, three secretaries, a butler, a house-keeper, a cook, a chauffeur, a dresser, and a rota of ladies-in-waiting. By late January 1996, Diana employed just two secretaries, Angela Hordern and Victoria Mendham; Paul Bur-rell, who acts as butler and housekeeper; Darren "Shady" McGrady, her cook; and Helen Walsh, her dresser. With so few public engagements, a lady-in-waiting is asked to attend only occasional events.

"Just another changing of the guard," Diana quipped when asked why everyone was deserting her. But her flip reply concealed a worried woman, for she hated to think that she had been responsible for her staff leaving her. It made her feel yet more lonely and unloved.

After the Queen's demand for an early divorce, Diana had come to some conclusions as to what she would demand in her settlement. She was determined to keep the title "Princess," and though she recognized that she could not continue to be "Her Royal Highness, the Princess of Wales," she still wished to be known officially as "Her Royal Highness, Princess Diana," although she was certain the Queen would not allow her to keep the title.

She would demand either a substantial London mansion, costing perhaps $5 million or, as a permanent arrangement, the apartments she now uses at Kensington Palace. She also de-

manded another house in the country, a large country estate
with land, costing perhaps another $5 million.

The Royal Protection Squad encouraged the Queen and her
aides to permit Diana to remain in her Kensington Palace
apartments because her security and that of the two princes
could be more efficiently managed. With the IRA renewing
their bombing campaign, and targeting members of the Royal
Family, in February 1996 security had once again become all
important. For the same reason senior police officers did not
want Diana and the princes to be given another home in the
country, fearing they could become an IRA target.

Diana told her solicitor Anthony Julius to demand a tax-
free, personal annual income of $2 million a year after all
expenses on the understanding that the upkeep of her homes,
staff salaries, cars, and all ancillary expenses would be met by
the Duchy of Cornwall, Prince's Charles's private estate. She
also demanded that all costs relating to Wills and Harry,
including their education, clothing, and holidays should be met
by Charles.

Most important, she demanded the settlement be guaran-
teed for her lifetime, whether she remarries or not.

Diana recognized that the question of custody of Wills and
Harry is quite different from that of any other British children
caught up in their parents' divorce settlement because they are
heirs to the throne. Diana accepted that as heirs to the throne
they are the responsibility of the monarch who has jurisdiction
over them.

Diana, for example, understands that she would not be
permitted to take Wills and Harry out of the country except
with the express permission of the Queen and, after her death,
King Charles. She knows, and accepts, that she would never be
permitted to live abroad with her sons.

However, Charles and Diana agreed that the arrangements
for access to the children, which have been in force since the
separation, will continue. They are both determined that their
divorce should have as little effect as possible on the two boys

and that Wills and Harry should see both parents as frequently as possible.

The Queen instructed her lawyers Farrer & Co. to include a clause in the divorce settlement that Diana must agree never to write, speak, or communicate any further information concerning the monarchy, the House of Windsor, Prince Charles, Wills and Harry, her marriage, or her divorce settlement. The Queen is determined to do everything possible to prevent another BCC *Panorma*-type debacle.

The Queen wanted Diana removed from the House of Windsor so that the full focus of attention could once again be trained on Prince Charles, as it was before Diana came on the scene in 1979. She knows that rebuilding the nation's respect and admiration for the monarchy will be a long, hard process, but she is a most patient woman, and a most determined one.

The Queen realized only too well that Diana will still be holding center stage, still grabbing the headlines, and will probably remain the most popular Royal for many years to come. She also understood the damage the Princess of Wales had inflicted on the monarchy during the past few years. Today, one-third of all voters believe the monarchy to be irrelevant, and more than half want to see less pomp, ceremony, and lavish lifestyles.

During her sixteen-year reign as Princess of Wales, Diana has caused the greatest upsurge of pride and passion in the British Royal Family. But in the latter years she has also inflicted severe wounds to the reputation of Prince Charles, to Queen Elizabeth, and to the monarchy itself. For that she will never be forgiven.

Diana was as eager to be rid of the House of Windsor as every member of that family wanted to be rid of her. But Diana never wanted to be forced out of the family, as she has surely been. She wanted no separation; she wanted no divorce; she wanted to remain a part of a family with her beloved Wills and Harry. Abandoned, she faced the future as a royal outcast with no family and very few friends.

# 22

## The People's Princess

———— ❦ ————

DURING THE SCHOOL SUMMER HOLIDAYS of 1996 Wills and Harry were watching television at home with their mother. They were in the lovely, sunny drawing room overlooking Kensington Palace Gardens when a news bulletin flashed on the screen showing young children maimed by land mines in Angola.

"Mummy, look at this," said William, then fourteen. Diana came over to view the screen. "Isn't that terrible. Why do they leave mines around for children to tread on?"

At first Diana wasn't sure how she should answer that question, but as she watched she, too, felt anger as the TV reporter talked of the hundreds of thousands of mines left by armies in Angola, Afghanistan, Cambodia, and Bosnia.

"They should pick them up after any war," she told William.

"Why don't they?" he asked with the naïveté and innocence of a teenager.

"Usually," Diana replied, "because the armies don't map out exactly where they lay the mines, and when the war is over the mines are just left in the ground."

"But that's awful," William said. "That's cruel. It shouldn't be allowed."

Diana told that story to many people during the final year of her life, for her son's recognition of the ghastly, horrifying effects of the indiscriminate laying of land mines made her realize that, if possible, the production and laying of antipersonnel mines should be stopped.

It was the beginning of a campaign which Diana swore she would not end until all the major nations of the world which manufactured and sold these mines, including America, Britain, France, and Germany, agreed at the very least to ban their production and sale to third-world countries. She would say, "I will go anywhere in the world, I will talk to anyone if it means the banning of those awful mines. I owe it not only to my children but to every child in the world who has died, been maimed, or lost a limb because he accidentally stepped on one of these vicious weapons."

Diana asked her secretary to find out details and to gather as much information as possible from any charities actively working to rid the world of antipersonnel mines. And then, in her inimitable way, she set to work.

But Diana was learning. On many occasions in the past she recalled the obstacles placed in her way to prevent her sponsoring some charity or other. When Diana decided to throw her weight behind support for AIDS victims back in the late 1980s, there were those who cautioned her against it.

With a flick of her head, Diana would say, "They tried to stop me," and she was referring to those nameless, faceless advisers to the Queen. "They don't believe that I should help AIDS victims. They think it is not the *right* type of charity for a princess of royal blood to support." Almost spitting out the words, Diana went on: "They tried to talk me out of the idea. They tried to explain that AIDS was principally a disease caught by homosexual men until I told them all about AIDS, pointing out that many heterosexual men and women caught the disease from needles and other people."

Diana ignored the advice and won acclaim throughout the world for bringing compassion and humility to the lives of those dying from HIV and AIDS-related illnesses, and she continued to do so until her death. But now she realized that to achieve a worldwide ban on the production and sale of land mines she needed heavy political support. She turned to Elizabeth Dole, head of the Red Cross and the wife of Robert Dole, former U.S. senator and the one-time Republican candidate for president. She had been running such a campaign for some years. They talked on the phone, and Diana said she was only too willing to do anything that would help.

Together, Diana and Elizabeth Dole became a formidable team. And in January 1997, Diana visited Angola and posed for pictures with pitiful children maimed by mines, pictures that were reproduced in newspapers around the world. Pictures flashed across the world showing Diana comforting and nursing land mine victims, and the very fact that she was now openly pushing for a ban brought a renewed demand from ordinary people to join the campaign. Almost overnight, politicians in all the major nations producing and selling arms realized they had a battle on their hands. Diana wasn't the only person campaigning for a ban, but the world's most loved and admired woman had now become the focus of the global movement to rid the world of antipersonnel mines.

And in August 1997, only three weeks before her death, Diana interrupted her summer holiday to fly to Bosnia to continue the campaign. Once again Diana was using her political common sense. She knew that talks pushing for a ban would be resumed among politicians from many countries in September 1997, with the hope that the conference scheduled in Ottawa for December 1997 would bring about a treaty banning mines. In Bosnia she visited one of Sarajevo's largest cemeteries. As she toured the cemetery, she came across a young woman standing in prayer at the grave of her child, a land mine victim. Diana, who could not speak the woman's language, slowly walked up to her and placed her hands on the woman's shoulders, comforting her. There was no need for words. The young Muslim mother looked up into Diana's eyes, and both shed tears.

On other occasions during that visit, the last duty she would ever perform, Diana would hold people, both young and old. She would comfort them simply by holding their hands or stroking their faces, showing she cared, sharing their grief in a most remarkable manner. She wasn't posing for photo opportunities or exploiting the injured and their relatives; her motives were entirely innocent, concerned only with bringing some understanding to those bereaved and maimed by their terrible wounds. And to the people it showed. Such scenes during those three days embodied Diana's attitude throughout her short life. "I am a humanitarian," she would say in all innocence. "I always have been, and I always will be."

In those words Diana laid down her own epitaph, for that, above all else, is what she really thought about herself.

During her tour of Bosnia's battlefields and graveyards, Diana talked to the relatives of many victims and heard harrowing tales. She saw dreadful wounds, heard horrifying stories, and yet managed to maintain the demeanor of a professional but sympathetic nurse. And throughout those few days of intense and heartrending moments Diana never lost her concentration. She had become a professional at bringing hope and compassion to people from all walks of life, but she principally brought her touch of magic to the disadvantaged and ordinary people who needed someone to lift their spirits, which Diana did with gentleness and understanding.

From the moment Diana learned that she was officially divorced—in July 1996—it seemed that she had come to terms with her new role in life. She had more spring in her step and showered her boys with even more affection and warmth than before. "I think they need me now more than ever," she would say disarmingly, "and I need them, too."

Diana's frailty and vulnerability no longer seemed to worry her as it had during those early years when she appeared so shy in anyone's company. "I just want to curl up and die," she would say when she walked into a room full of dignitaries and their wives, who would turn en masse and inspect her from head to toe, checking not only the clothes she was wearing but also her demeanor, her mood.

"They make me feel so small," Diana would complain to friends, "and some of them look at me as though I'm not good enough to be married to the Prince of Wales. At first I tried to be kind and considerate to them, to understand their jealousy,

but in the end I knew it was impossible to win them over. On
occasions, when I left a group of them, they would immediately
begin talking about me in voices loud enough for me to hear.
And not many of the things they said were complimentary."

But in the two years before her death, a new Diana
emerged, a young woman who was more challenging and more
confident. She said of her sons, "They make me feel wonderful.
They give me confidence, tell me I look great, and, sometimes,
give me funny looks when they see me in something they don't
like." She would ask them, "Shall I not wear that again?
Usually William would be kind, saying that I didn't look too
bad in the outfit. Harry would be more brutal, often answering
no and adding, 'I think it would be better if you didn't wear that
again, Mummy.'

"I loved them for their honesty and their openness, because I
want them to grow up able to look people in the eye and feel
proud that they are not bound by protocol, tradition, and
bullshit!"

And yet in her private world Diana still suffered from a lack
of confidence. On weekends she would telephone friends,
asking, in a tentative manner, what they were doing, hoping
that one of them would suggest getting together so that she
didn't have to spend Friday night through Monday morning
alone in the confines of Kensington Palace, watching television
and videos or flicking through magazines.

She would often stand at her drawing room window on
Saturday or Sunday looking out across the acres of Kensington
Palace Gardens and watching families enjoying themselves,
mothers pushing prams, children out with their parents, and
couples sauntering along hand in hand. Those were the weekends when her boys were at boarding school or spending time
with Prince Charles; times when she felt the bitterness of
loneliness, and the desolation of a life on her own.

And then there were the weekends when Diana had the
boys, particularly during the school holidays when she wanted
to escape from the confines of the palace with Wills and Harry.
But Diana was not like any other mother, nor, unfortunately,

were her sons like any other sons. She had tried to make their lives as normal as possible by taking them for a burger at the nearby McDonald's, a walk away from Kensington Palace, and making them stand in line. She had occasionally taken them to the cinema and again insisted they stand in line like everyone else. She took them to adventure parks, zoos, museums, and art galleries, walking around like everyone else, seeking no privileges. But the task was becoming increasingly difficult because people would stop and stare, point and make remarks, walk up and talk to them, and small knots of people would gather, exactly the opposite of what Diana wanted for her Wills and Harry.

"Why can't people leave us alone," Diana would plead in frustration to her friends, although she knew the answer. "It's me, isn't it?" she would say, and a look of depression would sweep across her face because she was feeling guilty that she was unable to bring up her sons the way she wanted, providing as normal a childhood as possible. But she knew that later in their life they would be constrained by the chains of royalty.

Annabel Goldsmith was a friend of Diana's for a number of years, with children older than William and Harry. She often entertained Diana and the boys at lunch or tea following the separation from Charles. She said, "The phone would ring often on a Friday afternoon, and a shy Diana would first of all ask how I was and what was happening in my life and in the children's lives. After a few minutes of small talk she would ask what we were doing for the weekend, and I knew immediately that she wanted somewhere to go, to take the boys, to find a haven where there would be privacy and fun for them. We were always happy to have them over, for it was always such fun, the children enjoying themselves, messing around, rushing around, playing together,. sometimes arguing like other children anywhere in the world. And Diana would muck in like any other mother, helping to prepare the meal, checking whether the children were all well fed, and helping to clean up afterward. What I remember of those days was the fun and the laughter and seeing the real Diana enjoying herself as naturally as any mother, laughing and smiling and joking with everyone, and totally without side, behaving perfectly naturally."

Many people who saw Diana in such circumstances during the last year felt that she had adapted to life outside the Royal Family and was learning to cope with single motherhood. She would on occasion complain of her solitude, of being without a man with whom she could share the ordinary joys, someone to talk to, a shoulder to cry on, and someone to bring laughter into her solitary existence. She sought solace with William and Harry. She adored the time she spent with them, the moments she described "as the most precious of her life."

At Eton, William was maturing fast, and in their last year together, Diana found him, like all fourteen-year-olds, desperate to grow up and become a man. It seemed that William was coping well, indeed enjoying life at school, and though a few foreign paparazzi had invaded his privacy while at Eton, snapping shots of him whenever he ventured outside the confines of the school, he had managed to deal with them quite well. And he had the total support of his friends, who, given the opportunity, would chase the paparazzi and threaten to throw stones at them or smash their cameras if they dared to impinge on William's privacy. At times, discovering and chasing paparazzi became something of a game, but his friends believed it their duty to protect their pal, the heir to the throne.

Naturally, Diana's relationship with William was changing, and they would discuss and sometimes argue points on a range of topics. William loved to have grown-up conversations with his mother, but when with other people he would usually confine himself to a quip or an odd remark, usually intended as a joke. Diana liked that.

But young Harry, still at Ludgrove, his preparatory boarding school, missed his mother and would sometimes become homesick. When home Harry still loved to be cuddled by Diana. It seemed he needed the physical contact with her. Though in his twelfth year, he would sit next to her watching television or when she was reading a book with him, and he didn't like returning to school after a weekend with his mother, though he would always try to stop himself from crying.

And then there was always the great bane of her life, the ever-present paparazzi and the tabloid journalists who would watch her every move, following her on their motorbikes and scooters, working as a team with their mobile phones, making sure she could not escape their tentacles, no matter how hard she tried.

Diana was determined to enjoy the summer holidays of 1997 with the boys. She discussed plans with them, and William, who for years had been bitter about the constant media attention toward his mother, was keen that they should escape to a hideaway where no paparazzi could find them. As a result, when the offer came from Mohamed Al Fayed, the millionaire owner of Harrods, the Knightsbridge department store, to loan them his villa in St. Tropez in southern France and unlimited use of his luxury yacht, *Jonikal,* Diana was more than happy to accept his hospitality and his generosity.

Mohamed Al Fayed had known Diana's father, Earl Spencer, slightly, and following his death had invited Diana's step-mother, Raine Spencer, daughter of the novelist Barbara Cart-land, to become a member of the Harrods International board of directors. He had suggested to Raine that his eldest son, Dodi, would be available in St. Tropez if Diana or her sons required any assistance.

Diana and the boys had always enjoyed their beach holidays until the summer of 1996, when photographers tracked them down and kept them pinned in their villa, not even able to venture out for a swim in the pool or a stroll on the grounds, because the photographers staking out the villa shot pictures constantly whenever they left the privacy of the house. The photographers totally ruined the holiday for Diana, and even more so for Wills and Harry. They totally disregarded their privacy in the most outrageous fashion and, even when asked, refused to stop taking pictures.

The constant media pressure during that two-week period

angered William to such an extent that Diana decided to break off their holiday and return home to Kensington Palace. As a direct result of that invasion of their privacy William would react with great ferocity and venom at the death of his mother twelve months later.

Diana calmed William's fears with the news that their holiday retreat in St. Tropez was not only well hidden but would also be patrolled by Mr. Al Fayed's security staff, who would make sure no photographers would get within a mile of the villa. Having just passed three difficult school examinations, William was in a positive mood when they set off for their holiday in the Mediterranean sun. Harry was looking forward to spending time with his mother and in the pool.

It was while on holiday in St. Tropez that Dodi Fayed entered Diana's life.

Dodi Fayed was born in Alexandria, Egypt, in April 1955, the son of Mohamed Al Fayed and Samira Kashoggi, sister of the world-famous arms dealer and billionaire Adnan Kashoggi. Adnan laid the foundation of the Fayed fortune by putting Mohamed in charge of his furniture interests in Saudi Arabia. When Dodi was only two years old, however, his parents separated, and he was to lead a rootless life, educated in various boarding schools in Switzerland with homes in France and Egypt and holidays spent on yachts in various Mediterranean harbors.

Dodi, whose given name was Emad, spent two years at Sandhurst, Britain's military academy for officers, and served for a short while in the air force of the United Arab Emirates, but the military was not for Dodi. The life of an international playboy beckoned, and he had the support of his wealthy, doting father. He dabbled in movie production, and among his credits as a producer are *Chariots of Fire* (1981), the pop music film *Breaking Glass* (1980), and *The World According to Garp* (1982).

And Dodi, with his spectacular array of classic autos, including Ferraris and Rolls-Royces, dated some of the most beautiful and alluring women in the world, including Brooke

Shields, the model Marie Helvin, Patsy Kensilt, Princess Stephanie of Monaco, the singer Linsey de Paul, and Koo Stark, who had once dated Prince Andrew. His only sortie into marriage was in 1986, when he wed the model Suzanne Gregard. Eight months later they were divorced, and Suzanne was believed to have received a $1.5 million settlement.

Dodi had never met William or Harry, but they had no reason to question why this stranger was sharing their retreat, staying in the Fisherman's Cottage near the beach, about one hundred yards from the main house. Diana had introduced him as the owner of the pink-washed villa, the Castel de St. Thérèse, and of the yacht *Jonikal,* which he had put at their disposal for the duration of their Mediterranean holiday.

And Dodi was fun to be around. Fit, athletic, and with a constant smile on his face, he was good holiday company for both William and Harry. Here was someone who let his hair down, would spend time in the pool fooling around, having fun, and encouraging the boys in whatever they wanted to do. And yet he was also quiet, never demanding or argumentative. Instead of telling the boys what to do he offered gentle encouragement. Diana liked that. He had no children of his own, but both William and Harry seemed to enjoy his company.

They would often have lunch together under the sun shades on the patio still dressed in their swimming trunks. Diana would usually wear a sarong over her bikini or swimsuit. She would invite Dodi to join them. The talk was usually fast and furious, and the boys would gobble up their food in minutes before returning to the pool once again. Their holiday would be truly informal, something they enjoyed, and so very different from their boarding schools and life at Balmoral, which they found stiff, formal, and very boring. And they loved being aboard the *Jonikal,* for, with Dodi and his crew, the two boys were allowed to run riot, so unlike the times they were aboard the royal yacht H.M.S. *Brittania,* when they would always have to behave impeccably, walking around the decks, sitting properly and dressing correctly for breakfast, lunch, and din-

ner. On *Brittania,* there were no al fresco, casual dress meals.
And the boys were forbidden to go below to chat with the crew.
On *Jonikal* they were free to roam the yacht and do as they
pleased.

On her return from St. Tropez, Diana would tell her
friends, "That was the best holiday I have ever had. It was
wonderful, and the boys had a great time."

A few days after returning from St. Tropez, a chauffeur-
driven car arrived from St. James's Palace, Prince Charles's
London home, a stone's throw down the Mall from Buckingham Palace. The boys were excited, once again looking
forward to their holiday with their father in Scotland. Though
they always enjoyed being with Diana, both boys didn't like the
time they spent at Diana's apartment at Kensington Palace
because they felt imprisoned there, unable to enjoy any freedom
for fear of the hated paparazzi as well as the tourists who
frequented Kensington Palace Gardens, trying to get a glimpse
of Diana at home.

Diana went outside to the car with the boys to say goodbye
and, as usual on such occasions, kissed them on the cheek. She
was careful not to be too affectionate with them in public
because she knew that such displays embarrassed them, especially in front of their school friends. She wanted to hug and
kiss them goodbye but she nearly always managed to prevent
herself. Harry, on this occasion, however, threw his arms
around his mother's neck, all but pulling her to the ground with
his enthusiasm. As they drove away, they turned and waved
through the back window of the car. It was the last time they
would ever see their beloved mother.

As William and Harry journeyed north to spend a month
with their father and his parents, the Queen and Prince Philip,
at Balmoral Castle in Scotland, they had no idea that their
mother was contemplating taking another holiday alone with
Dodi, cruising the Mediterranean on board the *Jonikal.*

Both William and Harry thoroughly enjoyed their time
with Prince Charles in Scotland. They adored fishing in the
River Dee under his expert tuition, helped always by a friendly

gillie. They loved to ride their ponies, cantering across the thousands of acres with their father. And they enjoyed stalking the deer, spending all day walking miles through the heather and gorse, up hills and down valleys and criss-crossing the dozens of burns (streams) they would encounter. They also enjoyed shooting, though they knew their mother totally disapproved of the sport. As to their father, it didn't matter to them whether the weather was cold and raining or sunny and bright—they were attracted by the sheer enjoyment of the wild open spaces of the Scottish Highlands.

During Diana's second Mediterranean cruise with Dodi the two became lovers, enjoying seven days together, relishing the peace and tranquillity of slowly cruising the blue waters of the Mediterranean, swimming together in the sea, and spending their nights enjoying lovely food aboard the luxury yacht. They would sit and talk until the early hours, sometimes walking the decks still warm in the August heat before going to bed, then rising the next day for a late, intimate breakfast on deck. And, blissfully for Diana, for most of the cruise they were able to escape the pursuing paparazzi. Only once did a photographer manage to shoot some fuzzy pictures of the couple, but one was most revealing, showing them embracing and kissing. It was the proof the world wanted that Diana had a new man in her life.

Indeed, Dodi was more than "another" man in her life. Diana was falling in love. She would say later, "I have found the man who will look after me. Dodi is sweet and gentle and so loving. And I can't resist him. I find him attractive and so exciting."

Diana also realized that Dodi, with help from his wealthy father Mohamed, had the money to care for her. She understood only too well that she needed a man of substantial wealth to safeguard the privacy she yearned for but seldom managed to achieve. Dodi could provide security guards and safe havens, an apartment in Paris, a home in London, a secluded villa in the south of France, as well as a luxury yacht. And there was more. Dodi had the use of a private jet and a helicopter and a fleet of chauffeur-driven cars. Diana had always enjoyed luxury throughout her life, and everywhere she traveled with Dodi she would want for nothing.

As the tabloids realized that Dodi might be destined to play an important part in Diana's life, reporters began to look into the playboy's past. The inevitable media trawl threw up questions over a string of allegedly unpaid bills and taxes in the United States. An American model, Kelly Fisher, announced that she would sue Mr. Fayed, to whom she claimed she had been engaged, for breach of promise and distress, after he allegedly jilted her to pursue his friendship with Diana.

After grainy photographs of "the kiss" between Diana and Dodi circulated around the world, Diana threw caution to the wind. Now, all of a sudden, she was happy to reveal to everyone that she was seeing Dodi on every possible occasion, that she was staying with him in his apartments in London and Paris, dining with him in whichever capital city they were visiting. And she was even happy to be seen holding hands in public.

To many, such behavior would be normal and natural. But not to Diana. In the aristocratic world in which she grew up, such behavior would be tolerated only when couples became engaged or married, and though in private a blind eye was turned to every intimacy or loving caress, in public such overt loving tenderness was met with frowns and disapproval. Throughout her life Diana had hated and rebelled against such hypocrisy.

On Friday, August 29, 1997, Diana and Dodi had arrived on board the *Jonikal* at the Cala di Volpe, an Italian resort favored by some of Europe's richest families for its secluded position on the northeast coast of Sardinia. As they disembarked from the yacht's tender onto the resort's jetty, photographers in a small boat appeared with their cameras at the ready.

Diana and Dodi decided to go for a swim in a small secluded cove within the resort's private grounds, but the paparazzi, in a speedboat they hired to search for the couple, discovered them and began taking pictures. The crew of the

*Jonikal* tender approached the photographers, asking them to leave Diana and Dodi in peace and to stop taking pictures. One or two photographers refused to cooperate, and so the crew members blocked the view of the couple, making it impossible for the paparazzi to take any further pictures. That incident made the couple realize that they would get no peace on the Costa Smeralda, so they decided to fly to Paris for a final night together before returning to London.

Diana had planned to be back in London on Sunday because Wills and Harry were to spend a few days with her at Kensington Palace before their return to school that week. Instead of staying one more night on the *Jonikal,* shortly after lunch on Saturday the couple left for Paris from Olbia Airport near the resort in a Harrods Gulfstream IV jet.

Dodi had talked to Diana about the former Paris home of the late Duke and Duchess of Windsor in the Bois de Bologne, which his father leased for $6,000,000 and had spent $35,000,000 refurbishing. The mansion had private apartments on the top floor for the use of Mohamed Al Fayed's family and friends.

The casually dressed couple, looking bronzed, relaxed, and happy, arrived in Paris in midafternoon and were driven immediately to the Ritz. They would shop in the area while Diana searched for presents for the boys as she did whenever she returned to see them after an overseas trip. The paparazzi, however, had not given up the chase.

In Paris, photo agencies had been informed by their Italian photographers that Diana and Dodi had left Sardinia and, after phoning various Paris airport control towers, the agencies discovered that the Harrods Gulfstream was due to land at Le Bourget, outside Paris, that afternoon. When Diana and Dodi stepped onto the tarmac, the paparazzi were already there, clicking away. On the drive into the center of Paris, however, photographers in a black Peugeot swerved in front of the couple's Mercedes and braked hard, forcing them to slow down. This enabled the paparazzi on their motorbikes and scooters to catch up with the car and take pictures. Later, however, the Mercedes driver was able to lose the photographers, and Diana and Dodi arrived at the Ritz undetected and went upstairs to the Imperial Suite.

During the next hour Diana had her hair washed and styled in the suite, and around 6 P.M. the couple left the hotel and shopped together for an hour in the streets around the Champs Elysées, undetected by the paparazzi. It is not known what presents Diana bought for Wills and Harry, but it is known that Dodi slipped out of the hotel alone just before 7 P.M. to Repossi's, the exclusive jewelers near the Ritz, in search of a diamond ring that he and Diana had seen in Repossi's Monte Carlo branch when they stopped off in the principality for a few hours during their Mediterranean cruise. Later that evening, a ring was delivered to Dodi at the Ritz.

At around 7 P.M. Diana and Dodi left the hotel and traveled through the dense Paris traffic to Dodi's apartment off the Champs Elysées, a fifteen-minute drive from the Ritz. The paparazzi were waiting for them. Two hours later the couple left, once more captured on film, and they made their way back to the Ritz for a late dinner. Though some of the other diners that evening were blissfully unaware that the world's most photographed woman was sitting at a corner table near the back of the restaurant, other guests spent much of the time staring at them. After the main course, Diana became uncomfortable and the couple went upstairs to their suite to complete their meal.

The hotel staff made plans to distract the thirty or so photographers who had gathered outside the hotel. The strategy devised involved the use of a decoy car parked in the Place Vendôme, in hopes that the photographers would believe that the couple were still inside the building, allowing them to leave by a rear door onto the narrow Rue Cambon.

The paparazzi thought they had the couple cornered. This was a photograph they wanted: Diana and Dodi had never before been photographed together late at night. All the photographers present that night knew that a good photograph of the two of them together might earn them in excess of $1 million. They were aware that the famed photograph of "The Kiss" had earned one photographer around $5 million. The photographers would use their considerable resources to ensure that this picture did not escape them. That was why they split their forces that night, some guarding the rear entrance, always in contact through their mobile phones.

The paparazzi of Paris are well known for their persistence. They will often ride pillion on the back of a motorcycle driven by an expert rider, weaving in and out of the traffic, making sure they can keep up with the fastest cars. They will trail the French president or prime minister, snapping away as they draw up level with the official car to get the picture they want. On occasion, even television cameramen will ride pillion, standing on the pedals and leaning forward against the rider for support while they film the hunted victim.

At about thirty minutes past midnight on Sunday, August 31, Diana and Dodi emerged from the hotel's rear entrance while the decoy car at the front of the hotel sped off, taking with it some photographers. The couple stepped into the back of a black Mercedes 280SEL. Dodi looked around to see the photographers running toward the vehicle, and he held Diana close, so that her face could not be seen by the photographers. As a result of their embrace, neither Diana nor Dodi attached their seatbelts.

Dodi's personal security guard, a former British Army paratrooper, Trevor Rees-Jones, got into the passenger seat of the Mercedes and at some point in the short journey connected his seat belt. Fearing the paparazzi, Dodi asked the deputy head of security at the Ritz, Frenchman Henri Paul, a forty-one-year-old former member of the French navy, to take the wheel. Paul never bothered to attach his seatbelt. The car sped off as fast as possible down the Rue Cambon, heading south to the Rue de Rivoli. The paparazzi gave chase.

The traffic was thick, which made it difficult for Henri Paul to keep ahead of the pack of motorcyclists. He was able to speed a little around the vastness of the Place de la Concorde, next to the River Seine. To Diana's left, on the other side of the river, was the Eiffel Tower, enormous and brightly lit. To her right, the approach down the Champs Elysées, mapped out with lights on either side of the road like an airport runway, could be seen the Arc de Triomphe.

The Mercedes sped to the far side of the Place de la Concorde, one of the busiest traffic circles in Europe, and swooped at the southwest corner down the Cours de la Reine toward the road which runs along the Seine and leads to the underpass next to the Pont de l'Alma. Henri Paul saw his chance to increase the distance between his car and the pursuing photographers, and he put his foot flat to the floorboards of the Mercedes. The car, capable of speeds of up to 136 mph, responded, and within a few hundred yards, the Mercedes was traveling in excess of 120 mph. On that stretch of narrow, winding road leading to the Pont de l'Alma the speed limit is 37 mph.

Drivers entering the tunnel first veer toward the left before straightening out. The road has a slight camber, and there are no guardrails, only concrete posts on the driver's left side and a concrete wall on the right.

That night the driver Henri Paul had been drinking heavily. Police blood tests subsequently showed that his blood alcohol level was 172 milligrams per 100 milliliters of blood, three times higher than the French legal limit. Moreover, Monsieur Paul was also under the influence of two drugs that drivers are advised to treat with caution.

The French prosecutor's office said in an official statement that a search for toxic chemicals in M. Paul's blood had revealed "therapeutic levels of a medication whose active ingredient is fluoxetine, and subtherapeutic levels of a second drug whose active ingredient is tiapride." Fluoxetine is the active ingredient in Prozac, the commonly used antidepressant. Official guides to medicine say the drug has a number of side effects, including drowsiness, nervousness, anxiety, confusion, dizziness, thoughts of suicide, movement disorders, and violent behavior.

Tiapride, the drug found in "subtherapeutic" traces, is commonly prescribed to treat behavior disorders and involuntary twitching, as well as to manage acute alcohol withdrawal symptoms. Pharmaceutical journals state that this drug can alleviate distress, improve abstinence and drinking behavior, and facilitate reintegration within society following detoxification.

Exactly what occurred that night is not known for certain, but for some reason Henri Paul lost control of the car while traveling at high speed, crashed into the concrete pillar on his left, and then careening head on into the thirteenth concrete pillar. That second impact spun the car around 180 degrees and hurled it across to the other side of the road, where it smashed into the concrete wall before coming to a stop. The Mercedes was a tangled mass of steel, the roof caved in almost to the level of the hood.

· Dodi Fayed and Henri Paul, who were both on the left side of the vehicle, died instantly. Diana was severely injured, and Trevor Rees-Jones, a fit twenty-nine-year-old, though belted in, suffered internal injuries and severe facial injuries.

Diana was alive and may have been semiconscious as she lay sprawled on the backseat. At first it appeared that she was not badly injured, for her face was unharmed by the crash, and she seemed to be drifting in and out of consciousness, though confused and very agitated. The paparazzi were the first on the scene, leaping from their motorcycles and swarming around the Mercedes, desperate for pictures of the Princess and her lover.

One photographer wrenched open a door while others took pictures, another lay on the hood to get a better shot. Not one of the paparazzi bothered to call the police, ambulance, or fire brigade though all were equipped with mobile phones. When they had sufficient "quality" pictures some took off with their prized rolls of film while others stayed around to photograph the arrival of the emergency services and to take pictures of the injured Princess being removed from the wreckage and taken to the hospital.

Indeed, police called to the scene complained later that photographers had pushed them out of the way, demanding the right to take more photographs. Police later described the paparazzi actions that night as "virulent and disgusting," saying they had deliberately prevented the police officers from aiding the victims.

Dr. Frederic Mailliez, who was passing the crash scene on his way home from work and stopped to help, reported that Diana was unconscious, moaning and waving her arms about when he saw her. "First I helped free her respiratory tract, but her head was lying on her shoulder in a position in which you cannot breathe if you are unconscious, so I lifted her head and tried to help her breathe with oxygen."

One unnamed photographer claimed Diana had spoken a few words, saying, "Oh my God," and repeating twice, "Leave me alone, leave me alone." Surprisingly, the first official reports to reach Britain—ninety minutes after the crash—said that the Princess had suffered only a concussion, a broken arm, and cuts to her thigh.

Within fifteen minutes an ambulance arrived on the scene, and because it was understood that Diana had suffered a heart attack while lying in the wrecked car, the ambulance drove very slowly to La Pitié Salpétrière, a leading Paris hospital, requiring an hour to complete the journey.

Once examined by a team of doctors and surgeons, the severity of Diana's injuries rapidly became known. She was suffering from heavy blood loss, broken ribs, and multiple lacerations. Recovery from her main injury, a tear in the pulmonary vein, which carries freshly oxygenated blood from the lungs to the heart, is rare, and possible only through immediate hospital treatment. Even if her life had been saved, heart surgeons believe it is likely she would have suffered from permanent brain damage as a result of the loss of blood circulation.

First attempts to revive her by external heart massage took place at the scene of the accident, and she was unconscious when she arrived at the hospital. Once inside the hospital she suffered another heart attack and an urgent thorocotomy (surgical opening of the chest) revealed the major laceration to the left pulmonary vein. A patient who suffers such severe leakage in a major blood vessel often bleeds to death very quickly.

After establishing that Diana was suffering from internal bleeding, a team of up to twelve doctors carried out the thorocotomy through the breastbone to the left side of her chest, giving access to the heart and lungs. The surgeons found the leakage and repaired it. Throughout the operation Diana was given about twenty pints of blood and fluid, pumped into her as fast as possible. While surgeons worked to repair the laceration, others took turns pumping her heart manually, attempting to keep the blood flowing through her body.

Despite these heroic attempts to save her life, including two hours of internal and external heart massage, the doctors were unable to restore circulation and Diana, Princess of Wales was declared dead at 4 A.M. Paris time on Sunday, August 31.

Her death sent shock waves throughout the world. A stunned British public awoke on Sunday morning to the horrifying news, and many were unable to comprehend that the Princess, whom ordinary people had come to love and admire, was dead. In America and throughout Europe thousands who in some extraordinary way had felt close to the Princess, burst into tears when they heard the news. Never in the history of mankind had so many people reacted with such instant sorrow.

Within days, six photographers and a dispatch rider were charged with manslaughter and accused of failing to help the victims of an accident, charges which in France carry a maximum sentence on conviction of five years in prison and a fine of $75,000.

Prince Charles told William and Harry of the crash—and the death of their beloved mother—when they awoke the next morning, explaining that it had been a terrible accident. He then talked by phone to Diana's younger brother, Earl Spencer, at his home in South Africa. Charles agreed that no decisions would be made about Diana's funeral until Earl Spencer returned to London.

Charles flew from Scotland to Paris with Diana's elder sisters, Lady Jane Fellowes and Lady Sarah McCorquodale. Sarah had already visited Diana's home at Kensington Palace and selected a black Catherine Walker full-length dress for her burial gown. The three, accompanied by two government officials and bodyguards, flew in a Bae 146 plane of the Royal Squadron to the Villacoublay military airfield near Paris and drove under escort to the hospital. Diana was dressed there, and her body was placed in a coffin before the return flight to RAF Northolt outside London.

Even in death the Royal Family were bitterly divided over Diana and her funeral. The Duke of Edinburgh, Charles's father, was strongly opposed to a state funeral, arguing that Diana was no longer a member of the Royal Family and therefore did not have the right to a state funeral. Incredibly, he believed that Diana's body should not rest in a royal chapel at the Court of St. James's, Charles's London home, but in an ordinary mortuary in London.

Charles was incensed, and he angrily attacked his father for daring to treat Diana, his former wife and the mother of Wills and Harry, in such a despicable fashion. Philip tried to interrupt but Charles refused to let him speak, giving vent to his fury, telling his father in no uncertain terms that he would make the decisions and, in effect, telling him to hold his tongue. Prince Charles has never had a good relationship with his father, and the two have hardly spoken a word to each other for eighteen years, primarily because Philip is jealous of his eldest son, the heir to the throne. The Queen intervened, telling Charles that he should make the decisions about the funeral arrangements with Earl Spencer and senior palace advisers.

But the Royal Family were heavily criticized for not leading the nation in mourning. Belatedly, six days after Diana's death, the Queen was forced to react to the crescendo of public criticism as the media urged her to speak out on behalf of a grieving nation. Her live speech, the first in thirty-eight years, was received by most as a gesture "too little, too late." She did, however, say, "No one who knew Diana will ever forget her. Millions of others who never even met her, but felt they knew her, will remember her." But the Queen never mentioned the word *love,* the one word all wanted her to say of her former daughter-in-law.

People from all over the world flocked to London for Diana's funeral, many remembering her spectacular wedding at St. Paul's Cathedral in July 1981 when they had shed a tear, never imagining that sixteen years later they would openly weep at her funeral. They didn't come because Diana was a great person, or because they had respect for her station in life. Nor did they come because she had been a member of the Royal Family.

They came because she had managed to make them love and admire her for her good deeds and her informality and the compassion she showed to others less fortunate. They came to salute her and to thank her for bringing the attention of the world to the poor and the disadvantaged, to AIDS sufferers, lepers, orphans, cancer patients, and those maimed by land mines. And they brought their tears. Those who lined London's streets stood silent for most of the funeral, only the weeping and crying could be heard above the hushed silence that hung over the city. Over thirty million Americans and two and a half billion people worldwide watched as the cortege slowly moved toward Westminster Abbey. They were impressed by the two young princes who walked in the funeral procession, their heads bowed. With them was their father, Prince Charles, their uncle, Lord Spencer, and their grandfather, Philip.

The words of Earl Spencer, relayed over loudspeaker systems, caught the mood of the nation. Diana's brother spoke from the heart with a savagery that startled members of the Royal Family, politicians, and the great and the good privileged members of the congregation of two thousand.

The Earl attacked the Royal Family for failing to protect his sister, for stripping her of her title "Her Royal Highness" at the time of her divorce, and he warned them not to suffocate her two sons in duty and tradition. He attacked the tabloid press and the hated paparazzi, accusing the media of "sneering at her genuinely good intentions."

No one ever applauds at funerals of this importance. But at the end of the eulogy, the silence turned to clapping and to cheers from the crowds in the streets outside the abbey. The ordinary people—Diana's real people—began to applaud, and the clapping was caught up along the two-mile funeral route. Unbelievably, inside Westminster Abbey the congregation, too, five hundred of whom worked for Diana's charities, took up the applause until everyone, the whole city, seemed to be applauding Lord Spencer's sentiments.

For the entire Royal Family the events of that day were the most embarrassing they have ever been forced to endure. In life, Diana had fought with them against stuffiness, protocol, and tradition, and the family had expelled the brightest flame the Windsors had ever known, branding her a loose cannon.

But in death, Princess Diana triumphed. The people showed that Diana was the one member of the Royal Family they truly loved, not caring about the rest of the Windsors who had betrayed her. And neither her triumph nor her memory will ever fade. She will always be remembered as England's rose, young, radiant, and compassionate. The People's Princess.

## Earl Spencer's Eulogy for His Sister, Diana

I stand before you today, the representative of a family in grief in a country in mourning before a world in shock.

We are all united not only in our desire to pay our respects to Diana but rather in our need to do so.

For such was her extraordinary appeal that the tens of millions of people taking part in this service all over the world via television and radio who never actually met her, feel that they too lost someone close to them in the early hours of Sunday morning. It is a more remarkable tribute to Diana than I can ever hope to offer her today.

Diana was the very essence of compassion, of duty, of style, of beauty. All over the world she was a symbol of selfless humanity. All over the world, a standard bearer for the rights of the truly downtrodden, a very British girl who transcended nationality. Someone with a natural nobility who was classless and who proved in the last year that she needed no royal title to continue to generate her particular brand of magic.

Today is our chance to say thank you for the way you brightened our lives, even though God granted you but half a life. We will all feel cheated always that you were taken from us so young and yet we must learn to be grateful that you came along at all. Only now that you are gone do we truly appreciate what we are now without and we want you to know that life without you is very, very difficult.

We have all despaired at our loss over the past week and only the strength of the message you gave us through your years of giving has afforded us the strength to move forward.

There is a temptation to rush to canonize your memory, there is no need to do so. You stand tall enough as a human been transported back to our childhood when we spent such an enormous amount of time together—the two youngest in the family.

Fundamentally she had not changed at all from the big sister who mothered me as a baby, fought with me at school and endured those long train journeys between our parents' homes with me at weekends.

It is a tribute to her level-headedness and strength that despite the most bizarre-like life imaginable after her childhood, she remained intact, true to herself.

There is no doubt that she was looking for a new direction in her life at this time. She talked endlessly of getting away from England, mainly because of the treatment that she received at the hands of the newspapers. I don't think she ever understood why her genuinely good intentions were sneered at by the media, why there appeared to be a permanent quest on their behalf to bring her down. It is baffling. My own and only explanation is that genuine goodness is threatening to those at the opposite end of the moral spectrum. It is a point to remember that of all the ironies about Diana, perhaps the greatest was this—a girl given the name of the ancient goddess of hunting was, in the end, the most hunted person of the modern age.

She would want us today to pledge ourselves to protecting her beloved boys William and Harry from a similar fate and I do this here Diana on your behalf. We will not allow them to suffer the anguish that used regularly to drive you to tearful despair.

And beyond that, on behalf of your mother and sisters, I pledge that we, your blood family, will do all we can to continue the imaginative and loving way in which you were steering these two exceptional young men so that their souls are not simply immersed by duty and tradition, but can sing openly as you planned.

We fully respect the heritage into which they have both been born and will always respect and encourage them in their royal role. But we, like you, recognize the need for them being of unique qualities not to need to be seen as a saint. Indeed to sanctify your memory would be to miss out on the very core of your being, your wonderfully mischievous sense of humor with a laugh that bent you double.

Your joy for life transmitted wherever you took your smile and the sparkle in those unforgettable eyes. Your boundless energy which you could barely contain.

But your greatest gift was your intuition and it was a gift you used wisely. This is what underpinned all your other wonderful attributes and if we look to analyze what it was about you that had such a wide appeal we find it in your instinctive feel for what was really important in all our lives.

Without your God-given sensitivity we would be immersed in greater ignorance at the anguish of AIDS and HIV sufferers, the plight of the homeless, the isolation of lepers, the random destruction of land mines.

Diana explained to me once that it was her innermost feelings of suffering that made it possible for her to connect with her constituency of the rejected. And here we come to another truth about her. For all the status, the glamour, the applause, Diana remained throughout a very insecure person at heart, almost childlike in her desire to do good for others so she could release herself from deep feelings of unworthiness of which her eating disorders were merely a symptom.

The world sensed this part of her character and cherished her for her vulnerability whilst admiring her for her honesty.

The last time I saw Diana was on July 1, her birthday in London, when typically she was not taking time to celebrate her special day with friends but was guest of honor at a special charity fund-raising evening. She sparkled of course, but I would rather cherish the days I spent with her in March when she came to visit me and my children in our home in South Africa. I am proud of the fact apart from when she was on display meeting President Mandela we managed to contrive to stop the ever-present paparazzi from getting a single picture of her—that meant a lot to her.

These were days I will always treasure. It was as if we had

to experience as many different aspects of life as possible to arm them spiritually and emotionally for the years ahead. I know you would have expected nothing less from us.

William and Harry, we all cared desperately for you today. We are all chewed up with the sadness at the loss of a woman who was not even our mother. How great your suffering is, we cannot even imagine.

I would like to end by thanking God for the small mercies he has shown us at this dreadful time. For taking Diana at her most beautiful and radiant and when she had joy in her private life. Above all we give thanks for the life of a woman I am so proud to be able to call my sister, the unique, the complex, the extraordinary and irreplaceable Diana whose beauty, both internal and external, will never be extinguished from our minds.

# Index